Notes & Apologies:

✻ If you received this issue as part of a *Believer* subscription, you will find inside your poly bag a limited edition 2025 calendar, featuring original work by acclaimed artist Nina Chanel Abney. Abney has had solo exhibitions across the country, and her work is held in the collections of major institutions, such as the Whitney Museum of American Art and MoMA. In a statement describing her canvases, she says they "propose a new type of history painting, one grounded in the barrage of everyday events and funneled through the velocity of the internet." The striking piece made for this calendar is characteristic of Abney's oeuvre, which addresses race, celebrity, religion, politics, sex, and art history, and forgoes "linear storytelling in lieu of disjointed narratives." As she puts it, "The effect is information overload, balanced with a kind of spontaneous order, where time and space are compressed and identity is interchangeable." Please send photos of your calendar hanging in hospitable places to *@believermag* on Instagram. Photos of your calendar hanging in inhospitable places are also acceptable.

✻ The cover of this issue features, clockwise from the bottom left, Martine Syms, Annie Leibovitz, Hilton Als, and An-My Lê.

✻ The incidental drawings in this issue are by Gabrielle Bell. They were made during Draw Me Draw You, a themed drawing night in which artists pose for each other. The main theme for these was loneliness.

✻ Inside this issue, you'll find a sixteen-page, conveniently perforated gift guide, which includes recommendations for tried-and-true, and occasionally very large, items from over forty working artists. Among these gift ideas are knives, pens, paper towel mega rolls, holy wafers, a cathode-ray tube TV set, and a bottle of grappa. We hope you discover something within this catalog that enriches the practice of the creators you hold most dear.

✻ Subscriptions to *The Believer* include four issues, one of which might be themed (like this one, for example) and may come with a special bonus item, such as a giant poster, free radio series, or annual calendar. View our subscription deals at *thebeliever.net/subscribe*.

Dear Believer,

In "Fear as a Game" by Elisa Gabbert (Summer 2024), she writes, "What's unusual about *Tetris* is that you can't beat the game; the levels just keep speeding up until you 'die.'"

Not 100 percent true. International headlines were made when a young man "beat" the original Nintendo *Tetris* in December 2023. Here are the first lines from his Wikipedia page: "Willis Gibson (born January 27, 2010), also known online as Blue Scuti, is an American classic *Tetris* player from Stillwater, Oklahoma. He is best known for becoming the first person to 'beat' the game on December 21, 2023, after he triggered a killscreen on the previously unreached level 157, crashing the game." The historic playthrough can be seen on YouTube.

Hope this helps!
S. Matt Read
New Bedford, MA

Dear Believer,

I've often thought about what my most dreaded way to die is. Having a moderate fear of heights, I've considered falling to my death to be in at least my top (bottom?) three. This is not just because of what would likely be the horrifyingly interminable descent, during which you'd be sentenced to a mental speedrun of every regret in your life, all the while knowing that at any moment, you will be shattered and gooified. It's also because, just moments before, you'd have to peer from that monstrous height and feel your soul slide down your bones, pooling inside your feet. There must be a devastating moment when you realize it's over and there's nothing but the plunge ahead. And what a mess you'll leave at the bottom too.

But Elisa Gabbert's essay "Fear as a Game" (Summer 2024) made me rethink all this. Gabbert discusses her acrophobia and why we seek out the thrills of controlled danger: "How strange, that life can seem pointless once survival is mostly a given." She mentions the call of the void, that disturbing (if brief) desire that we sometimes get to jump as we look down from somewhere up high.

What if we hear that call because we know it'd be the greatest thrill in the world, especially if we fell from somewhere spectacularly beautiful, like, say, Angel Falls? No cumbersome parachutes or ropes or weird suits. Just you, as you've been in your life.

Yet the majority of us will never listen to that call. And for good reason. We hopefully have fulfilling lives that we want to experience, with loved ones we'd be heartbroken to leave behind. We have missions, both enjoyable and burdensome, that we'd like to see through. Gabbert writes, "Kierkegaard thought anxiety arose from possibility—a reaction to radical freedom, the 'dizziness of freedom.'" The freedom to end one's life is too daunting for most of us.

But what if we were relieved of that choice? What better way to finally heed the call of the void? To see Angel Falls, upside down, on the way down after a swan dive. If people travel far and pay a lot to ride a roller coaster in some sweaty swamp, this would surely be infinitely better.

And, yes, you'll leave behind a bloody mess. But you'll be way too dead to feel it by then, so who cares?
Chris Jesu Lee
New York City, NY

Dear Believer,

After seeing the sort of witty deprecation suffered by violists in Jude Stewart's schema piece (Summer 2024), I was stirred toward a sense of solidarity. As an accordionist, I know a thing or two about playing an instrument that invites sarcastic commentary, often requiring a secure ego, a self-deprecating disposition, and a stiff upper lip. I sometimes think of Gary Larson's *Far Side* comic depicting an angel handing out harps at the gates of heaven, and, below, the devil handing out accordions at the gates of hell. But I think there's something honorable in choosing an instrument that's underappreciated or maligned. Plus, if they're not impressed when you start playing, at least it pleases them when you stop.
Sofia M.
Hartford, CT

A PAGE

Acrophobia 3
Activist 13, 27, 67, 75, 100
Ad nauseam 117
Advocacy 64
Akil Kumarasamy 56
Alan Herman 114
Aleksei Kruchonykh 10
Alfonso Cuarón 54
Align 32, 50, 53–54, 73
Amanda Dannáe Romero 122
Amanda Rosa 125
Anachronisms 43
Andrea Barnes 124
Andrea Settimo 21
Annie Leibovitz 1, 32–39

AL: I had a whole slew of very, very conceptual years. Of course, there's no going back after you start working like that. Now I'm kind of like a dinosaur when it comes to what I do, which is sort of a sitting portrait.

An-My Lê 1, 78–92

"HOW DO YOU MOVE BEYOND THE SPECIFICITY OF YOUR OWN STORY?" *p. 82*

Ansel Adams 59, 99
Archive 2, 12, 51, 60–61,
.... 64, 97–101, 106, 108, 115
Art Agnos 106
Artificial 23
Associations 81

B

Baby Ikki ....
.... 110–111, 113, 116, 117
Banksy 7–8, 27
Barbara Kasten 51
Baroque 30
Barthes 24, 42
Benjamin Garcia 28
Benjamin Tausig 128
Bernal Heights 97–99, 101
Billie Holiday 21
Blackness 43–44, 47, 49, 51
Bob Newhart 119
Branch Davidians 120
Bryce Woodcock 9
Bucky Miller 124

C

Capitalism 104
Carmen Winant 33
Carrie Brownstein...17
Casserole dish ....
..................101–102
Cézanne... 48–49, 127
Charlemagne 48
Charles Schafer 103
Cheese log 119
Chelsea Ryoko Wong 6
Chicago 10 13
Chinatown 50, 96, 98, 103
Cindy Sherman 22, 27, 38
Claire L. Evans 51
Colonialism 119
Commerce 96, 104
Connoisseurship 47
Constellation work 57–58
Constructivism 10
Continuity 54, 56, 81
Courtney McClellan 126
Cringeworthy 21
Cubo-futurism 10–11
Cyndi Lauper 115

D

Danny DeVito 115
David Salle 26
Descending 53
Dialogue 24, 59–60, 113, 119
Distortions 49
Donald Judd 121
Dorothea Lange 96, 99
Drag City 111
Drippy 108
Dualism 11, 26, 74

E

Ed Roberts 67, 75
Eileen Myles 125
Embroidery 86, 88–89, 91
Ephemeral 125
Epistolary 41–42
Equilibrium 85
Equivocal 42
Ethos 42, 45, 47, 126
Eric Bogosian 113
Erin Wylie 126
Estelle Araya 125
Estrangement 111

F

Feminist 15, 131
Fetishization 89
Flannery O'Connor 46
Fluxus 21
Formalism 11
Freedom Rides 13

G

Gabrielle Bell 1
George Abraham 100
Gertrude Stein 23, 28
Gesamtkunstwerk 25
Gestures 70, 79, 81
Glitzy 65
God 23, 28, 59, 61,
.... 100, 113, 117, 121, 130
Goethe 43, 44–45
Gooified 3
Grace Wales Bonner 47

H

Hack 110, 118
Hannah Krafcik 123
Hannah Langer 59, 106
Hayden Bennett 111
Heidegger 24
Herb Caen 101
Hilton Als 1, 41, 85
Humanism 42
Hunky 106
Hybridization 87
Hyde Street 98
Hypocrite 8

I

Impenetrable 23, 26, 68
India Claudy ....
.... 13–15, 19, 127
Infantilism 116–117
Infirmity 47
Intangibility 43
Isabel Ling 131

J

Jackson Pollock 69
Jeff Koons 26

Jim Crow 13
Jimi Hendrix 21
John Cage 106
John Coltrane 25
Jordan Wolfson 26
Joseph Stalin 11
Judith Heumann 64, 67
Judy Baca 12–15
Juliana Luna 108–109
Juliano-Villani 26

K

Kabuki mask 27
Kara Walker 38
Karen Rosenberg 47
Kazimir Malevich 10–11
Kiss 56
Kitschy 120
Kristian Hammerstad 7, 17, 32,
.... 42, 50, 64, 78, 96, 110
Kyle Hilton 10

L

Labor 19, 29, 73–74,
.... 89, 115, 126
Lanterman–Petris–Short Act 64, 67
Lascaux 26
Leon Trotsky 11
lê thị diễm thúy 79
Lille Allen 123
Lindsey White 124
Los Tres Grandes 12
Lynette Yiadom-Boakye .41–44, 46, 48
Lynn Hershman Leeson 28, 52

M

Malcolm X 49
Margaret Ross 61
Marginalized 70, 103
Marianne Moore 47
Martine Syms 1, 50–61

MS: For a long time, I would have a very, very, very clear idea of what I wanted to make and what I was trying to achieve. A couple years ago, that stopped being that interesting to me, and it just became more fun to go in blind.

Compiled by Yasmina Kacila; portrait illustrations by Kristian Hammerstad

Martin Yan......................................105
Megan Posco 108–109
Metaphysical 10, 54, 126
Met Cloisters 109
Merce Cunningham........................106
Mercurial...30
Michael Heizer.................................81
Michael Hunter.......................97, 106
Michael Smith.......................110–121

"THE RAINBOWS AND UNICORNS, I THINK THEY'RE GOING TO YIELD SOMETHING."
p. 120

Mika Rottenberg..............................23
Mikhail Matyushin 10
Monica Datta....................................10

N
Natalie Ng 98
New age 56–59
Niccolò di Pietro Gerini....................9
Nick Hornby......................................7
Nicole Lavelle 95
Nietzsche 25, 130

NippleJesus.......................................9
Nixon 103, 112
Non-objectivity 10
Nonlinear....................................51, 54
Nonaction 13

O
October Revolution..........................11
Off-kilter..126
Orange-tipped jade plants................97
Orlando Whitfield..............................7
Ottessa Moshfegh............................23

P
Pat Metheny 23
Pepper Stetler..................................63
Performative.......................17, 60, 87
Perspectives.................14–15, 26, 103

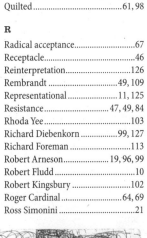

Quantum 54, 60–61, 130
Quilted......................................61, 98

R
Radical acceptance..........................67
Receptacle.......................................46
Reinterpretation.............................126
Rembrandt 49, 109
Representational 11, 125
Resistance 47, 49, 84
Rhoda Yee......................................103
Richard Diebenkorn 99, 127
Richard Foreman 113
Robert Arneson 19, 96, 99
Robert Fludd...................................10
Robert Kingsbury 102
Roger Cardinal 64, 69
Ross Simonini 21

"WHAT CAN A WORK OF ART TELL US ABOUT OUR WORLD, IF THE BEST WE CAN DO IS CELEBRATE ITS MYSTERY?" *p. 70*

Peter Voulkos......................96, 99
Pettiness..22
Phenomenology 44
Picasso 25, 27, 127
Pietà 9
Porn 79, 88–89, 121
Post-conceptual................................8
Power 21, 23, 49, 70,
.... 89, 91, 114, 124
Productivity...........66, 69, 74–75
Proficiency.......................................66
Proto-suprematist 11
Proust...121
Punto de Oro 13

Q
Qahwah House 111
Quaker..112

Ruth Braunstein 104, 106

S
Sara Carmichael.........................18, 27
Sarah Rose Sharp 123
Scenester..22
Seth Price...................23, 28, 111, 116
Shambolic..17
Shtick 117–118
Signals.......................................79–80
Six Gallery.....................................100
Smiling flowers 28
Sorbonne 8
Sparkly 22 Miracles 27
Sprüth Magers..................................52
Starfucker..................................50, 57
Steve Paul 114
Stradivarius 121

Strong Opinions 24
Studio Museum...........................45, 47
Sublimating 57
Subversion 103
Suprematism 10

T
Taboo 21
Thich Quang Duc..............................84
Thingness 23
Timothy H. O'Sullivan 86
The Dirty Show..............................117
The Katzes 67–70, 74–75
Tom Bolin.......................................125
Tom di Maria 67
Tom Hayden 13
Tomi Um..130
Toni Morrison...................................47
Transcendentalism...........................21
Tretyakov Gallery.............................11
Trina Calderón 12
Trump University................................8

U
Unabomber's Cabin 118
Unimpeachable 42
Unintentional obscurity 26

V
Vibrant..15
Victim 42, 81–83
Violet Schafer 102–103
Virginia Woolf.............. 25, 29, 38, 44
Vladimir Lenin..................................11

W
Waifs 96
Walt Whitman 79, 85, 92
Wayne Thiebaud 100, 127
Whimsy 104
White Cube..8
Whiteness...49
Wittgenstein................... 43–44
Works Progress Administration.......12
Wyna Liu 128

Z
Zaria Ware 77
Zaum..10
Zia Anger 56

Famous Art Heist and its Estimated Value: The Scream by Edvard Munch, stolen in 1994

$120M

Bottom left illustration by Gabrielle Bell; center artwork by Nicole Storm

THE ROUTINE: CHELSEA RYOKO WONG

AN ANNOTATED RAMBLE THROUGH ONE ARTIST'S WORKDAY

8 a.m.

It's already hot out. Wake up against my own will.

8:30 a.m. → **9 a.m.**

Read the news to see if the world is on fire.

The world is on fire.

10:30 a.m.

Grab clean paintbrushes and head to the studio.

11:30 a.m.

In the studio. Send emails. Friend drops off a bottle of fermented hot sauce.

4 p.m. → **4:30 p.m.**

Break my health pledge and effort to curb greenhouse gases. Eat a plate of carnitas tacos.

Paint.

6 p.m.

We're in a heat wave. Leave the studio early and meet friends at the beach.

9 p.m.

Find out it's a phenomenon called earthshine.

10 p.m. → **10:30 p.m.**

Go home. Sit on the stoop.

Roast a chicken.

8–11 a.m.

11 a.m.–2 p.m.

2–7 p.m.

7–9 p.m.

9 p.m.–12:45 a.m.

9:30 a.m.

Shower. Put contacts in; I can see again.

10 a.m.

Translate the label for my Japanese cabbage peeler. Cut my cabbage open in anticipation. I don't have meaty cabbage. I have only *disappointing spring cabbage*. Guess I'll just slice it. Cook three vegetarian dishes with prized vegetables from the farm stand. Commit to "being healthy!"

12 p.m. → **12:30 p.m.**

Research Portuguese tiles for a painting. Sketch.

Paint. Watch paint dry. Inhale veggies. Paint.

7 p.m.

Watch a glorious sunset and swear I can see the outline of the dark side of the moon.

8 p.m.

Yes, and I see Venus too.

12:30 a.m. → **12:45 a.m.**

Skip around *The Paris Review*.

Good night.

Photos by the author

STUFF I'VE BEEN READING

A QUARTERLY COLUMN, STEADY AS EVER

by Nick Hornby

BOOKS READ:
* *All That Glitters: A Story of Friendship, Fraud, and Fine Art*—Orlando Whitfield
* *All the Beauty in the World: The Metropolitan Museum of Art and Me*—Patrick Bringley
* Other books to be discussed at a later date

BOOKS BOUGHT:
* *All That Glitters: A Story of Friendship, Fraud, and Fine Art*—Orlando Whitfield
* *All the Beauty in the World: The Metropolitan Museum of Art and Me*—Patrick Bringley
* *The Ladies' Paradise*—Émile Zola
* *Headshot*—Rita Bullwinkel
* *The Spinning House: How Cambridge University Locked Up Women in Its Private Prison*—Caroline Biggs
* *All I Ever Wanted: A Rock 'n' Roll Memoir*—Kathy Valentine

I am very worried that I am about to fogey-ize myself. It was bound to happen eventually, I guess. I have been amazingly cool for a long time, as you of all people, dear *Believer* readers, can testify, but one of the two books I have recently read about art has pushed me over the edge into disapproving old age, and I doubt there's any coming back. The two books are Patrick Bringley's *All the Beauty in the World* and Orlando Whitfield's *All That Glitters*. The former is about the art collected in the Metropolitan Museum of Art in New York; the latter is about the contemporary art market. So two books about art that begin with the word *all*, but only one contains the word *beauty*; the other is a shorthand warning about money. *All the Beauty in the World* is, yes, beautiful, but also wise and sad; *All That Glitters* made me feel a bit sick.

It's not Orlando Whitfield's fault; not really. His book is compelling, with a real villain, an art dealer called Inigo Philbrick, at its center, and you may recall the name. Philbrick was arrested in 2020 for fraud and jailed for seven years. He was released in early 2024, after serving four of them. *All That Glitters* is the story of Whitfield's relationship with Philbrick, from the time they studied together at Goldsmiths in London until the time of Philbrick's disappearance, when it all got to be too much for him—he had told too many lies, promised too many things to too many people, owed too much money. And yet all his crimes seem to be a quite straightforward consequence of the way the contemporary art market operates: borderline criminality is baked in.

Here is how Philbrick and Whitfield operated. Walking home one evening, Philbrick spots what is now known to everyone as "a Banksy," a piece of street art on a pair of metal doors. It depicts a rat wearing a baseball cap and carrying a beatbox. He sends a photo to Whitfield, who joins him at the site, and they plan what to do—because, of course, something has to be done. You can't just leave it there for the enjoyment or indifference of passing foot traffic. The next morning, Philbrick hears back from a London auction house, and his contact there tells him that the auction house would pay eighty grand for it. This is right at the beginning, *before* the beginning, even, of our protagonists' careers as gallerists in the art world. They are both still students.

If Banksy's rat belongs to anyone, apart from the public, then it belongs to the owners of the building, so Philbrick suggests they bung the building manager fifteen grand and pay to replace the doors. They don't have the fifteen grand, of course, but that doesn't seem to matter. A conversation with the night manager is unsatisfactory. They show him what they are interested in doing, but he won't let them speak to his boss. And before they know it, the Banksy is gone and the doors are being replaced. Philbrick calls Whitfield. "They fucked us! The fuckers. They fucking fucked us, dude. The door. It's fucking gone." I am not sure that Philbrick and Whitfield were fucking fucked, really. The thing they wanted to steal was stolen by someone else, is all.

But this is a world full of thieves, chancers, con artists. An artist called Adam installs a glass divider in their gallery—that is his entire show. ("A previous show of his, in New York, consisted of a woman he hired from Craigslist to travel to the vicinity of the gallery twice a week. No one but the woman knew when or if she would be there.") When the billionaire collector Marc Steinberg sent his business manager to do an audit of the art fund Philbrick ran for him, Philbrick had to reproduce one of the works of art, because he'd sold the original, and the money had been "transferred out of the fund." Luckily, the artwork in question was a bunch of rubber welcome mats, so Philbrick sourced a hundred of the same ones from a hardware store and re-created the piece. He got away with it. The business manager "had no idea

what the fuck he was looking at," Philbrick said, chortling, but one has sympathy for the guy. Who can tell, really, which rubber welcome mats are phony and which are real?

Did you know it was possible to own only a percentage of an artwork? I was naive enough to believe that if you purchased something, it was yours, but the rich don't do things like that. They are interested only in the value of a thing, not in the thing itself. (And the value of most contemporary art is created and then inflated entirely by the important art dealers. Did you ever have the dream that a piece of art by a young artist you bought would, over the course of time, become worth a lot more than you paid for it? Well, it won't. Not unless Jay Jopling, founder of the uber-influential gallery White Cube, or Larry Gagosian, says so.)

Sometimes you can own 50 percent of a piece, or more, or less. Does that mean you have to hand it over every few months to its co-owner, so they can put it on their wall? No, of course not. They are not interested in displaying the art, just as they are not interested in displaying their hedge funds, so it sits around in a climate-controlled customs warehouse. One of Philbrick's crimes was to sell more than 100 percent of an artwork. On at least one occasion, co-owners thought *their* painting was in *their* warehouse. It is amazing how important the "post-conceptual" artist Christopher Wool—whose works are worth several million—is to their schemes. Wool's work often consists of large words on a canvas. *HYPOCRITE. AUTHORITY. PRANKSTER.* They do not, to my mind, reveal their meanings slowly.

The book describes the fever-inducing relationship between Philbrick and Whitfield, from college to prison. Whitfield is clearly not cut out for the task of lying to and stealing from the super-rich. He's too thoughtful, and his mental health suffers, and he ends up in a hospital with a Xanax addiction. But for a long time there was a part of him that wanted to be Philbrick, whose unaffordable lifestyle (private jets, clubs, villas, Miami galleries) is of no interest to us here at Believer Towers, right? Whitfield pulls himself out of it eventually, and now works in a world that is in every way the opposite of the bizarre universe of White Cube: he helps restore works of art, painstakingly and with love. "Why did you do this?" the federal judge asked Philbrick at his trial. "'For money, Your Honour,' Inigo replied.' 'That simple?' 'That simple.'" Depressingly, this is an answer that a great many people in this book, dealers and artists, would give, if they were honest.

I read *All the Beauty in the World* not long after finishing *All That Glitters*, and though the comparison is unfair to Whitfield, whose book really is worth reading, I feel like I'm being asked to choose whether to attend Trump University or the Sorbonne. Patrick Bringley was a security guard at the Metropolitan Museum of Art in New York, and his book is about his job, and why he took it, and what he thought while he was there, and it's beautiful.

Bringley wasn't always a security guard. Before he worked at the Met, he worked at *The New Yorker*. He was set for a conventional smart-white-boy career. But then his older brother, Tom, died at the age of twenty-six, of cancer, and he no longer had the stomach for it.

Every single chapter of this book contains something illuminating about art history, or people, or the lives of others, but the third chapter, titled "A Pietà," is as lovely and sad a piece of writing as I have read this year. Tom is dead, and while visiting relatives, Patrick and his mother sneak away to visit the Philadelphia Museum of Art. They split up, and when Patrick finds her again, she is looking at a picture by Niccolò di Pietro Gerini, a fourteenth-century Florentine:

> Against a featureless gold background, it depicted a young man who was very beautiful but bluntly dead, supported bodily by his mother, who hugged her son as she would if he were living—a scene that is called a Lamentation or Pietà. My mother has always been a good one to cry—at weddings, at the movies, but this was different. She cupped her face, and her shoulders shook, and when I met her eyes, I saw she wept because her heart was full as well as breaking, because the picture inspired love in her, bringing both solace and pain.

ITEMS THROWN AT THE MONA LISA

✶ A stone (1956)
✶ Twenty to thirty droplets of red spray paint (1974)
✶ A teacup (2009)
✶ Cake (2022)
✶ Pumpkin soup (2024)

—list compiled by Bryce Woodcock

Shortly after this piercing moment, Bringley remembers the guards at the Met. "Could there really be this loophole where I could drop out of the forward-marching world and spend all day tarrying in an entirely beautiful one?" He applies for the job, gets it, and is there for the next decade.

Bringley is a brilliant observer of the paintings and the artifacts and the life of the museum—the guards who become his friends, people from all over the world, and the visitors, with their cranks and misapprehensions and delights. On his last day, he gets to have a conversation he has had many times over the years: he has to disappoint a young woman who wants to see the *Mona Lisa*. "What? You don't have, like, a copy of it?... Well, where are your da Vinci paintings?" No luck there, either. There is only one da Vinci in the US, and it's in DC. You can understand the poor woman's bafflement. You've made all this effort to go to an enormous place full of old masters, so you might as well get everything ticked off all at once. Otherwise, what's the point?

There are nuggets throughout the book that you'll want to remember: the signs behind the scenes that say YIELD TO ART IN TRANSIT, a slogan I want on a T-shirt, and surely a motto for *The Believer*; the advice Bringley receives that twelve hours on a wooden floor is the equivalent of eight hours on stone, podiatrically speaking. I didn't know the Met owned thirty thousand baseball cards, left to the museum by a man named Jefferson Burdick, who didn't like baseball but loved cards. The one depicting Honus Wagner, who played for the Pittsburgh Pirates in the first years of the twentieth century, is worth somewhere in the region of seven million dollars, if recent auctions are any indication. And I didn't know about the Met Cloisters, way up in Manhattan beyond the George Washington Bridge, which specializes in medieval art and architecture. It's the setting for another exquisite chapter in the book. Bringley's then new girlfriend (now his wife and the mother of his children) lives up that way, and they have a magical early date there. His brother's funeral took place on the day they were supposed to get married, and the writing is suffused with pain and hope.

This is really a book about love—of art, of people—written with love. There aren't many of those. Bringley loves his visitors, loves his wife and kids and family, loves his colleagues, and all this love is contained and channeled into his love for the art. And he is a terrific art critic, writing unpretentiously about craft and context, rather than vaguely about mood and meaning.

A long time ago, I wrote a short story about a security guard at a museum. (The story is called "NippleJesus," and it's in an anthology called *Speaking with the Angel*.) I wrote it because it seemed to me that the relationship between a work of art and the person who looks at it all day, every day, has to be a profound one. The penultimate chapter of *All the Beauty in the World* is about two shows at the Met, one by Michelangelo and one by a group of quiltmakers from Gee's Bend, Alabama, and Bringley adores and admires both of them: there's no difference between them, as far as he's concerned. Maybe he is one of the few people in the world to understand that. ✶

RESURRECTOR

A ROTATING GUEST COLUMN IN WHICH WRITERS REEXAMINE CRITICALLY
UNACCLAIMED WORKS OF ART. IN THIS ISSUE: *BLACK SQUARE*

by Monica Datta

In 1915, long before the release of *Spinal Tap*, and longer still before sculptor Anish Kapoor purchased the rights to Vanta-black, the Polish Russian artist Kazimir Malevich first exhibited *Black Square* in Saint Petersburg, at *The Last Futurist Exhibition of Paintings 0,10* (called simply "zero-ten"). The number indicated a "point zero" for a new arts movement, suprematism—from whence all possibility might begin—and for the ten featured artists. "Up until now… painting was the aesthetic side of a thing, but never was original and an end in itself," Malevich wrote in a handout accompanying the exhibition.

Malevich's very first black square appeared in the design of a stage curtain for the production of a 1913 cubo-futurist opera called *Victory Over the Sun*, for which Aleksei Kruchenykh and Velimir Khlebnikov wrote the text, Mikhail Matyushin composed the music, and Malevich designed the set and costumes. Written in Zaum—a phonetic, trans-rational language created by Russian futurist poets—the work attests to the values of suprematism, setting it against the artistic movements that preceded it, as well as its utilitarian, technologically charged contemporary, Soviet constructivism. In the opera, the characters seek to abolish discursive reasoning by capturing the Sun (encasing it in concrete, to be given a lavish burial by the Strong Men of the Future) and ending time as it is known; the play culminates in an aviation catastrophe, with the world in darkness. The opera was not well received by the public at Luna Park, the amusement park in Saint Petersburg where it premiered in 1913, or by critics, but it announced the genesis of a uniquely Russian approach, one unbound by the traditions of Western Europe.

At *0,10* two years hence, the gallery-goer might first have been struck by the presentation of *Black Square*, in the upper right corner of the wall, at the sacred site traditionally dedicated to icons in Russian Orthodox households and known as "the red corner," usually located in the eastern part of the building. They might have been outraged not only because of the work's simplicity—it is a 79.5-centimeter-square canvas bordered thickly in gray and white, filled in with black paint—*but because it was not even a square.* Measure the piece in any direction and find nothing in the image that is truly orthogonal. Because it is not a picture of a square, per se, *Black Square* is free from the constraints of representation, an absolute zero.

According to Malevich, neither critics nor the Russian public understood the piece. "This was no 'empty square' which I had exhibited but rather the feeling of non-objectivity… Yet the general public saw in the non-objectivity of the representation the demise of art," he wrote. His friend Matyushin (a painter as well as a composer) was especially harsh: in letters to Malevich he declared that the work demonstrated a "lack of restraint," "lack of maturity," "insufficient understanding," and an "incomplete break with 'Cubo.'" Alexandre Benois, a leading art critic of the day, "denounced Suprematism with biblical horror," wrote Aleksandra Shatskikh in *Black Square: Malevich and the Origin of Suprematism*. Benois, Matyushin, and Dmitry Merezhkovsky—who referred to suprematism as "another step of the coming Boor"—maintained such opinions. This would galvanize Malevich, who found such views outdated.

The curator Andrew Spira writes that, in fact, imperfect black squares—and even rhomboids—had long existed in art, from the English physician Robert Fludd's attempt at capturing infinity in *The Metaphysical, Physical, and Technical History of the Two Worlds* (from 1617, nearly three hundred years earlier), to the black Yorick-death page in *Tristram Shandy*

Illustration by Kyle Hilton

(1759), to Gustave Doré's *History of Holy Russia* (1854). It is not clear how many of these works were known to Malevich, but if they relied on traditional black-and-white dualism—contrasting lightness with darkness to correspond respectively to good and evil, knowledge and ignorance, heaven and hell—Malevich stated definitively that *Black Square* indicated the beginning of life, of possibility, of true abstraction in art.

After *0,10*, Malevich would go on to compose some of his best-known works, such as the *Supremus* series, which reflected the optimism—utopianism—of the new Soviet era, rejecting the bourgeois constraints of cubo-futurism and expressionism. Critics and fellow artists warmed to Malevich's theories on form and color in the years following the October Revolution. By the 1920s, he had received patronage from the Soviet government, and became a teacher at, then the director of, the Vitebsk Popular Art Institute, replacing Marc Chagall.

The death of Vladimir Lenin, the fall of Leon Trotsky, and the appointment of Joseph Stalin as general secretary of the Communist Party began to change Malevich's work, along with his travels to Poland and Germany between 1927 and 1929, where he became acquainted with the artists of the Bauhaus, who became his champions. These adventures during Malevich's komandirovka, or state-sanctioned professional trip, ultimately contributed to the end of his adulation in the eyes of the government, but that was not all. Around 1930, Stalin became more forceful in ridding society of noneducational, elitist, and apolitical work; in the process,

Malevich lost his job, his works were seized, and he was no longer permitted to make art. Shortly afterward he was accused of being a Polish spy and was threatened with execution but was ultimately imprisoned for two months for the crime of "formalism."

Under Stalin, formalism was an atheist's cardinal sin: it was used to describe art that was concerned mainly with aesthetics and technique. Unlike art made in the style of social realism, formalist art did not serve the ideological or political goals of Soviet communism. Malevich's willful abstraction and anti-representational work fell under this charge.

After his release from prison, Malevich was again permitted to paint but was forbidden to pursue abstraction: the works from the last five years of his life are increasingly representational—and often pay homage to life before the revolution—but he continued to sign his work with a black square. *Black Square* was featured heavily at his burial: on his arkhitekton casket, on the front grille of the hearse,

and on his gravestone in the Moscow suburb of Nemchinovka, which would be destroyed during the Second World War; currently, an apartment building sits on his gravesite. In the same town, after a long battle, the Kazimir Malevich Memorial Center was demolished unceremoniously in 2019, the 140th anniversary of the artist's birth; authorities cited the lack of title documents for the land and the building.

Alas, I have never seen *Black Square* in person, and geopolitics make it increasingly unlikely I ever will: it is housed at the Tretyakov Gallery in Moscow, though versions of it have traveled to the English-speaking world on several occasions. The work is incredibly fragile, due largely to its five decades of neglect in Soviet storage. When I look at images of *Black Square*, I see a leopard in the fine craquelure, then Koko the legendary simienne of my childhood, who had a robust vocabulary and a pet kitten called Lipstick.

In 2015, imaging specialists Irina Voronina and Ekaterina Rustamova found—in a series of X-rays, infrared scans, and high-resolution 3D surface color recordings—many mysteries to be read in the flaking material. In addition to two colorful paintings that had been painted over—one cubo-futurist composition, one proto-suprematist—they discovered Russian-language text referring to earlier works featuring black squares, including a print with a racist title by the French writer Alphonse Allais. The levels of regret, indecision, and false starts that make up an artist's life were laid bare in new ways; indeed, this was no ordinary square of black paint. ✱

THE PROCESS

IN WHICH AN ARTIST DISCUSSES MAKING A PARTICULAR WORK

Judy Baca, *Generation on Fire*, 2023

rtist Judy Baca created the mural The Great Wall of Los Angeles *over five summers (between 1974 and 1983) with four hundred collaborators from the Social and Public Art Resource Center (SPARC), an organization she cofounded that is made up of youth, artists, and community members. Running along the walls of the Tujunga Wash, a tributary of the Los Angeles River in North Hollywood, the mural is half a mile long and features the erased history of local communities. With a grant from the Mellon Foundation, Baca and SPARC are now expanding* The Great Wall's *chronology. These "sites of public memory," as they are described by Baca, are visual records of our authentic historical narrative. The new sections are being painted indoors, as opposed to on site, thanks to innovative mural processes and technologies. Baca and I discussed* Generation on Fire, *a new segment of the wall that focuses on the '60s.*
— Trina Calderón

THE BELIEVER: Tell me about the origins of muralism in Los Angeles and how you came to work as a muralist.

JUDY BACA: I've been involved in the mural movement since its beginning in Los Angeles, as the director of the first citywide mural program. The precedents for this work in the twentieth century are Los Tres Grandes [leading Mexican muralists David Alfaro Siqueiros, Diego Rivera, and José Clemente Orozco] and, of course, the Works Progress Administration. The WPA mural programs came to be, in part, because of George Biddle writing to Roosevelt saying: *Look what the Mexicans are doing down here in terms of creating a giant public education program and painting on public buildings.*

On the Mexican side, Los Tres Grandes were supported largely by their government's mural program, which was directed by the secretary of public education, José Vasconcelos. He created a program that gave them sites to paint public pieces on. Their intention was to educate the public about the precepts of the revolution, which was about land, family, and liberty. While the revolution in some ways failed, the artwork was a way of carrying those concepts forward. Here in the United States, the WPA was unfortunately kind of shortsighted. It was a wonderful program, but it didn't continue long enough. It wasn't until 1974 that the city of Los Angeles began a mural program, which was when I proposed it to the city council. We began a public program that contracted artists to do works in their communities with the support of community members.

The Great Wall was a result of that program. It had been on a production hiatus because we didn't have the public monies to continue it after the '80s. The last time it had been worked on was in '83.

BLVR: How did you begin to imagine this new segment of the mural, *Generation on Fire*?

JB: The process is always kind of procedural, and it's something that we have used since the beginning of *The Great Wall*. Researchers, historians, thought leaders, and people from the community help determine the content. This particular section came out of an interview I did with Tom Hayden. I asked Tom to give us a general view of how he would describe the 1960s, considering his significant acts during that period, both as a member of the Chicago 10 and later as an elected official. He said very definitively, "We were a generation on fire." What he meant was that there were thousands and thousands of self-described revolutionaries, and the tone of the era was people thinking they could create change. It was more acceptable, or more the norm, to consider yourself an activist—compared with today, when it's common for young people coming out of universities to be focused more on entertainment and social media, and basically nonaction. People in that time came together across race and class and began to take action to end the war. To change what was the white male world. That's how Tom described it, and that's what the image is about. On one side, there are people carrying the I AM A MAN signs from the marches in Selma, Alabama, and underneath them are the actual Jim Crow laws. Reverend [James] Lawson told us the most important thing about the '60s was the end of Jim Crow—even though we also know that Jim Crow shifted to the prisons. When we picture the Jim Crow laws, everybody thinks they came primarily from the South, but California had extreme Jim Crow laws too. California's laws were aimed primarily at Asians, Latinos, and Mexicans. So when young people march alongside the mural, they'll be learning the history as they go along, and the reality of these Jim Crow laws will come into view.

And then, on the other side of this discrimination, you see the "generation on fire," with their arms linked, with fire in their chests. Above them is the Freedom Rider bus. We have named the people who took the Freedom Rides—some of them ended up at the lunch counters here in Los Angeles.

BLVR: Yes, you can see their names right outside the bus windows. After you've conceptualized this image, what's the next phase of your process?

JB: No painting—no mural—I have ever done is painted directly on the wall without a drawing. After our research has established a defining metaphor, we go to the design team. The design team are artists I work with who propose images or sketches. We look at all these ideas and select an option we like. From there, the image comes into my digital mural lab, and I begin to manipulate the ideas into what we call the Punto de Oro system, which is based on the Mexican division of space and musical ratios. No arm flies in any direction and no head turns without being coordinated by this ratio, which creates a sense of musical time within the piece. Then those final drawings are solidified and I make sure they fit with the other pieces of the mural, so it all flows. From there, the drawings go into colorations. The drawings are printed on giant nonwoven fabric material. The prints are in blue. We do a monochromatic treatment of the pieces—meaning we're creating three-dimensionality with

FAMOUS ART HEISTS AND THEIR ESTIMATED VALUES

✷ The Oratory of San Lorenzo in Palermo, 1969, $20 million
✷ The Montreal Museum of Fine Arts, 1972, $10–20 million
✷ The Kunsthal Museum, 2012, $26 million
✷ The Van Gogh Museum, 2002, $30 million
✷ The Nationalmuseum, 2000, $30–45 million
✷ The Mahmoud Khalil Museum, 2010, $55 million
✷ The São Paulo Museum of Art, 2007, $55 million
✷ *The Scream*, 1994, $120 million
✷ The Musée d'Art Moderne, 2010, $107 million
✷ Isabella Stewart Gardner Museum, 1990, $500–600 million
✷ *Mona Lisa*, 1911, unvalued

—list compiled by India Claudy

one color, a phthalo blue. From there we begin to color-mix based on the colorations. We're looking at a color treatment that is predetermined. And then we begin to paint. It's a far cry from a spray-can artwork.

BLVR: What is the origin of this newer mural process, and why did you feel the need to use this new technology?

JB: I began the first digital mural lab in '93, to look at how new technology could give us the capacity to put a mural on a building in advance of actually putting it there. It became clear that, in just a minute, we could advance hundreds of drawings virtually and see things from different perspectives. So we began to use these technologies to speed up our process, which had been laborious. Then I began to play with the idea that our drawings could be refined through digital capacities, using programs like Painter, Photoshop, Illustrator. We are now able to take our stylus and draw directly on the screen. That's advanced in the last five years, profoundly. More and more, it's becoming totally intuitive and functional to use the technology to accelerate our work and to reduce the cost of doing that work.

BLVR: Along with all these new tools, how did you develop the nonwoven cellulose fabric that can adhere to a wall?

JB: There were other people who were trying it. I think Kent Twitchell did his orchestra piece in downtown Los Angeles [*Harbor Freeway Overture*] with this nonwoven material. We saw it working. People in Philadelphia started to work with it too. I was working with building facade materials, die-bond materials that were metal for the creation of my Denver International Airport piece [*La Memoria de Nuestra Tierra*] twenty years ago, so that the work could be produced off-site and then installed. It created accessibility. We didn't have to dangle off an eight-story building to put it up. The nonwoven material we're working with now is very similar to what is used on the inside of clothing—to stiffen a collar, for example. The fact that it's nonwoven means it's pretty indestructible. You look at FedEx envelopes: you can't tear them. There are new materials that are foolproof. The adhering of that material, the nonwoven fabric, onto the concrete is like a layer of paint, and it's submerged in the same clear Rhoplex or emulsion that the

pigmentation gets. It goes on lightweight and adheres to the wall. It looks exactly as if it were painted there.

BLVR: How long will it take to adhere *Generation on Fire* to the wall?

JB: Probably one day. It depends on the wind factors. It depends on how much equipment we have, how many people we can put on it, but it can go up quickly.

BLVR: What are some of the challenges you find working like this, as opposed to the old school way of working with paint?

JB: One of the challenges I recognized in the museum [painting the mural sections in a Los Angeles County Museum of Art exhibition] was that we were painting only seventy feet at a time. That meant I couldn't look down the wall and see three hundred and fifty feet or more of the mural at one time. If a certain red—let's say in the first hundred feet of the mural—had to be echoed three hundred feet later, I couldn't see it in advance. I had to imagine it, either on the computer or in drawings. That is one of the things I'm kind of missing: the capacity to see the overall view of the mural.

VARIOUS CRITICAL INTERPRETATIONS OF GRANT WOOD'S *AMERICAN GOTHIC*

✮ A positive portrayal of rural American values
✮ A negative portrayal of rural American values
✮ A source of encouragement during the Great Depression
✮ A sign of mourning during the Great Depression
✮ An image of Americans preventing the devil from entering their home
✮ A critique of Puritans
✮ A commentary on Americans' devotion to the home
✮ A satire of the Midwest
✮ A celebration of the American dream

—list compiled by India Claudy

And the other thing is that you're not in full daylight. That's great because you're not dying in the heat, but the other part is that the light is different for color mixing.

BLVR: You have to reset your eyes, possibly go outside, and come back in to try and recalibrate the way you're looking at it?

JB: If I hadn't had so much experience on the site, I probably couldn't have done it, but I could kind of calibrate, knowing the difference. I know what bright California sunlight at midday looks like.

BLVR: That would be a Valley girl skill set.

JB: Yep.

BLVR: The color palette in *Generation on Fire* is bright. Could you talk about how you chose the colors?

JB: We do color trials and we mess with it then. You can't mess with it on the wall, because it's too expensive. If you have to repaint figures—pants, for example—you're running up

---

VARIOUS MEDIA THAT HAVE PARODIED GRANT WOOD'S *AMERICAN GOTHIC*

★ *The Rocky Horror Picture Show*, film
★ *The Music Man*, film
★ *Miss Piggy's Treasury of Art Masterpieces from the Kermitage Collection*, book
★ *Desperate Housewives*, TV show, opening titles
★ *Green Acres*, TV show, opening titles
★ *The Simpsons*, TV show, "Bart Gets an Elephant"
★ *The Dick Van Dyke Show*, TV show, "The Masterpiece"
★ *Pee-wee's Playhouse*, TV show, "Miss Yvonne's Visit"
★ *SpongeBob SquarePants*, TV show, "Artist Unknown"
★ 1963 commercial for Country Corn Flakes
★ 2023 commercial for Google Android

—list compiled by India Claudy

hundreds of dollars in expensive paint. The colorations are done with an understanding of the Mexican mural palette, gravitating away from a European color style. I'm much more interested in what the Mayans did, much more interested in pre-Hispanic work and the Mexican muralists' use of color—with the exception of Orozco: his colors were too muted. But in Renaissance paintings, or in Italian or Flemish paintings—think of all the paintings that are classics—they begin with a muted background. They might begin with an olive green base and then bring up color from that. What we are doing is the reverse. We are looking to bring the most vibrant colors possible, and that partially has to do with the sun it will be exposed to, because we know it's going to fade. The second part of it is that we're looking at something that is becoming profoundly different from the European precedent.

BLVR: How does your feminist perspective inform your process?

JB: My point of view is to have wide-open arms to contributions and people. I accept the input of many, and then help coalesce that into a statement that is inclusive and incorporative. I don't set myself up like the white-boy artists historically did in the United States, where they didn't feel any sense of responsibility to the community. I don't set myself up as the sole master of the work of art. I look for the inclusion of every mastery that is around me. I'm creating a dance in public that is unified and that our brushes can pass between each other. That's the gift that I bring. As an artist, I am a feminist and I'm also a Chicana. I am a person that is of this land and is bringing up the story from the land because it's where I was born and raised. I'm not a visitor. I have made a life here. I was born in Watts, grew up in Pacoima. In this work, I'm making something that tells the story of a river that was turned to concrete, and the recovery of that river, and the stories of the people.

BLVR: It's beautiful because it's multiple perspectives, told through your eyes, which can embody all of them.

JB: All together. Yes, this is a woman's perspective. It's the creation of family and community, and it's fully inclusive. ★

RAVEN CHACON
ISHAN CLEMENCO
MANON DE BOER
CLAIRE FONTAINE
ISABEL NUÑO DE BUEN
CARLOS REYES
ANA VAZ

The Blinding Light

CURATED BY
DIEGO VILLALOBOS
JANUARY 11–APRIL 19, 2025

Isabel Nuño de Buen, *Untitled 1*, 2023, glazed ceramic, yarn, transparent paper, paper, graphite, charcoal, watercolor, muslin, hand dyed fabric, hand made cords, 17 x 4 x 1 3/4 in. Courtesy of the artist and Chris Sharp Gallery, LA.

ASK CARRIE

A QUARTERLY COLUMN FROM
CARRIE BROWNSTEIN, WHO IS BETTER
AT DISPENSING ADVICE THAN TAKING IT

Send questions to advice@thebeliever.net

Q: *What is an appropriate amount of time to stay at your friend's art show if you're not interested in the social aspect of that kind of thing? I'm all about showing up to support people, but I find the conversations at these events so tedious and performative. And I hate who these events make me become: I find myself trying to fit in, while also judging my friends, who are all of a sudden talking differently and putting on airs. Should I just suffer through them?*

—JD, Los Angeles, CA

A: I went to college in a small town where we had to make our own fun. Lots of what we did was reimagine and emulate big-city functions like art openings, musicals, and fashion shows. Our events were scrappy, shambolic, and wonderful. They worked because we intentionally aimed for gilded and saw no value in actual gold. But when there's a lack of self-awareness, these gatherings can feel performative and contrived. That being said, I now live in a medium-sized city, and the last time I attended one of these events, and felt my skin begin to crawl when confronted with a mid-Atlantic accent and Truman Capote cosplay, I started to think that maybe everyone—even in New York or Paris or London—is simply acting out an idea of what it means to be a party-goer or an art aficionado or an intellectual. So what is the appropriate amount of time to stay at your friend's art show? However long you can stand to pretend along with the other fakers.

Q: *I've gone on a number of art museum dates, but I'm not sure how good of an idea they are. They're starting to feel like screening tests that invariably detect a problem. On one occasion, I was with someone I seemed to have a lot in common with, but we ended up clashing over most of the canvases—he saw laziness where I saw fleeting beauty; he saw bold defiance where I saw petulant rebellion. It got so tense that we ended up leaving early.*

Another time, my date paused at nearly every painting to say something like "This painting is so me!" She projected herself onto everything, from portraits to landscapes, relating each one back to herself. Her constant self-comparison gave me the ick, and I decided to call things off.

These experiences have me wondering if the art museum brings out the worst in my dates, or in me. Should I stop taking future dates there, or is this actually a good way to gauge someone's character?

Jess
Chicago, IL

A: Clashing over art should not be a deal-breaker, as long as there is mutual respect in both delivery and intent, a willingness to entertain opposing views, and perhaps the concession that a right or wrong

Illustration by Kristian Hammerstad

interpretation is beside the point. On the other hand, "This painting is so me!" is an absolute deal-breaker and your reaction was entirely appropriate. (At the very least, you've spared yourself from ever having to hear the words "This breakup is so me!")

As to your question, I do wonder if museum-going is best left for further along in a potential relationship. While gently sparring over a painting or sculpture can be stimulating, it can be irksome too. Also irritating, I would think, is the constant affirmation and parroting of our own views. Plus, you need to be wary of the mutual desire to establish common interests early on, often while obfuscating more nuanced or even contrary predilections. And while you posit museum-going as a test of character, perhaps you're simply struggling with the age-old quandary of whether opposites attract or if shared interests prevail. Or, to be less trite, maybe you deem yourself someone with good taste and are thus looking for someone else with good (i.e., your own) taste. No shame there! I probably wouldn't date anyone who'd never heard of Poly Styrene or Elaine May.

So might I suggest a deeper examination of what you're looking for when you say "character." My hunch is you could replace "museum" with just about any context, and face the same conundrum: finding a romantic partner, someone who really sees you and loves you for who you are, is really, *really* hard. It's often easier to look for faults and reasons not to try. Therefore, maybe gauging good character is less about how a date responds to David Wojnarowicz and more about how vulnerable, silly, sexy, gross, smart, and just plain stupid you can be with someone, and finding someone who can be those same things around you. No judgment, no ridicule. A person you can trust not only with your excellent taste in culture, but with your heart. If art matters to you, witness it with someone who matters to you as well. Sigh. This answer is so me! (I'll show myself out.)

Q: *I'm a painter who specializes in abstract art. I started taking on pet portrait commissions for extra cash, and it's become a successful and time-consuming hustle. For the first time ever, I'm close to making a living solely off my art. But I'm sick of transferring images of grimacing pugs onto canvas, and I have so little energy now for trying to create meaningful work. And I can't help but wonder: Can people even take my art seriously anymore? Where do I go from here?*
Chase
Philadelphia, PA

A: Would it help if I told you I am writing this answer beneath a framed oil portrait of my first dog, Tobey, a German wirehaired pointer mix with black-and-white ticking, a regal snout, and a bristly beard? In the painting, he's in profile under a gray, cloudy sky, surveying the landscape, a pause before the pursuit. After Tobey died at the age of fifteen, I commissioned the portrait from an artist in England whom I found on Etsy. Whenever I look at the painting, which I do daily (unlike other artworks in my home), I am

---

POSSIBLE FORGERIES DISPLAYED IN MUSEUMS

✶ *Kouros*, attributed to a sixth century BCE Greek sculptor, at the Getty Museum
✶ Three Etruscan terra-cotta warriors, attributed to a fifth century BCE Etruscan sculptor, at the Metropolitan Museum of Art
✶ *La bella principessa*, attributed to Leonardo da Vinci, at the National Museum of the Republic of Kazakhstan
✶ *Christ at Emmaus*, attributed to Vermeer, at the Museum Boijmans Van Beuningen
✶ *Netherlandish Proverbs*, attributed to Pieter Brueghel the Elder, at the Fleming Museum
✶ *Amarna Princess*, attributed to thirteenth century BCE Egyptian sculptor, at the Bolton Museum
✶ *An Allegory*, attributed to Sandro Botticelli, at the National Gallery
✶ The Rospigliosi Cup, attributed to Benvenuto Cellini, at the Metropolitan Museum of Art
✶ *The Faun*, attributed to Paul Gauguin, at the Art Institute of Chicago

—*list compiled by Sara Carmichael*

aware of how Tobey is both near and far, just as in life he was unabashedly domestic and alarmingly wild, unwilling to sacrifice either. He was mine but never really mine. And, Chase, there is more: I have gifted no fewer than five pet portraits to friends and family, all from different artists, the most recent a birthday present to my father for his eightieth birthday. Unfortunately, a portrait requires a photo, and for the life of him, my dad can't take a decent picture of his two dogs. So I imagine the portrait will end up being a pair of dark, amorphous blobs atop a comfy chair. Still, they are his pet blobs and he adores them. Suffice to say, we'd all save these paintings in a fire.

As to where to go from here: If you feel uninspired by the pet portraits, it's worth striking a balance between commissioned and self-generated work. Perhaps set limits for yourself on the number of commissions per month and how much time you spend on them per week. Dedicate certain days for your own pieces, and during those hours work with the same diligence you employ when working for others, even if it's not generating income. It's easy to fall into the trap of romanticizing the art we're not creating and deriding the art we are, yet both require labor, the actual making and doing. Tend to all of it: from that caretaking comes the seriousness.

Last, please remember that in the end we don't determine what work of ours will be meaningful to others. We can make art with the best of intentions, with years of learned and practiced skill, with all sorts of high-minded, theoretical, and intellectual goals in mind, yet we cannot predict which of our deeds and endeavors will matter or last, if any. I hope you take some solace in knowing that while you might wrestle with your own definition of what it means to be a serious artist who makes meaningful work, no one hanging your painting of their beloved pug on their wall has any doubt.

———————————————

Q: *I've taken up watercolor painting in the past year, and the practice has become a nightly routine. It's been a way to privately process thoughts, feelings, and events through a medium that is new to me, adding color and dimension to my reflections that journaling could never capture. I've built up a portfolio of work that, unlike my mortifying journal entries, I'm proud of and feel eager to share with my artist friends. But I struggle with the idea of sharing something imbued with so much personal meaning that could be completely lost on others—not to mention my sensitivity to the fact that the watercolor medium is considered inferior in serious art circles. Do you have any advice for working up the courage to share my (amateurish) art with those around me?*

Shy Watercolorist
New Hope, PA

A: Congratulations on being one of the few remaining people with quandaries or reservations about sharing! I quit Instagram after seeing a woman's video of her husband enjoying a glass of her breast milk with a plate of chocolate chip cookies. Anyhow, your restraint and thoughtfulness bode well for weathering your artistic debut. While I know your art is personal and that you want it—and yourself—to be understood, the first thing you'll need to let go of is the desire to prescribe interpretation. Impossible! Instead, remind yourself that putting art—amateurish or not—into the world is an act of expansion and susceptibility; it's about letting go, being vulnerable, and exploring rather than explaining the mystery that is you. It's connection and communication, which I sense you're up for. Yes, it takes courage, but you've already done the hardest part, which is dedicating yourself to a creative nightly routine and sticking with it. There is nothing inferior about that! ✷

———————————————

A PARTIAL LIST OF TOILETS IN MODERN AND CONTEMPORARY ART

✷ *Fountain* (1917)
  by Marcel Duchamp
✷ *His and Her's* [*sic*] (1964)
  by Robert Arneson
✷ *Toilet: Life Size* (1964)
  by Robert Arneson
✷ *Soft Toilet* (1966) by Claes
  Oldenburg
✷ *Fountain (Buddha)* (1996)
  by Sherrie Levine
✷ Bjarne Melgaard's bathroom
  installation at Luxembourg
  & Dayan (2012)
✷ *America* (2016) by Maurizio
  Cattelan (installed in one of the
  Guggenheim's public restrooms)

  —*list compiled by India Claudy*

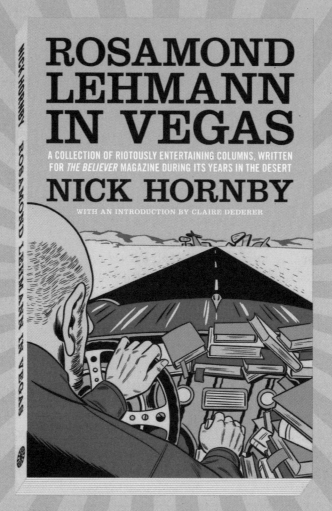

THE JOY OF PERSONA

ON THE MEDIUM OF ARTISTIC PRESENCE

by Ross Simonini

THE ACCEPTANCE OF PERSONA

Every artist expresses persona. For performers, the public face is inside the art. The work of Charlie Chaplin, Billie Holiday, Ana Medieta, or Jimi Hendrix cannot be separated from the undeniable power of persona.

For artists who send their work into the world, persona may be less apparent. Writers, painters, and composers will have little relationship to an exterior self unless they actively choose to engage it. Such private-minded artists may find the very subject of persona to be taboo, distasteful, and cringeworthy. They might bristle and scoff at the possibility that they, too, have constructed and worn masks for many years.

In such cases, persona becomes a hideous relative, ignored, avoided, or acknowledged only when absolutely necessary, in a huff of obligation. Negligence may lead someone to believe that persona has been extinguished, but it has not.

If an artist releases art into the world, they have already created immortal persona. When we expose ourselves and ask for the world's attention, we give birth to strange new forms of self, shadowy doppelgängers who will live on even after our death.

Punk, hip-hop, Fluxus, surrealism, goth, transcendentalism, the Beats—many of the most potent artistic movements are defined as much by the artists as by the work itself. Any exhibition of art is also an exhibition of its creator. Denial is futile.

I was once a persona hater—which, at times, could be a form of persona in itself. To me, dealing in public facades was, in the best cases, an irritating distraction. In the worst cases, it was an

Illustration by Andrea Settimo

Untitled #654. © 2023 by Cindy Sherman. Gelatin, silver print, and chromogenic color print. 40 × 28 in. Courtesy of the artist and Hauser & Wirth.

would a creative person not be a creative person?

The term *persona* was coined by Carl Jung as "a complicated system of relations between individual consciousness and society." Jung says the mask is essential to human interaction, and without it, we suffer. But we can also find trouble if we overly identify with it. For Jung, integration is the only path forward.

In the century since Jung invented the concept, the word has developed a stench of pettiness, as if persona were only for the swindlers and fakes. It is often associated with the kind of superficial traits that rarely support meaningful human exchange: seductive charisma, affected coolness, self-absorbed confidence. These qualities look best from afar, on camera, or through the rose-colored lens of history. Up close, they refuse intimacy.

I am bored by the contemporary persona archetypes: the narcissist, the scenester, the "on brand" celebrity, the campaigning politician—all of whom are trying to transform themselves into perfect icons. Encounters with such forms of persona are often repulsive. Like a wax figure, they stand still, uncanny, dead.

Artistic persona, the subject of this text, encourages the contradictions of our changing selves. Instead of a fixed image, consider persona as a field of infinite expression, as unresolved and irreducible as human perception—"a complicated system," as Jung says. For this reason, I avoid the traditional grammatical usage of *a persona,* and consider it as a fluid substance, forming and re-forming to the manipulations of the artist.

inauthentic scheme, at direct odds with the mission of artists: to seek and present truth.

To define some terms: *persona* is constructed, while *personality* tends to be a more passive phenomenon, shaped by genetics and the vicissitudes of life. Persona is an invented, enhanced, and performed version of personality, which, I came to understand, makes it a natural material for artists, for whom invention, enhancement, and performance are the primary means of working. Why

Artistic persona does not require self-obsession, only an acceptance of the true nature of artistic exchange, in which evidence of the self is always present, even if hidden or ignored. The line between self-expression and selfishness is razor thin, but persona, when worked thoughtfully, is a tool for profound connection. Bob Marley's physical energy amplified his music. Gertrude Stein was an extraordinary writer but is still best known for the effects of her magnetic social presence in 1920s Paris. Like a sonata or a painting, the presentation of self can be a window into consciousness and a generous display of vulnerability.

For me, communication is the fundamental pleasure of art. While I enjoy fetishizing a sculpture for its sensual thingness, I ultimately want to feel a relationship to the vitality that produced the object. This is true even in my relationship to the natural world: a mountain stirs up awe not just because of its material presence, but because of the universal forces that lifted it into being.

THE TRANSMISSION OF PERSONA

Persona is artificial, which is to say, it's created by humans. So is paint. So is a piano. So is a seventy-thousand-year-old arrowhead. This does not corrupt persona or make it inauthentic, whatever that word means. The word *art* has the same root as *artificial*. One of art's few defining characteristics is that it is made, in part, by people—not by a deity or wilderness or chaos. (Animals and plants, as aesthetically expressive as they are, do not make what we usually call art.)

Still, there is a feeling, especially among artists, that a successful sculpture is like a tree in the wild—unspoiled by human effort. It's a hope that our art contains a higher truth than we do. For many people, this might even be the purpose of art: to transcend the messy human being and present a clarified natural harmony.

"I wish the art I make to have nothing to do with me," the artist Seth Price writes. "The goal is to capture something beyond the human."

Mystics call this channeling. For the mystic, the artist is not the creator but a medium through which creativity flows. Human personality is bypassed and a divine power is responsible for the art. Some arrive at this idea misanthropically, through a disgust at humanity, while others see this process as a visitation from the genius, or genie. The writer Ottessa Moshfegh once described channeling to me as hearing a radio wave in her mind. The musician Pat Metheny explained improvisation to me in nearly the exact same words.

This is a common experience among artists, and yet it's reasonable to think that this energetic transmission, even if divine, is shaped by the person through which it travels, just as a radio signal vibrates distinctly in different speaker cones. The artist may not be the total creator, but they are certainly a collaborator, leaving some trace of their earthly presence. You might call this trace a personal style.

Moshfegh and Metheny, for example, both have distinct artistic styles, despite their process of channeling. They both have spent their lives studying the techniques of their craft and would certainly take credit for the distinctive quality of their novels and music. Likewise, each artist expresses persona, dressing, speaking, and opining in ways that are as idiosyncratic as their art. In this way, channeling need not exclude persona. Inward and outward exploration lead to the same place. God, as the mystics say, is already inside us.

Persona is a transcendental phenomenon and it, too, can move through us as selflessly as the transmission of art. It eludes scientific measurements. Like art, it shows itself through matter (e.g., speech, fashion, gait, countenance, behavior) but is an expression of deep feeling. It is a counterpart to genetics, a conscious way of freeing ourselves from the flesh through imagination. Persona can even exist online, or in art alone, without any physical body to support it. Unlike the soul (permanent, impenetrable), persona is not who we are, but what we create.

THE COLLABORATION OF PERSONA

Build a good name.
　　—William Burroughs's advice to a young Patti Smith

The alternative to persona would be a constant public exposure of our most intimate parts at all times. Is our soul on display everywhere we go? Should it be?

For artists who value privacy, persona may, in fact, allow for further protection of the self. Richard Tuttle said to me, "The only way I could survive growing up was to construct a persona."

The artist Mika Rottenberg once told me, "All artists are control freaks."

Self-Portrait at the Age of Twenty-Eight. *1500 by Albrecht Durer. Courtesy of Creative Commons.*

created a portrait of the author as a perfectionist.

Neither art nor persona can be entirely controlled by the artist. Once art is unleashed into society, it becomes a dialogue, and the audience becomes a collaborator. This is apt, because art and persona both come from a desire to connect with another life, and they will always be shaped by misinterpretation. They will never be understood as the artist intended.

In "The Death of the Author," the literary critic Roland Barthes argues that readers should utterly ignore the opinions of the artist when reading a text. Similarly, the philosopher Martin Heidegger believed that the only information we need to know about a philosopher are the dates of their birth and death. He was clearly anti-persona, which makes sense for the author of *Being and Time*, a book that tries to describe broad, abstract laws of reality, rather than reveal any facts about the author.

But Heidegger was a Nazi, and the people who are aware of his fascism likely outnumber those who have read his vast and daunting tome. So is it possible to approach this book without an awareness of his personal life, however impersonal the words might be?

For years, I believed in such intellectual possibilities. I told myself a fable of pure art. It's a scenario that many artists imagine: when art enters the world, it is experienced in a state of isolation, without undesirable context or awareness of the artist's life. In this idealized situation, the audience is ignorant of all things the artist feels do not serve the art, but knowledgeable about everything that does.

The manipulation of self is often one of the few things in life we can reliably control, and still, the subconscious will always interfere.

Vladimir Nabokov required that all interviews with him be conducted in written correspondence, so that he could edit every word before publication. Eventually, he collected them in the book *Strong Opinions*, as his own document of persona, and whether he intended it or not, he had

This desire for total control eventually leads to something like the white-cube gallery, a place that attempts to present art as if it were floating in space, disconnected from culture, observed with pristine amnesia. Pure artifice.

I could scrub my presence from this essay, remove this first-person perspective, and speak from an omniscient, ambient voice. Instead, this essay contains some part of me, presented in a bundle of sentences, edited with care. This is how the assembly of persona slips into our lives—not as some grand strategic plan, but in the gradual development of an artistic vocabulary: *I would never wear that outfit, or play that instrument, or behave like her, or use that word to end this locution.*

The boundaries of our persona are defined through an accumulation of choices. If I hid my presence, as another writer might, the authorship would still be here, in my tone, in the movement of my thoughts, and even in what I refuse to reveal.

THE BALANCE OF PERSONA

One thing is needful.—To "give style" to one's character—a great and rare art! It is practiced by those who survey all the strengths and weaknesses of their nature and then fit them into an artistic plan until every one of them appears as art.
—Friedrich Nietzsche,
The Gay Science

I became an artist to make art, but also to *be* an artist. I wanted the open schedule, the liberated social role, the romantic tropes. Mostly, I wanted to be connected to a long line of humans I admired, most of whom I'd never met and had experienced only as inspiring forms of persona. John Coltrane, Andy Kaufman, Virginia Woolf—these humans were artistic *beings*. They were ideal containers for their art, and I loved them for it.

The artists I loved were not all good people, in moral terms, but they were good figures, in aesthetic terms. In the documentary *Cy Dear*, the artist Giosetta Fioroni describes her friend the fellow artist Cy Twombly in a seemingly critical way, as "interested in only himself, meaning his person, his own emotions, his own travels, his own movements," only to conclude by saying, "He was truly a masterpiece."

Through these artists and others, I learned that the human, the art, and the lived life all form a kind of complete statement. I have since thought of these elements as the subject, object, and verb. Together they form a full sentence of an artist's expression. The viewer, too, experiences the art (object) in relationship to persona (subject) and to how the artist lives (verb), which inevitably influence how the art is made. Reconciling this trinity and keeping it in balance becomes a Gesamtkunstwerk, a total work of art.

Picasso said, "It's not what an artist *does* that counts, but what he *is*," which is why he spent his energy creating both his pictures and his legend. He exhibited his paintings and life in tandem, in galleries and in cafés. Now when I look at a painting by Picasso, I *see* Picasso, the man (striped shirt, confident smirk, macho bravado) alongside the story of his life (war, bulls, affairs). It all happens in one look. My mind and eye merge.

For any artist who achieves success, this is inevitable. Kahlo, Dalí, Kusama, Warhol. It's nearly impossible to view these artists' works and not think about the way they acted, lived, and thought. Rene Ricard, describing Basquiat in New York, wrote that "one must become the iconic representation of oneself in this town."

The conflation of subject-object-verb is equally true of composers and writers. Think of Hemingway, Stein, Baldwin, Beethoven. If one looks back to the history of art, this kind of public trinity might have seemed escapable—it wasn't—but now, in the age of the internet, it's undeniable that the artist, art, and life are ineluctably wired together. Celebrity is now a spectrum, not a binary.

The philosopher Boris Groys considers this an era of narcissism, a term he defines as "understanding one's own body as an object, as a thing in the world—similar to every other thing." He writes this in his book *Becoming an Artwork*, whose title is another way of saying the same thing.

THE NEED OF PERSONA

I have never loved a work of art because I consider it only a residue. What attracts me is the thought of the artist… The work is a deposit from which the artist has already detached himself.
—Lucrezia De Domizio Durini on
Joseph Beuys

In our current moment, people are often more fascinated by persona and the artist's life than they are by the art. This can be a lopsided experience.

An artist's personal activities—social media, politics, sexual peccadilloes—increasingly dictate whether their art is appreciated or ignored. What we narrowly call an artist's identity (race, nationality, gender) drives many of the most important critical perspectives toward art, sometimes utterly defining its interpretation.

Artists who actively fold their identity into their work may enjoy subject-verb interpretations. Others may not want their art affected by their private lives, or attributes they inherited at birth. Instead, they might prefer to brew up a new identity, something as eccentric and full of possibility as their own body of work.

I, too, am sometimes compelled more by the artist than by the art. A bold interview with an artist can show me how to see a picture. A writer's creatively lived life can inspire me more than the same person's impenetrable new novel. Hearing the poet Anne Carson speak about literature makes me love her work even more. In this way, a well-balanced persona acts in service of the art. But ultimately, the full art experience feels complete only when subject, verb, and object all hum with vitality.

The artist Jordan Wolfson is well known for his persona, which is, like his sculptures and videos, alternately vulnerable and pugnacious. He admires the way pop musicians navigate persona as part of their work, and how their audiences are willing to conjoin artist with art. He considers David Bowie a master of the malleable self, able to continually bend his appearance and behavior to his changing music.

"People develop persona over time," Wolfson said to me. "We all have the seed of it. And if you feed it—as, say,

Jeff Koons did with his *Made in Heaven* series—it can grow."

The artist and writer David Salle often analyzes persona in his criticism. He describes the paintings of Philip Guston and Marsden Hartley by referencing their "fully fleshed, meaty" bodies, pointing to the physical aspects of persona. He regards the success of sculptor Urs Fischer as largely due to "the force of his personal charisma." (Conversely, the critic Benjamin Buchloh dismissed the work of Joseph Beuys for being too dependent upon charisma.) Salle isn't ignoring the art by writing this way. He understands that each picture is, in part, a self-portrait. All art reflects the artist just as every character in a dream is the dreamer in disguise.

THE PROBLEM OF PERSONA

*I look inside and my model is
really myself.*

—Louise Bourgeois

Recently, a queue wrapped around the block for the opening of Basquiat's exhibition *Made on Market Street* at Gagosian Beverly Hills. A month later, another line formed at Jamian Juliano-Villani's show *It* at the gallery's New York location. Do people love this art so much? People certainly appreciate it, but I believe persona brought the crowds.

For years, Juliano-Villani has actively nurtured her image alongside her paintings. She live streams while eating a midnight spaghetti dinner. She talks to online followers while trying on new outfits and opining about the art world. She includes herself in her art as a character, transforming her presence into a literal icon. During one of

her many interviews, she said she'd been "cosplaying for 10 years… This is the cartoon version of me… It's like all up here." [*Points to head*]

Juliano-Villani cultivates big art-star persona, but even the little-known artist must deal with the presentation of self. The invention of persona begins the moment an audience encounters a new artist. Even with no other stimulus, the art and its context (when, where, et cetera) can conjure an image of the author. Again: once attention is paid, persona is there.

Only through *unintentional* obscurity can exhibiting artists avoid persona. Few artists desire this now, but in the past, anonymity was often a required condition of making art. Before the rise of individualism in the Renaissance, artists did not sign their work, and music was anonymously composed. Ancient forms of art, such as Egyptian or Aztec, were made by groups of writers or artists, and might not exhibit enough traces of a single hand to hold singular persona. This art aimed to capture the expression of a community, not of a person. Contemporary viewers may find it difficult to imagine persona behind the painted beasts in Lascaux, but someone was in that cave and they were trying to communicate.

Intentional obscurity, on the other hand, is a common method of avoiding persona—refusing social media, or press, or published photos—but this usually backfires, turning the artist into a mythical hermit. Martin Herbert's book *Tell Them I Said No* is a document of this phenomenon, chronicling the efforts of Lee Lozano, Cady Noland, David Hammons, and other visual artists who actively erase evidence of themselves from the world. In all these cases, refusal draws attention to the thing refused. Secret identities stimulate fascination from viewers, and the artist's absence becomes primary to the art. The effort of erasing persona is additive, not subtractive.

Every Trisha Donnelly sculpture I've seen is, in some way, an artifact of her retreat from the media. Every lover of J. D. Salinger knows of his grumpy, reclusive ways, and several years ago, an entire documentary film was made about the many attempts to track down the author's whereabouts.

Perhaps the most effective method for backgrounding identity is not a dramatic physical exodus, but a public dulling of the self. This kind of neutrality is how many artists respond to the problem of persona, but this, too, can harm the work. Ambivalence is a generally unattractive quality in a person, and a boring presence can drape over art like a wet blanket, dragging against the work's own energetic momentum.

Other artists may distance themselves from persona out of fear that they might begin to identify with such outwardness. This may be a noble effort, but fear, too, can disturb the art.

Attempts at flatness also won't matter if artists achieve fame. Of the artist Jasper Johns, the photographer Hans Namuth once said, "Jasper doesn't pose," which is to say that Johns doesn't *act* like a man with persona. But this anti-posture has not hindered public interest in his life. In fact, this very quote is taken from Michael Crichton's biography on Johns, a testament to the infatuation Johns has inspired in one of his close friends.

THE POSSIBILITIES OF PERSONA

I am trying to get to that place where nothing matters except the flow of this persona.
—Ebecho Muslimova on Fatebe, the alter ego in her work

Persona is not an obligation. The artist has the right to fully ignore their social identity, but this does not mean persona can be erased for the beholder. Instead, it can be warped, accented, refined, or faded like any other material, and each artist can develop their own technique for transforming it.

Some artists may use their presence to confuse. Cindy Sherman displays a crowd of varying personae in her photographs, which ultimately destroys any idea of a real Cindy Sherman. The artist Hanne Darboven wrote her personal correspondence with an intention to publish it, and according to writer Alex Bacon, she used these letters to invent her biography as a character within her oeuvre, harnessing the medium of private revelations to create public persona.

For many artists, the altered self is neither additional nor ornamental, but necessary. Like the Kabuki mask, persona allows someone to step outside their ordinary consciousness to make something beyond their abilities. A mask may help an artist to maintain distance from the intensity of the process, or to access something their personality cannot knowingly express. Such transformations can occur privately in the studio, explicitly in public, or even unconsciously.

The artist Nora Berman uses the digital avatar "Sparkly 22 Miracles" for her seven-hour-long, endurance-length online performances. The artist Madam X employs her pseudonym for mystical purposes, feeling that this name points to the true appellation of the maker, a parallel spiritual being.

False identity can relieve the artist of culpability. Graffiti writers assume monikers. Political activists wear disguises. The Guerrilla Girls dressed like gorillas to avoid arrest. The Brontë sisters and George Sand used male names to avoid misogyny. Stage names are

---

WORKS OF ART THAT GAINED VALUE AFTER BEING DAMAGED, DEFACED, OR VANDALIZED

★ *Love Is in the Bin* (2018) by Banksy, between $1.4 million and $25 million
★ *Le rêve* (1932) by Picasso, between $48 million and $155 million
★ *Erased Rauschenberg* (2017) by Nikolas Bentel, between $10,000 and $21,000
★ *Salvator Mundi* (1500) by Leonardo da Vinci, between $1,000 and $450 million
★ *L-Isoleucine T-Butyl Ester* (2018) by Damien Hirst, between $30,000 and $304,000
★ *Black on Maroon* (1958) by Mark Rothko, between $6 million and $27 million

—list compiled by Sara Carmichael

MNEMONIC DEVICE

by Benjamin Garcia

For
glory, god, & gold. Or
was it god that came first? For
god, glory, & gold. If you mine god,
you'll find gold. Not the glory of god, but the
glory of gold. Hail to the god of glory. Hail
to the fervent allure of god galore. And gold's
gaudy gore. Ore of gold in the aura of god. The
glory on high of the god of glut. This god of ours,
this god of late hours. Inlays the gog like gold
within gears: of synagogue and demagogue and
demigod. The golden glottal glory of god, the
godly glory of guttural gold. The glory of god's
gold. The one true god of the golden glow, the
one begotten god. The godly golden
gotten glory is the goal. Glory, god,
& gold. My god, I have not
forgot.

---

common for pop musicians who command audiences larger than their birth-name personalities can handle.

Filmmaker Lynn Hershman Leeson wore the name Roberta Breitmore for five years, until she exorcised that persona in a ritual. Duchamp used R. Mutt and Rrose Sélavy to refuse his past. The artist Lutz Bacher never revealed her real name. Nor has the writer Elena Ferrante.

Some artists tell lies to create confusion around their personal lives, offering conflicting biographical information. For years, the trickster-artist Maurizio Cattelan sent the curator Massimiliano Gioni to be interviewed as a fake Cattelan. The artist Terence Koh often provides differing birth information to keep his past a mystery.

Clowning is a way for performers to expose and hide themselves in plain sight. The artist Pope.L spent an entire career placing himself in shameful situations—balancing a pie on his flaccid penis, shitting onstage, and crawling through New York City gutters. It's almost impossible to critique a persona mired in so much embarrassment.

Albert Oehlen wrote an autobiographical film, *The Painter* (2023), in which an actor portrays Oehlen as a fool, struggling to paint, snapping at interviewers, and prancing through his own exhibitions with arrogant delight. When I watched it, I knew it wasn't Oehlen onscreen, but now I can't help but think of the film's pompous buffoon when I step into the artist's exhibitions.

THE FREEDOM OF PERSONA

Persona need not be aesthetically connected to any aspect of the work. Some artists use persona to rub against the art, creating a nice, satisfying dissonance between subject, object, and verb.

Georges Bataille dressed like a gentleman while writing depraved sexual horror. David Hammons is an artist of the streets, scouring them for trash, but he regularly positions his objects in a high-class stratum of society, at the bluest-chip galleries, among the wealthiest collectors.

Agnes Martin, a painter of meditative serenity, who lived in ascetic simplicity, also enjoyed driving her expensive BMW at top speed through the desert. Takashi Murakami, best known for depicting a bright world of smiling flowers, often appears on social media with his face sagging in depression and wet with tears, in a display of his struggle with mental health.

These variations of persona bring new colors to the art, but they are never the whole art. Persona is just one among many materials: oil, marble, video, content, form, self. The real art is always below the surface.

Gertrude Stein called this the "bottom nature" of people, an essence that comes through in art, regardless of the material. The soul can be decorated by masks but it can never be fully covered.

Seth Price wrote a novel called *Fuck Seth Price*, purposely working in the tradition of autofiction, a genre of literature dedicated to the simultaneous depiction and abstraction of persona. In it, the fictional Price says, "Appearance is a red herring… regardless of the artist's exterior or persona, it is the inner self that manifests in the work. And you can really *feel* it emanating." It's an idea that's almost completely at odds with Price's previously mentioned goal of creating art that has "nothing to do with [him]," but artists have no need for uniformity of thought, and Price knows that contradiction will help to enrich the unsettling disorientation at the heart of his work.

THE INTENSITY OF PERSONA

The word *persona* suggests extroversion, but the manipulation of the self can be as subtle and intimate as our mundane, daily transformations. Each of our interactions—with a family member, a service worker, or an employer—requires minor shifts of facial expressions, vocal tone, and body language. William James said that we have as many selves as we have social relationships. Jasper Johns said, "I think I am more than one person."

Another word for these permutations of persona could be *attitude*. Attitude can be felt anywhere in art, such as in the application of material—Helen Frankenthaler's easy pours of paint; Rashid Johnson's frantic scratches into melted black soap.

When I see a Wolfgang Tillmans photograph, hung with a humble binder clip, I feel his persona. When I listen to James Blood Ulmer's liquid guitar tone, I hear an entire worldview.

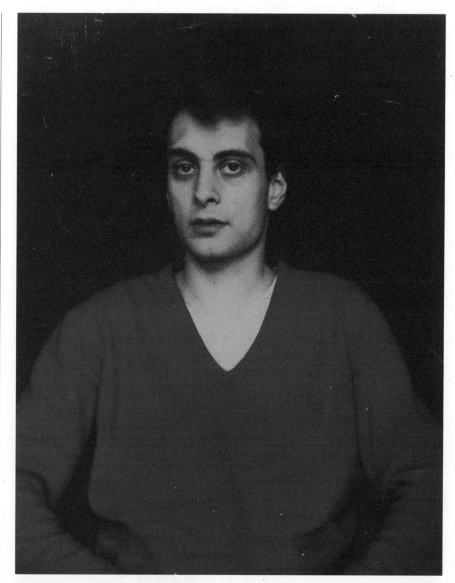

Untitled. © 2010 by Rudolf Stingel. Oil on canvas. 131 × 102 ¼ in. Courtesy of Gagosian.

The artist can also *hide* a brushstroke, or perform music with mechanical exactitude, creating something so impeccable that it appears that no human intention was ever present. But this kind of labor inevitably points to the kind of thinking that would focus on such details. Precision and virtuosity are evidence of persona.

THE SUCHNESS OF PERSONA

The various forms of persona are not mutually exclusive. The artist Rudolf Stingel, for example, exudes polyphonous persona, using many approaches at once: rough, abstract smears of paint; refined, photorealistic self-portraits; and an avoidance of the media. His manifestation of persona is both gentle and bold, with elements of absence and presence creating a dynamic, expanding tension.

Recently I stood in front of Stingel's *Untitled* (2011) in Los Angeles, a painting loosely slathered in golden streaks. Beside me was a man I'd met a few minutes before, who looked upon the picture and described his impression of Stingel—the artist, not the painting—as a "slicked-back hair, wine-drinking, cigar-smoking, big-bellied real estate mogul… I love that archetype!" He laughed. "Nice and baroque."

I'm not sure how he arrived at this image of the artist, but it seemed as clear to him as the painting before us. Despite the clear persona in his mind, he professed to have a limited knowledge of Stingel, as do I, since Stingel doesn't make himself particularly well known. Many New York artists I know don't even realize that Stingel lives in New York, instead imagining him in some faraway compound. I believe Stingel cultivates this sense, as he only very recently allowed photography in his studio, after several decades in the city. Like this, he grows the legend of the wizard behind the curtain.

Stingel rarely conducts interviews, and in one of the few talks I found online, he was salty and terse, and seemed barely tolerant of the situation. In response to one question, he retorted, "If I was thinking about these things I might as well shoot myself." However, in another interview, he was cordial and responsive to the interviewer, as if he were a totally different person.

His art, too is mercurial. His most significant work includes both self-portraiture and a series of pieces designed to remove his touch, such as those made by the carvings of viewers. Like this, Stingel's relationship to persona mirrors his slippery relationship to the category of painting, which, for him, includes carpets, Styrofoam, and floor-to-ceiling installations. In his life, work, and persona, Stingel projects an ongoing, relentless state of becoming.

THE DANCE OF PERSONA

Self-consciousness is the enemy of all art, be it acting, writing, painting, or living itself, which is the greatest art of all.
—Ray Bradbury

Inventive persona is never one thing. It's not a crass caricature or a dating profile. It's an ecosystem of impressions, forever in flux. The richest persona never settles into easy description and always slips from our understanding.

Dieter Roth, the polymath, once said, "I experience my person as a nebulous persona," and indeed, he taught his methods to his children and grandchildren, who carry on Roth's projects and use his name long after his death, as if his person had always been immaterial. This is the kind of understanding that liberates persona from egoic self-control and allows it to spill beyond our limited selves. Persona is a clumsy partner in our dance with culture, moving with the same organic, ever-changing steps as we do.

Last spring, I attended a talk with the artist Nairy Baghramian, who discussed her own negotiations with the art press. She spoke of the lack of critical discourse in the art world, which has led to her receiving an increasing number of interview requests, and to a resurgence of the belief that the only person who can address questions about an artwork is the author.

"The artist's persona," she said, "can work against itself… But it's not all about me. I would rather talk about other artists. I don't want to defend my work."

To address this problem, her talk included a viewing of Richard Serra's film *Hand Lead Fulcrum* (1968), which, she explained, was created by Serra to answer questions he had been asked about his own work. The film explains nothing.

The artist's persona need not be a way to explain art, but a vehicle for expanding it. Like the filmmaker David Lynch, Baghramian prefers to refuse to answer questions about the meaning of the work. Instead, she becomes a foil for her art, a means to building

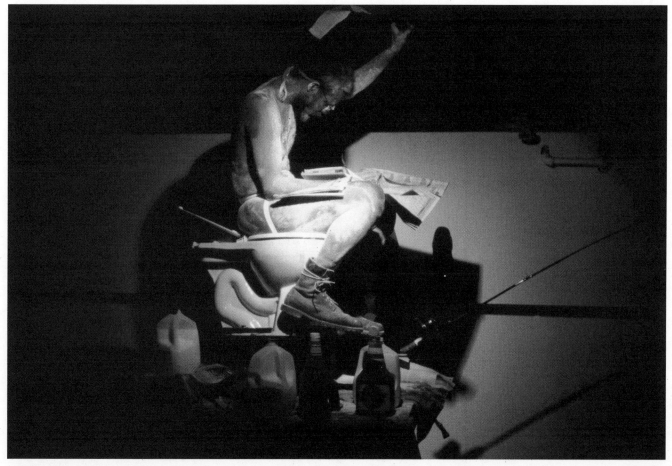

Eating the Wall Street Journal. © 2000 by Pope.L. Digital c-prints on gold fiber silk paper. 1 of 5 prints. 6 × 9 in. Courtesy of the Estate of Pope.L and Mitchell-Innes & Nash, New York.

further mystery and complexity. "We should not have to be the work," she told me. "That's boring. The persona should be constructed."

This is how persona can be less like a single work of art than an entire body of work—a constellation of choices spread across time. Life is change, and creative thought is motion. Beyoncé naturally transformed from pop singer to country icon. Donald Glover metamorphosed from nervous, skinny comic to slick, grinning celebrity. Miles Davis invented new genres every few albums, always with a fresh, dazzling wardrobe. We watch as these musicians defy the expectations of their role, whether they are jazz musicians or pop stars.

These expectations are in us all. Art, as free as it can be, still brims with standards. There is no such thing as a blank canvas. Always in the back of our mind is the landscape, the portrait, the still life, and whatever appears on any canvas must resist or submit to those expectations.

This is also true for persona. Even the most self-effacing personality must contend with that old, dusty archetype of the starving, tortured artist. Painters, sculptors, poets: the world looks to these artists as society's sources of authenticity and truth, which, as the tale goes, is found only in the darkest, harshest depths. The true artist must venture into hell and, through great suffering, bring back gleaming wisdom for the rest of us.

Who is responsible for this story? Is it van Gogh? Sylvia Plath? Kurt Cobain? And should we all have to perform this role until the end of time? Who needs us to? And what do we become when we pry off the mask of the serious artist, mix up a fresh palette of persona, and allow ourselves to just play? ⋆

ANNIE
LEIBOVITZ

[PHOTOGRAPHER]

"WHEN I STARTED WORKING FOR *ROLLING STONE*, I REALLY THOUGHT I WAS DOING JOURNALISM. AND THEN I QUICKLY REALIZED I WASN'T, BECAUSE I HAD A POINT OF VIEW."

Objects belonging to Jasper Johns, captured in photographs by Annie Leibovitz:
A Jetlife model airplane
A framed tarantula
N525 Sennelier pastels

In many ways, I am an unlikely choice of interviewer for a subject like *Annie Leibovitz. While I am trained as a photographer and still utilize photography across my work, for the most part I no longer author my own pictures. So I was skeptical when the call came: Were the editors of* The Believer *sure they wanted me for the job? Wouldn't the magazine do better with someone more closely aligned with Leibovitz's work—straddling the art, reportage, and editorial worlds as it does? But deep down I felt this request was tugging on my young self: As a teenager growing up in 1990s Philadelphia, I obsessively collected Leibovitz's pictures from magazines, taping them up all over my walls, such that the walls, in fact, disappeared under their many layers. Gap ads, Rolling* Stone *magazine covers, and, most of all, pictures from the "got milk?" campaign filled my little room by the hundreds. I was, it might be noted, unaware that these were her pictures. At that point, I didn't know anything about who made the images I was obsessed with, images I wanted to live with and inside. I had*

Illustration by Kristian Hammerstad; images courtesy of the artist and Hauser & Wirth

only my teenage desires to guide me. And they propelled me toward her at full tilt.

Almost three decades later, on this occasion, I miraculously got the chance to speak to Leibovitz, the person who had informed my own burgeoning photographic consciousness, curiosity, and ambition. I once heard someone say that we are all born with Beatles lyrics in our heads, so deep is their creative mark on the world. The same might be said for Leibovitz's pictures (as evidenced by my own teenage image-collecting pursuits): she has been making this work for so many decades, and with such consistency, innovation, and panache, that it feels hard to imagine the cultural landscape without her impression.

Leibovitz grew up in Connecticut in a large Jewish family; her father was in the air force, and her mother was engaged in art and dance (Leibovitz herself often refers to photographing as a kind of choreography). After graduating from art school at the now-closed San Francisco Art Institute—and living on a kibbutz in Israel for several months—she quickly became the chief photographer for Rolling Stone in 1973. Leibovitz has photographed at a wild pace ever since, making some of the most iconic portraits of the twentieth and twenty-first centuries: from John and Yoko in bed; to incarcerated people in Soledad State Prison hugging family members; to a young Whoopi Goldberg in a bathtub full of milk; to Demi Moore, nude and pregnant, on the cover of Vanity Fair. In addition to regularly shooting covers and features for that magazine and Vogue, Leibovitz has had exhibitions at the Brooklyn Museum, Crystal Bridges Museum of American Art, and the National Portrait Gallery.

Our conversation unfolded over Zoom on a warm October morning (I was in the Midwest, and she was in New York City), and after a handful of rescheduling emails. It centered on artistic process—sketching, editing, and more—while also delving into her new show at Hauser & Wirth, titled Stream of Consciousness. The show includes seventy images, from throughout her career, and largely centers creative thinkers and makers as subjects. We also discussed my work— a surprise to me!—with regard to my use of archival photography and how we relate to images in relation. We talked about Leibovitz's decision not to publish pictures of her children, attending synagogue, camera phones, photographing Kamala Harris in the final weeks of the 2024 presidential campaign, and why she feels photojournalism is the most exciting work happening in the field.

—Carmen Winant

I. WEAK IN THE KNEES FOR HOCKNEY

THE BELIEVER: Ready to start?

ANNIE LEIBOVITZ: Let me get some water here. I just drove in at six o'clock this morning from upstate, so I'm a little bit…

BLVR: Tired?

AL: And then I had a call with these publishers; my rabbi, Rabbi [Angela] Buchdahl, needs a photograph, so it was great to have a conversation with her publishers about what they would like to do.

BLVR: What temple do you go to?

AL: Central Synagogue [in New York City]. My three daughters were all bat mitzvahed there.

BLVR: How nice—and that you are photographing your rabbi too.

AL: She is an extraordinary woman. You know, she's Korean American, actually. Her sermons are quite extraordinary. I mean, the only reason I'm still at this synagogue is because of her. You look forward to her, to what she's going to say. Where do you live now?

BLVR: I live in Columbus, Ohio.

AL: I read about you, and that was part of the reason I put the interview off. I went, Oh shit. She's serious. She's fucking serious.

BLVR: You're giving me too much credit, I think.

AL: No, no, no. You are a serious artist, and, you know, I crawled into bed the night before and started to do my due diligence, and I called [my studio manager] Karen Mulligan. I said, "I can't do this tomorrow morning. First of all, she's

Louise Bourgeois, New York City

too serious." I mean, I think it's interesting what you're doing, the way you're using photography.

BLVR: I appreciate that. I'll carry it with me.

AL: Certainly. The older I get, and with the accumulation of the work I have, it is so interesting to see the relationships between the photographs. That's kind of what I'm interested in in the show I'm having at Hauser & Wirth. The gallery world, it's such a strange animal, you know?

BLVR: I have questions for you about this, so don't get too far ahead of me! But first, I want to ask you about photographing

such famous subjects. These are people that are used to being photographed; I imagine that makes your job both easier and harder. How does your process differ, if at all, from photographing noncelebrities?

AL: I mean, I've been doing this, what, fifty years. It started with journalism. Or what I thought was journalism. I admired the photo story, you know? When I started working for *Rolling Stone*, I really thought I was doing journalism. And then I quickly realized I wasn't, because I had a point of view. I found that my work was stronger if I went with that point of view. So the work evolved. It started with these incredible years at *Rolling Stone*. When I look at that work, I see a young, insane, obsessed photographer. Just, you know, photographing everything in front of me, never going home, really just working all the time. It was a great school for observation and learning and becoming a better photographer. *Rolling Stone* and I grew up together, and eventually, with the magazine, I began learning how to photograph people. Coming from that place, it was very awkward making portraits at first, because you had an… appointment with someone. It wasn't as fluid as just being able to be around and watching something evolve or happen.

So what happened? My subjects were sitting for photographs, and I became a little bit more inventive and conceptual. I had a whole slew of very, very conceptual years. Of course, there's no going back after you start working like that. Now I'm kind of like a dinosaur when it comes to what I do, which is sort of a sitting portrait. I became very aware of what it is I am doing, and feel very responsible to it— to sitting photograph. I'm very interested in it and how to make it work.

As for working with people who are very, very famous and aren't very famous, I think you'll see, if you look through all my work, that it's a mixture. Also, in a lot of the work, I photograph people who aren't famous yet, and then they're suddenly famous. When I did Whoopi Goldberg [in 1984], she was unknown. I just went to her apartment in Berkeley and photographed her there. So I'm just saying, these people sometimes become famous after the fact.

BLVR: It's interesting: The way I set up that initial question was sort of a way to ask, What is it like to photograph famous subjects versus non-famous ones? But what I heard in your answer was a far more interesting distinction: between photojournalism and portraiture.

AL: Yes, yes. The reality is that I love photography—every part of it. There are so many ways to use photography. I mean, it's so big. I never wanted to be pinned down to one kind of style or work. I have a huge photography book collection. I have a few photographs that I own, Robert Frank and Cartier-Bresson, and people I grew up on whose work I loved.

I just went to a Carrie Mae Weems show up at Bard [College], and I couldn't believe it. To go through every single room and see how she used photography—it was just stunning to me to see the breadth of her ideas. I remember seeing her very early work, with the kitchen photographs [the *Kitchen Table Series*, 1990], and thinking, Oh my gosh, here goes art photography, whatever it is. But art photography always has been interesting, quite honestly. Hockney was the first person to do it, when he did his study on perspective. I remember being weak in the knees, thinking, That's how the eye sees—the way he collaged his pictures together. I was so frustrated with the frame of the camera then—that everything had to be in that frame. We learned with Cartier-Bresson and Robert Frank to compose in that rectangle, and to use the whole negative. But now it's so wide open, and it's so interesting, and it's such a great medium. It deserves to be, and it is, now, taken seriously. It is art. It's great to live through all that.

II. SITTING POLITICIANS

BLVR: As for sitting portraits, the most recent photograph of yours that I've seen published is the portrait of Kamala Harris on the cover of *Vogue*. I was thinking about that as you spoke.

AL: What happened with that was, in April 2024, Kamala went out to Arizona and did this incredible speech on abortion. She was on fire. It was amazing. I came into the office the next day and I said to Karen, "We have to photograph Kamala Harris. We just have to do this." The magazines I work with weren't ready to take her photograph. They weren't interested at that moment, but I said, "I don't care. OK, I don't care. Call her office. We want to photograph her. I want to do it. Let's do it." And it began, and they were really happy. We were trying to work out a time, and then, of course, she got nominated as a Democratic candidate for president. So then it got a little harder to fit in, time-wise. And at that point, *Vogue* was very interested in doing a digital cover.

We did finally have the session, and it went online in a couple of days. It just went right out there. To me, it's the beginning of a relationship with her that hopefully I'll return to when she's in the White House.

BLVR: That was the first time you'd ever photographed her?

AL: No, I actually worked with her when she was the attorney general of California. I really loved the photographs I did. I did her in the courtroom. How many years ago was that now?

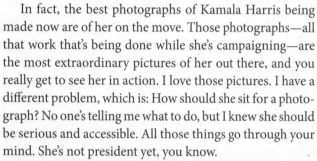

Jasper Johns's Studio, Sharon, Connecticut

In fact, the best photographs of Kamala Harris being made now are of her on the move. Those photographs—all that work that's being done while she's campaigning—are the most extraordinary pictures of her out there, and you really get to see her in action. I love those pictures. I have a different problem, which is: How should she sit for a photograph? No one's telling me what to do, but I knew she should be serious and accessible. All those things go through your mind. She's not president yet, you know.

But I'll tell you that the greatest photography going out right now is photojournalism and the journalism in our newspapers. I am obsessed with looking at *The New York Times* and *The Washington Post* to see all the work being done every single day.

BLVR: I can't help but notice that you haven't photographed Trump since he has been in office. I am aware you've shot him twice in the past: once with Ivana, his first wife; and then once with the very pregnant Melania. You'd talked about the desire

to photograph Kamala even before you were commissioned to do so, and I am wondering if that works in reverse—if there are people you don't want to image?

AL: Well, [the photojournalist] Doug Mills is doing such a great job with Trump. I look at his work every single day, and I admire him so much. He went through the White House years with Trump and now is out on the road; he's taking care of it for everyone. I also like my photograph of Trump and Melania so much—I can't think of where else I could go. I did think about photographing him when he was in office. I don't know. I'm just waiting for him to be all decrepit and squished and in a corner somewhere, to maybe go back. He's almost there.

III. THE MORTAR BETWEEN PICTURES

BLVR: As someone who has straddled those worlds—the world of photojournalism and the world of editorial work— what is your relationship to the art world? We are speaking

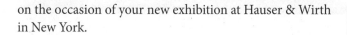
Jasper Johns's Studio, Sharon, Connecticut

on the occasion of your new exhibition at Hauser & Wirth in New York.

AL: I like the idea of working with a gallery, in part because they manage estates; Hauser manages the Louise Bourgeois estate, for instance. I have children, and I like the idea that, after my life, there's someone there to oversee stuff. And the gallery has never pushed me to do anything.

Bea Feitler, who was an art director I worked with, told me that you need to stop every now and then and look at your work and understand what you've done. I've said this nine million times, but I'm very engaged in looking back at my work. That's how you learn to go forward, how you learn what you want to do next. It's hard to believe, but many photographers don't do this. They go out and they shoot, shoot, and shoot—especially in journalism—and then they don't really get a chance to look back at everything they've done.

All my shows have always been about chronology. I've done books that reflect these chronologies, from 1970 to 1990, 1990 to 2005, 2005 to 2016. I do an edit first; then I do the book. The years from 1990 to 2005 were when I was with Susan Sontag, and it became my favorite book: *A Photographer's Life*. It has family pictures, and the assignments were, you know, put together with these photos.

The years from 2005 to 2016 were an attempt at trying to put some portrait work together. I don't think I'm a very good portraitist. I think I'm OK. So when it's just by itself, and you don't have the journalism to kind of knock it back and forth, it can look a little boring. [*Laughs*] I'm still taking the other kinds of pictures, the more personal ones, for myself. But I can't publish them, because my children, at a certain point—like ages twelve and thirteen—they said, "Mom, we don't really want to see our pictures published." I respected that. And I shoot, I still take pictures of them, but I don't publish them. My older daughter, when she was going to college, she would call me and we would FaceTime, and I had this whole series of screen grabs of her. It's really

Virginia Woolf's Writing Desk, Monk's House, East Sussex, England

fascinating, because the camera is not there. She's just talking to this phone, and it's as real as real can be. They're kind of amazing pictures of her.

BLVR: The question of chronology is interesting. That has been such an organizing principle for you, as you say, and you've strayed from it here, in this show. The very title is *Stream of Consciousness*.

AL: You know, the early conversations around the show were like, *Annie, you're such a contemporary photographer, you should just show your new work*. I put up a bunch of things on my work wall, and then I went through everything I had and I picked, like, ten pictures. Every day I would go by and look at the wall and at all the work in the last few years, and I finally said, I'm just going to pick my favorite pictures. I don't

care what year it was done in. I'm just going to start picking the pictures from the last ten years that really mean something to me. It was the first time I'd done this out of chronology, out of time. I actually really liked it, you know? It was an interesting exercise. I'm still more interested in history and chronology, but it was great to break away from putting things in order, which is the way I've been doing things my whole life.

BLVR: Maybe this goes against what you're saying, that you were just responding to what was jumping out at you. But I will say that I noticed a thread between some of the kinds of pictures and subjects. Among your picks are a lot of artists and writers and creative visionaries—people like Patti Smith, Kara Walker, Amy Sherald, Cindy Sherman. Do you think there's a thread there? It didn't strike me, for instance, apropos of the earlier questions, that there were a lot of politicians…

AL: Yeah, people commented early on that I have a lot of artists, that I could do an all-artists show. But the truth is, I'm just fascinated with photography as a subject and the process of how it all comes together. I just love process more than final things, you know? And I love these people. I admire them so much.

The other thing that's in there is this work I did in this book called *Pilgrimage*, which is all photographs without people in them. That work has turned out to be the kind of mortar between my photographs. There are quite a number of those pictures here. I am remembering a moment when Gloria Steinem had a fundraiser for Kamala Harris at her house. When I walked into her kitchen, I saw that she had my photograph of Virginia Woolf's desk on her kitchen wall. I was so moved by that. That was like *it*, you know? These person-less pictures—there is one of Edward Hopper's house that he was born in—they kind of hold things together.

BLVR: But all these pieces strike me as being such a different world than making pictures for a magazine, let's say. And I've heard some ambivalence in the last hour about how you approach it.

I am thinking about how the photographs you took inside the Frick Collection [in New York] operate this way as well. These pictures open the Hauser & Wirth show, right?

AL: Yes, they're at the beginning of the show: I ran a suite of four pictures of the Frick from the ceilings. Annabelle Selldorf—do you know who she is? The architect? She designed the Hauser & Wirth building, though I am the last person to find out about that. Annabelle is a really interesting architect. She was working on redesigning the interior of the Frick recently. *Vogue* was doing a story on her, and they asked if I would photograph her. I went up to her place in Maine. She was standing looking out at the at the ocean and she said, "I'm trying to figure out what the color of clouds is." I stood with her there as she tried to figure it out; she thought she would paint the ceiling of the museum's auditorium that color.

I ended up going to the Frick with Annabelle. This was problematic because the Frick didn't want me inside, because they had an exclusive with another publication. But Annabelle said, "You're coming in." I had only my phone with me; I shot with my phone. I just took a few frames and then walked out and then went back to my studio and studied the photographs. They were so cool, these photographs and the ceiling—the way it looked. Annabelle, whom I think of as always doing straight lines, was dealing with curves in this ceiling. And *Vogue* eventually ran two of them. I couldn't believe it. Photos from my camera phone; I couldn't walk in there with a real camera. My camera phone is amazing. It's not good for everything, but it's very good. If you use it horizontally, the sides get all cuckoo.

But that's when I thought about *Stream of Consciousness*. That's when the story about process really took hold. At the beginning of the show, I tell the story of Annabelle Selldorf.

BLVR: You know, I live in Columbus, Ohio, and I saw your show at the Wexner Center for the Arts in 2012. I've never forgotten that wall, with the bulletin boards and all the little prints, which I assume was meant to mirror your studio wall. In my mind, it was made up of all those shitty printouts, which I loved.

AL: Xerox-machine prints, yeah. It was the best part of the show, that wall. And I return to that wall repeatedly for ideas.

BLVR: That is interesting that it was also your favorite part of the exhibition. I felt that piece was a super generous way to share your work with an audience. To allow us access to process. We're able to step in and maneuver between the pictures.

AL: That's what I admire about your work—what you've done, you know, like the way you let the photos be there together. I really like what you're doing; I think it's a great way to work.

BLVR: That is very kind. Maybe that is a good place to end—on generative process, and on the space between pictures. Or rather, the way they relate to each other.

AL: That sounds good. I am sorry there was so much rescheduling in making this happen. I know you have two young kids, and I was worried about how that might affect you. By the way, you look exhausted.

BLVR: You sound like my Jewish grandmother! She used to say that to me as a greeting.

AL: Yes, it's a Red Badge of Courage. ✶

THE REALITY OF OUR SEEING

by

HILTON ALS

An epistolary essay on the terrains and fields of color in the work of painter Lynette Yiadom-Boakye

Dearest friend of my youth,

I've wrestled with, and then worried about, the form this piece should take for some time now, for days and weeks, really, because on some level I wanted to write to you out of the same kind of immediacy, not to say intimacy, that Lynette's images engender in me, and to get at that immediacy—the feeling of one voice addressing another—I finally settled on the epistolary form, just as Lynette's paintings can be viewed as letters sent from that currently under-explored land we might as well call the imagination, letters and thoughts from the depths of Lynette's imagination and strong hand, depicting figures some-times standing still and sometimes sit-ting upright in landscapes, terrains, and fields of color that are germane to Lynette's style, a style that, before you know it, floods your mind with her characters, let's call them that, who inhabit scenes where "nothing" hap-pens but the experience of being, and then there you are again, standing a bit away from the canvas, looking further at what Lynette has wrought, in, say, green unused areas—areas not filled with a vase or bed or person; patches of color that are "just" color—and just as suddenly, it seems, there is the green of your mind planting ideas and feelings about what Lynette has described with-out words but using a different kind of language, a language of brush and scale and colors the world has known before but not seen.

Looking at Lynette's exceptional new work in London recently, at the Corvi-Mora gallery in a show titled *A Mind for Moonlight*, I was with you, my friend, even though you weren't physically there, because I knew at once that you would exult in what Lynette has described as her lack of interest in and refusal to paint victims, an ethos that contributes to these new works painted on linen that breathes. As I stood in that gallery, with the pearly gray London light edging its way in, my vision, my mind, was transmogri-fied by the experience of looking, the intimate exchange between the thing seen, observed, and the thing itself. But I didn't know how to write to you about that moment, and how the world in Lynette's characters' heads filled my mind and made a world, too. What lan-guage could I use to describe what I saw at Corvi-Mora that afternoon. The eyes that illuminated the world inside a sub-ject's head, and then mine? This is an age-old problem that language never helps solve, ever, the problem of con-veying in one medium what it means to experience another. Because, essen-tially, those moments that change us, the long and short glances as we take in paint, for example, or a photograph, or words that become paragraphs and paragraphs that become thoughts and then a story, are inexpressible moments that we convince ourselves we can express through language, but that's just a trick of the mind, a kind of guise. By the guise of language I mean our propensity to adopt a role, a particular tone, when we talk about those paint-ings, those photographs, those words that moved us in the first place. I sup-pose one could call that tone author-itative, for want of a better word, but I would be a completely unreliable nar-rator if I started to imitate here or any-where, really, the language I learned in academia, or learned to imitate while a college student in the 1980s, when the goal was to be Rosalind Krauss, or Barthes, or someone other than your-self, certainly in terms of voice, a time when fracture—forced humanism—was essential in conveying the life of the text or the death of the author, I could never determine which as I read those various texts, an admixture of the per-sonal and knowingness, resulting in an unimpeachable intellectual and thus moral rectitude that wasn't so far removed from all those men Krauss, Barthes, and others had studied with to begin with, guys who didn't deal in the equivocal, saying painting was thus, a sculpture meant this, writing could be only that. What interests me here, writing about this today, with the memory of those Lynettes in London, is the failure of language, my language specifically, and how that failure marks the return of a kind of pleasure that was wrapped up in you, once, long ago, when we sat on hills, on green wet grass telling each other the story of color. The failure of language—my language—began in Harlem when I first saw Lynette's work. That was in 2010. Even then, I thought I would write to you indirectly, that is, in the voice of a critic, an academic wander-ing the halls of his own intellection, losing more and more contact with the feeling the images engendered, but I stopped myself then and I stop myself now, dearest friend of my youth, because that was not my voice, nor the voice Lynette's paintings engendered in me, work that would fill your mind with interest, too, and I thought of you when I first saw them, that would be in 2010, years ago now, when the world

Opening art by Kristian Hammerstad; images throughout courtesy of Lynette Yiadom-Boakye; Corvi-Mora, London; and Jack Shainman Gallery, New York

The Black Agronomical. © 2019 by Lynette Yiadom-Boakye. Oil on canvas. 98.4 × 78.7 in.

and I can't help but see in the spaces of these canvases, executed recently, a different kind of space, an isolation that goes inward more, and connects with others less, and this might not be what she intended at all but that is the artist's job: to give us something of their intention while not minding the beautiful intangibility and concrete need to connect that we bring to the work, a need and intangibility that are part of the experience of looking and that are not unlike the love we thread throughout letters, hoping to be heard.

When I first saw Lynette's work, I thought of you, and even though I hadn't seen you in a number of years by then—this was in 2010, as I have said—that experience was filled with you, and the stories you used to tell me about color, and how color has been used. Such a pleasant memory: us on the green, our backs turned to the fray below—mothers struggling sometimes happily, sometimes unhappily with their tired after-school children, messengers on frantic errands, office workers killing minutes, hours with a smoke or Diet Coke—as we talked about color sitting in our color: various strokes of brown and red that looked as realistic as the colored men in Lynette's paintings where blackness is not a solid, as it is, for instance, in Kerry James Marshall's paintings, but a color that changes with the light, with perception, as it does in life. We had two books, dear to us both, and for different reasons: Goethe's *Theory of Colours*, first published in English in 1840, and Ludwig Wittgenstein's *Remarks on Colour*, written 110 years later. What interested us: men of genius without color on their body writing about color, and

had yet to experience, at least consciously, what it's gotten itself into now, years before the British-born Lynette and my American self had ever considered let alone known that once again Empire would be linked to the Americas because of the madness of certain men, men who were born of this planet but who are not of it, smashing against the idea of humane behavior let alone intellection, treating them when they consider them at all as tiresome anachronisms, much more interesting to catalog and push out and define difference, catalog it and box it up on ships filled with the dispossessed swimming with hope in small crafts that invariably smash on the rocks in sight of liberty. I look at Lynette's recent paintings now, in light of life's current atrocities,

what did they make of that? Each of them taught us a way for color to be a freeing agent, not a prison. For Goethe, black was not a color, he didn't know everything, while Wittgenstein proposed certain things we loved to contemplate, jokes to play on the eyes, and how the eyes preconceive before looking. Wittgenstein asked, for instance, What if all traffic lights were brown? What if there was a tribe of color-blind people, how would we teach them what color was? For Wittgenstein, color was a story, and a way of unlearning what we thought we knew, such as racism having a color. To wit:

> We speak of a "black mirror." But where it mirrors, it darkens, of course, but it doesn't look black, and that which is seen in it does not appear "dirty" but "deep."

The dirtiness of black, of brown. A common assumption, one that is not above being rubbed out, killed, thought of as wrong. Indeed, we have heard of college students being arrested for reading while black. We have heard of a young man in Detroit being arrested for trying to garden while black. Colors can make for incomprehension, or sense, or violence. Wittgenstein could have been in North Carolina or Memphis or Staten Island looking at colored bodies when he wrote: "There is no such thing as phenomenology, but there are indeed phenomenological problems." The problem of color; it comes back to us again and again. As a young man, the writer James Baldwin was mentored by the painter Beauford Delaney, with whom he had a profound experience:

turning black from dirty to deep right before his very eyes. Baldwin wrote:

> Beauford and I would walk together through the streets of New York City.... the reality of his seeing caused me to begin to see... What I saw, first of all, was a brown leaf on black asphalt, oil moving like mercury in the black water of the gutter, grass pushing itself up through a crevice in the sidewalk. And because I was seeing it with Beauford, because Beauford caused me to see it, the very colors underwent a most disturbing and salutary change. The brown leaf on the black asphalt, for example—what colors were these, really?... And though black had been described to me as the absence of light, it became very clear to me that if this were true, we would never have been able to see the color, black: the light is trapped in it and struggles upward, rather like that grass pushing upward through the cement.

Looking at Lynette's paintings was like looking at that grass and that blackness struggling upward, and every stroke and positioning of her subjects resembled line after line of consciousness, lines of consciousness that stuck to my brow like letters in a letter, like stuck snow that melts and becomes another substance altogether, one that helps to grow the mind in a different way, like something watered, something beautiful, like a flower, Lynette's flowers.

And it's funny, my lovely, long-lost friend, to write Dear and Love to you

as a greeting or a salutation respectively, because we never used terms of endearment as a kind of show; they were in our hearts, always, but since we are far away from each other now, we must rely on form—distance drives us to these things—so let's just say Dear and Love for now as a way of shaping this letter you are in every line of, and as a way of giving a shape to a form that Virginia Woolf used so brilliantly in various ways, none more spectacularly than in her 1938 book-length letter about war, *Three Guineas*. But, of course, in my rush to share Lynette's work with you, I see, now, that I've neglected one of the basic tenets of letter writing, certainly in a public space, which is to tell the audience who *you* are. In *Three Guineas*, Virginia Woolf writes:

> In the first place let us draw what all letter-writers instinctively draw, a sketch of the person to whom the letter is addressed. Without someone warm and breathing on the other side of the page, letters are worthless.

Virginia was no stranger to drama, but in this case I don't mind her slight hyperbole, or really disagree with her adjective-heavy belief that what we recall in a letter implicitly is a portrait of the recipient too. If that's the case, think of this letter as a kind of self-portrait addressed to two recipients: you, a friend of my youth, and the artist Lynette Yiadom-Boakye. While much separates you from each other—you are a photographer and male and American, for starters—what unites you is much stronger than any of the superficial categories we are supposed to define one another by. What you share is a fierce commitment to invention culled out of the real, or the imagination fortified by the exigencies of truth, the discipline it takes to give dreams form, just as letters give forms to longing and observation.

A few facts: You were raised in Europe, and Lynette is a Londoner. She was born there in 1977. Her parents are from Ghana, and in the UK they worked as nurses for the National Health Service. In a 2015 interview, Lynette describes her parents as practical, "That's why they're wonderful." Every child wants to know and feel that the world their parents make for them is secure and reliable, and one can feel this steadiness in Lynette's work: What's more important than the world your parents make for you and that you then make for yourself?

An inveterate reader as a child, Lynette did not consider becoming a visual artist until her final year of high school; her first year of college was at Central Saint Martins, where she completed a foundation course, before finishing her undergraduate studies at Falmouth School of Art, in Cornwall, an experience that, says Lynette, gave her "the space to think" outside of London's busy artistic hub. In 2003, Lynette was awarded an MFA from the Royal Academy Schools, and it was during that time that the painter began to hone her style and ethos. For the most part she wanted to create a universe where black people could live in the everyday without being considered symbols of pain, suffering, or triumph, but, rather, as human beings subject to the exigencies of life. To that end, Lynette stripped her work of complicated narratives in favor of what the body could and did express in stillness, or in action, while simultaneously expressing the artist's deep interest in and commitment to color and form as they make up the world of the canvas. In short, Lynette is not blind to the question let alone to the reality of identity. And yet Lynette has done something profound with her work vis-à-vis the whole notion of categorizing—of bodies being "known" because of biography—by usurping the whole notion of portraiture, or the traditional notion of portraiture, wherein the artist marries an existing, preferably known face to the artist's sensibility. Instead, in her work, Lynette marries her sensibility—her love of color, for one—to bodies that wouldn't exist without her. The backstory in her imagined portraits is Lynette's mind, and what the paintings reveal about her mind.

But back to 2010. By then, I had not seen you, dear friend of my youth, for a number of years. Great sadnesses plagued you: one sadness being your inability to connect your work with a larger audience, and a sadness about love, and a sadness, too, about the ways in which the world treated your colored male self in all its difference that never felt different to me, or to you: you were always yourself to me, lovesick for love. It was 2010, a soft late winter afternoon, when I first saw Lynette's pictures. This was at the Studio Museum in Harlem. Curated by Naomi Beckwith, the exhibition was titled *Any Number of Preoccupations*, and the paintings preoccupied me at once, and rendered me silent, and were redolent of so many things, including Goethe's remarks on color. As a writer and an artist, Goethe was given to the fact of a thing and its interpretive value; a leaf was a leaf, and one's relationship to that leaf falling, falling to the ground, was of supreme interest: What did our minds see and our eyes invent when that foliage changed your perception of your inner life, and your hazy grasp of the so-called real world? Goethe's treatise on natural phenomena is worth having a look at, certainly, but his 1797 poem, also called "The Metamorphosis of Plants," reminds me of what the mind looks like, looking at Lynette:

> Thou art confused, my beloved, at,
>   seeing the thousandfold union
>
> Shown in this flowery troop, over
>   the garden dispers'd;
> any a name dost thou hear assign'd;
>   one after another
>
> Falls on thy list'ning ear, with a
>   barbarian sound.
> None resembleth another, yet all
>   their forms have a likeness;
>
> Therefore, a mystical law is by the
>   chorus proclaim'd;
> Yes, a sacred enigma! Oh, dearest
>   friend, could I only
>
> Happily teach thee the word, which
>   may the mystery solve!
> Closely observe how the plant, by
>   little and little progressing...

Looking at Lynette's paintings that afternoon in Harlem was a kind of progression. *Any Number of Preoccupations* was Lynette's first museum show in the US. (Two years before, she'd had a piece in the historic *Flow* exhibition curated by the museum's former associate curator

Prospect West of a Necromancer. © 2019 by Lynette Yiadom-Boakye. Oil on linen. 78.7 × 98.4 in.

Christine Kim.) In the Beckwith show, there were twenty-four paintings on view, ranging in size, ranging in the number of people the artist filled the canvas with, a range of colors and shapes that lifted me up spiritually while flooding me with giddiness in the way that pure, unadulterated joy can fill the body and make it something else, a receptacle of joy that wants to spill out into the world with its happy news without proclaiming itself just as Lynette does not proclaim herself—her autobiography—so directly in the paintings, which are metaphors about being in the way that actors are metaphors for real people. Despite the gorgeous flourishes in Lynette's work, there is restraint. Her people hold back, and peek out from the self-protective distance, saying: This is me, and then there's you, but how much of you do you share with me, a painting? Shall we call this interest in restraint part of her British character, or is it more a depiction of what the great Flannery O'Connor said when she observed, "The uneducated Southern Negro is not the clown he is made out to be. He's a man of very elaborate manners and great formality which he uses superbly for his own protection and to insure his own privacy," or is the elegance of holding back one sees in Lynette's work part of a particular ethos, one described by Marianne Moore when she wrote, "The deepest feeling always shows itself in silence; / not in silence, but restraint"—an ethos that affects the British artists Lynette now influences, ranging from painters to fashion designers like Grace Wales Bonner.

Dear friend, I thought of you, and our laughing together out of unrestrained joy and relief, when I saw Lynette's paintings for the first time, because here, in Lynette's paintings, was something we had longed for, talked about, and rarely seen: a distinctly colored world not defined by the standard narrative of the long gone guy, and the put-upon woman; a world, in fact, in which colored-ness was "just" a statement of fact, along with the rooms, mauves, reds, blues, spatial considerations, and so on, that made the painting. The release I felt looking at Lynette's work that afternoon— and on subsequent days and weeks and now years—can best be characterized as being released from race as a neurosis in art, an infirmity so insidious that one doesn't realize that one is reacting out of its various impulses—guilt, social responsibility, an earnest desire to understand more about the "other"—until it's too late, and you've seen nothing at all, not the painting or book or poem under review, because all you've been privy to or trained to see is your liberal imagination, that which takes a long view close-up of the so-called colored problem that is, after all, one narrative, right?

The colored problem has a body, and lives in so much despair. He or she or they grew up haunted by its ghetto past, and is prone to violence, not love.

I remember once talking to a woman I've known for a long time, and we were discussing something as harmless as school lunches—she was complaining about her daughter complaining about the food that was offered in her private school—and I said, "I don't remember having school lunches." And the woman—you don't need to know her race; in any case, it's fun, sometimes, to guess—the woman said, "That's because you were deprived." Of course, what I meant—what I knew, and remembered with love—was the fact that my mother always sent me to school with my own lunch. She didn't think school lunches were particularly nourishing, and by filling a brown paper bag with her food, my mother was offering me the discipline of care: she was thinking about me as she sliced the bread and wrapped the fruit, and I was thinking about her as I tore into the brown paper bag at noon, happy for her smell, and the taste of her care. But the woman I was talking to didn't consider that narrative, or even imagine it was possible. Her liberal thinking had colored her mind in ways that precluded love. I was black and poor and therefore deprived. The story of love was not part of that. My story aside, there was another story, or various stories, that I saw in Lynette's paintings at the Studio Museum that long-ago afternoon; the work was love staring me in the face; it was blackness not shaped by trauma or resistance to the general complications that come with being human, no one was maimed by their race, a misshaping that the world, let alone the world of culture,

has always associated with depth; it was the history of Western painting made into Lynette's painting, which confused a number of critics who put their liberal imagination before seeing, and who certainly didn't see what I saw that long-ago afternoon at the Studio Museum in Harlem: a woman of color making a world out of what the world had given her. In a review of the Studio Museum in Harlem show, Karen Rosenberg wrote:

> The man in the red robe looks familiar. It takes a minute to place some of the details—ah, yes, that louche cover-up, cocked elbow and rakish eye belong to Sargent's Dr. Samuel Jean Pozzi. But this stranger doesn't have a beard, and he sits rather than stands. At some point— it's hard to say exactly when—you realize that he is also black.

Huh. Shall we describe Rosenberg's claim as a kind of critical trauma, the weirdness that infects the liberal imagination when one feels one's liberalism— one's education—under attack because artists like Lynette defy certain expectations that are germane to connoisseurship, and because she manages to do this by jettisoning the very notion of what significance means to you: her bodies are not significant to others in the world, most likely, but they are significant to her and thus to the viewer, in the way black maleness was important to Toni Morrison, who said that when she was coming up she was confused and not a little annoyed by titles like *Invisible Man* and *Nobody Knows My Name*: she knew those guys' names, they weren't invisible to her. And that's what I felt, dear friend of my youth, looking at those figures

After Every Word. © 2019 by Lynette Yiadom-Boakye. Oil on linen. 51.1 × 62.9 in.

in Harlem: that Lynette had seen joy in guys like you and put the joy forward through the skein of her imagination.

I didn't think about Whistler the first time I saw Lynette's painting, but of course she loves Whistler, and of course there's Cézanne, too, but isn't every artist the product of an amazing amount of alchemy and isn't the development of their vision through those various influences part of the job? To discipline what they see and feel and make it theirs? Why should Europe be any less of an influence than Africa, or more specifically why should the African seen in European art be any less of an influence on black female sensibility? Does Europe own red—the red these figures were, a color one associates with the blood of conquest, of richness, Charlemagne in his red boots—does red belong to Europe more than it belongs to Lynette?

Just recently I was in London and I met a curator who talked to me about Cézanne, and a painting I didn't know very well, or remember very well: Cézanne's *Le Nègre Scipion* from 1867. In it, a young man sits with his back to the painter, his right arm tensed as it holds up a great deal of the young man's now weary strength. His form leans against another shape—an oval shape—thus calling attention to the length of his body, his arm, and the tension that exists between a fixed object (the oval or wall of the painting, so to speak) and that which can change in an instant: the human body. I'm sending you this image, dear friend of my youth, for a number of reasons, the primary one being to show (again) what we've always known: how the body's distortions become a kind of fashion, and whether you're looking at Manet's portrait of Jeanne Duval, or other pieces, distortion of spiritual form, of that black body's intent, occurs because Cézanne, Manet, and others put race before the art, thinking that's all they needed, that that different color made a canvas. In the process, they left out what Lynette put back: the human. No one is just skin. Every one of us is a story written in blood standing between this world and the next.

Lynette's paintings also drove a wedge between the black past and the human present. Her painting is a radical turning away from the ideology found in the precepts laid down during the Black Arts Movement. Founded in 1965 by Imamu Baraka (LeRoi Jones), the movement was established in reaction to Malcolm X's assassination. The bloody years. Martin, Medgar, Malcolm. And now the bloody years. Grenfell, Charleston, Lexington, Virginia. Back in the day, Baraka wanted to help create a cultural world that promoted revolution, and that told black stories to black audiences, a universe of blackness. During those years, I remember going to the East, a black cultural center in Brooklyn, with my older sister. I was a child. There, we heard music and watched plays, looked at paintings, and heard readings. And what struck me, aside from all the youthful enthusiasm in that rickety, beautiful building, was how much time was spent talking about white people. If they weren't so important to us, why did they take up so much of our time. Why was whiteness treated as the dominant power, if not the only power? So many artists of color are still there. They believe their work is a form of resistance, but what they're really showing, playing into, articulating, is how important whiteness is to them. And it's a power that the liberal imagination recognizes as such. In his brilliant essay "Within the Context of No-Context," George W. S. Trow writes:

The Decline of Adulthood: During the nineteen-sixties, a young black man in a university class described the Dutch painters of the seventeenth century as "belonging" to the white students in the room, and not to him. This idea was seized on by white members of the class. They acknowledged that they were at one with Rembrandt. They acknowledged their dominance. They offered to discuss, at any length, their inherited power to oppress. It was thought at the time that reactions of this type had to do with "white guilt" or "white masochism." No. No. It was white *euphoria*. Many, many white children of that day felt the power of their inheritance for the first time in the act of rejecting it, and they insisted on rejecting it and rejecting it and rejecting it, so that they might continue to feel the power of that connection.

In Lynette's work, the power of the connection is with you and the figures in the work and you and you again. There is spiritual uplift and glorious ordinariness. Her figures' skin is the most natural fancy dress in the world, on a par with these words, written by the Caribbean American author Jamaica Kincaid in her short story "Blackness":

The blackness is visible and yet it is invisible, for I see that I cannot see it. The blackness fills up a small room, a large field, an island, my own being.... The blackness cannot be separated from me but often I can stand outside of it. The blackness is not the air, though I breathe it. The blackness is not the earth, though I drink and eat it.... The blackness is not my blood, though it flows through my veins... In the blackness my voice is silent. First, then, I have been my individual self... then I am swallowed up in the blackness so that I am one with it...

What Lynette showed me is what our friendship has shown me, dear friend, despite your being away, I send her images to your mind, I know through love that you receive them: that even in separation, in not being the subject of her painting, we are all one with it because of the joy to be found in our actual or metaphorical blackness, that which we wear—as members of the same life dance with beloved friends we no longer get to see—a dance that goes round and round and round.

Your friend,
Hilton ✶

MARTINE SYMS

[ARTIST]

"THAT'S WHAT I LIKE ABOUT FILM: IT BENDS TIME AND SPACE."

Words and phrases Martine Syms has been using recently:
Manifest
Align
New age
Starfucker
Channeling

Imet Martine Syms at a microscopic art gallery in Los Angeles's Chinatown in 2012. We'd both been invited to give presentations to an audience so small we were essentially performing for each other, and although I can't remember what either of our talks was about, Martine's slides had a deep purple background—her signature color—and featured an elegant font I'd never seen before (a year later, the font, Lydian, was everywhere). At the time, she was calling herself "a conceptual entrepreneur." Thinking about it now, I'm not sure if she meant she was an entrepreneur only conceptually, or that she sold ideas. Both might have been true, but neither quite encompasses the artist she was then, and has since become.

Martine was born in Altadena, California, in 1988. She was homeschooled off and on by her parents and spent her teen years in Los Angeles's DIY art and music scene, volunteering at all-ages punk venues and experimental cinemas and shilling zines before going to the School of the Art Institute of Chicago. After graduating, she ran a speakeasy project space called Golden Age there for five years. When

Illustration by Kristian Hammerstad; images throughout courtesy of Martine Syms; Sadie Coles HQ, London; and Bridget Donahue, New York

she came back to LA, she founded Dominica Publishing, dedicated to exploring Blackness in visual culture. In 2017, she had her first solo show at MoMA; she was barely thirty. Since then, it's been a whirlwind: solo shows at the Art Institute of Chicago, the Philadelphia Museum of Art, and the Institute of Contemporary Arts in London; a Creative Capital Award, a Tiffany Foundation Biennial Competition Award, a Future Generation Art Prize, and a Guggenheim Fellowship; teaching at CalArts and earning an MFA from Bard College; commercial work for high-end fashion houses; and, in 2022, her feature directorial debut, The African Desperate, a witty, scathing, formally audacious send-up of art-school delusions.

In her work, Martine moves through mediums and ideas like a freeway moves through neighborhoods. That is to say, directly, easily, without much regard for the old world. For a long time, she had a show on NTS Radio called Ccartalk LA, on which she interviewed people as they drove though the city together. In Los Angeles, car routes are currency, and how you drive, she figured, reflects who you are. Martine drives a black two-seat convertible with a vanity license plate; on the road, as in her work, it's very clear who is behind the wheel. She draws heavily from her own life, merging selfie videos, personal notes, and clothing in nonlinear, stylish installations. She has a facility with both archival and new media, easily mixing virtual avatars, machine-learning-driven conversational bots, and augmented-reality overlays with home movies and amateur photography culled from personal and institutional archives.

This formal boundlessness has always reflected a cinematic vision—the product, perhaps, of growing up in a city where any place can become a location, and can cross the boundary between reality and fantasy. In the last few years, however, Martine has made that vision more explicit. Although she's created lots of video work and even a feature-length film, Incense, Sweaters and Ice (2017), intended for gallery exhibition, The African Desperate is her first movie for theaters. In the film, cowritten with poet Rocket Caleshu, she mines her own grad-school memories to satirize art education in America, which operates under a false premise of equality, which, as she told Artnet in 2022, "every single person knows [is] bullshit."

In the film, Martine's friend and longtime collaborator Diamond Stingily stars as Palace Bryant, a Black artist on the final day of her MFA program at an Upstate New York art school (the film was shot, mostly, at Bard College). The opening scene, of a loaded and cringey critique session with Palace's thesis advisers, sets the tone, and the film pulls no punches about just how exasperating the creative class can be. But like everything else Martine makes, it leaves open the possibility of transcendence. The African Desperate takes place over the course of a single long day, a convention that reflects Martine's fascination with time, which she has called her medium. If she's managed to make so much with the time she's had, it's because Martine knows something that nobody else does: that time isn't real.

—Claire L. Evans

I. "DOES THE PROCESS KNOW I'M TRUSTING IT?"

THE BELIEVER: You're big on cycles. You work harder than anyone I know, and then you have these periods of release afterward. Where are you in the cycle now?

MARTINE SYMS: Where am I in the cycle? I'm working on much larger projects than I ever have. And I'm not used to this kind of timescale, where I'm spending nine, ten months on just one part of something—there's gonna be much, much more to come. I think I have to figure out how to take breaks. I like to work in bursts, but it's just not possible on a project that's going to take me three years. I would die.

BLVR: Working on something you know is not going to see the light of day for that long, you have to have a speculative mindset. What is the world going to be like in three years?

MS: I'm having a hard time with it, honestly.

BLVR: Think about how much has happened in the past three years.

MS: Yeah. But creatively, I have to have periods when I'm just taking stuff in, because otherwise I'd get really stale. I have to sit with things. I used to work for the photographer Barbara Kasten. I was really young, and she was in her seventies. At that time, everybody my age was like: You make something, you put it on the internet immediately. I remember being very enamored by the way she would shoot something, put it up in her studio, and look at it for a while. And I'd be like, "Oh, is that one going in

Martine Syms's installation at the 2019 Whitney Biennial. Photograph by Gregory Carideo.

the show?" And she'd say, "No, I'm still thinking about it." [The artist and filmmaker] Lynn Hershman Leeson said to me once that after she had a kid, as a single parent, certain things just took longer than she wanted them to take. But she accepted it at a certain point, because she felt like time made everything better. I don't think time necessarily makes *everything* better, but I know what she means: you come back to something and you're like, This part of it was cool. What I'm writing right now, I started writing last year. I've come back to a lot of stuff I wrote last year that I thought was shit at the time. And it probably was, but now it's been recontextualized and I'm like, Oh, actually, the idea *was* there.

BLVR: When you start something new, do you have a sense of the shape you want it to take?

MS: For a long time, I would have a very, very, very clear idea of what I wanted to make and what I was trying to achieve. A couple years ago, that stopped being that interesting to me, and it just became more fun to go in blind, even with shows. The show I did last summer [*Loser Back Home*] at [the Los Angeles art gallery] Sprüth Magers, I was like: I don't know what this thing is going to be. I'm just going to let it become something. Certain things you have to plan, because there are other people involved. But to a degree, the unknowns are fun for me. Honestly, in art, I love an unknown; it's great. That's the whole point to me: I don't know what it's gonna look like, I don't know what it's gonna be, I just have this weird idea in my head: let's see where it takes me.

BLVR: I think about this with writing books—you can't let yourself imagine the cover or where it will sit, on which shelf.

Martine Syms's installation at the 2019 Whitney Biennial. Photograph by Gregory Carideo.

Because if you start thinking that way, it constrains you so much. Later, there's a transition that has to happen between "the document," which you and I talk about a lot, and the final form, which other people consume.

MS: Do you show people your doc, ever?

BLVR: My doc has never been messier. I'm trying to trust the process, but it is hard sometimes.

MS: Yeah, that's been one of my mantras this year, even though at times I'm like, Does the process know I'm trusting it? I'm trusting it *so* hard.

BLVR: When there's only one set of footsteps in the sand, that's when the process is trusting you. I always come away from hanging out with you with a new sense of what's possible. I feel like I can do anything, because you're so in control of what you do, and you really make things happen. I wouldn't call it manifesting, because that makes it sound like there's no effort involved. In your artist bio, you use the word *grit*.[1]

MS: I didn't write that, but yes. I use it. I identify with it, I suppose.

BLVR: You're really good at seeing things through.

MS: It's hard for me not to talk about astrology with regard to this. But you know I am a Taurus, and I'm a Capricorn moon, two signs that are like, *We're just gonna stick with this. We're just gonna climb this mountain.* Better be the *right* mountain, because we're not getting off it. I don't mind the word *manifest*. One of my friends says *align*, which I've also adopted. I'm aligning with the thing that I want. It's already there. I've already done it—I'm just aligning with it. And I get excited about projects too. That's what's hard about this long project: I'm finding myself losing enthusiasm for it. This acting teacher I once had, she was like, "I don't require myself to be excited." Take excitement off the table. If you decide you're going to do something, you're going to do it. You don't have to be inspired, and you don't have to be excited, and some days it's going to suck, but if you just take that requirement off the table, then you can show up and do it. And that's my thing with writing. At a certain point you just have to sit your ass down.

I've been describing myself as a "descending" kind of writer. I'm putting so much material in, and all the ideas are in that first draft. Some stuff works, some stuff doesn't, but it's gonna be too much, and I'm going to whittle it down. Whereas in screenwriting, there are some people who build it up. I don't think one's better than the other—ascending is maybe more efficient.

BLVR: Efficiency is totally overrated. You get to where you get to, however you get there.

---

1. On her website, Martine's bio reads: "Martine Syms is an artist who has earned wide recognition for a practice that combines conceptual grit, humor, and social commentary."

MS: Did I need to write those pages? No, but I did, and they'll find their way.

II. NO CLOCKS, NO SUBSCRIPTIONS

BLVR: You were talking about alignment before. I've been getting served all these Instagram videos for "timeline jumping." Do you know about this? It's people who genuinely believe they are somehow mentally moving from one timeline to another.

MS: I use that phrase a lot, but I don't know if I actually believe I'm jumping timelines. But I like the idea of it, in a sci-fi way.

BLVR: It feels right for you. You've talked about how when you were making *The African Desperate*, your crew "opened up portals" to get the film done.

MS: The quantum is very, very important to me. People are always like, *How did you do all those things in the same period of time?* I don't know, but I could show you—all the clocks in my house are covered. In any city I'm in, I like to go to the metaphysical bookstore, because you just find cool shit, or maybe meet some weird people. Before we started shooting *The African Desperate*, I bought this book called *Waking Up in 5D* because I liked the cover. When I first tried to read it, it made absolutely no sense to me—it was literal gibberish. We shot the film, we did all this other stuff, and maybe a month later I was back home, I saw the book and picked it up. Suddenly it all made *perfect* sense to me. I'm not even kidding. I know that sounds weird. It felt like I was reading a different book that was written for me in that exact moment.

It had all this stuff in it about time, which sometimes I refer to as my medium—that's what I'm playing with. That's what I like about film: it bends time and space. You can put things next to one another; you can make it seem like something happened in between. You can compress time, you can extend it. There's a very phenomenological aspect to it. But then also, when you're making films, weird things happen. What was that movie, *Roma*? Alfonso Cuarón recreated his childhood. You know how trippy that probably was for him? *He went back in time.*

But anyway, in this book, they talk about compressing time, or having a quantum experience with time. I used to get *The New York Times* every day. This book was like, *Cancel your subscriptions, cover the clock on your stove so you're not constantly being reminded of what "time" it is.* Like how I put that in quotes? And say you have to drive somewhere and you don't have enough time. You just say to yourself, I do. I'm going to make it. And honestly, that has opened up something for me.

BLVR: A more fluid way of existing in the world.

MS: Yeah, because I am very time-conscious. I'm clocking, counting basically all the time—so it was very freeing for me. I try to think about it as, like: There is no time. Even when I'm late on a project, and I have that feeling—I have that feeling all the time: I'm late! I had a dream the other night that I was supposed to do this whole project, and I just forgot about it. I'm always having a dream where I'm late for a flight. But now I'm just like: There's no time, so I can't be late.

BLVR: That's a great phrase, "There's no time." There's no time, as in "I'm in a hurry." But also there's no time, as in there is none. Part of the reason I stopped going to my weekly chess club was because it made time go faster. It was always Sunday again, Sunday again.

MS: When I was living upstate, the days would be so long. I would feel like, OK, I'm gonna do nothing today. By 1 p.m., I'm like, it's only *1*? Jesus. I'm going to the studio. I got up, I got groceries, I swam, I went for a hike, I read a book, and it's still only 1 p.m.?

BLVR: Your installation work is nonlinear. Videos overlap, audio bleeds, you create these architectures that allow viewers to pass between the works in different ways. How does that square with feature film for you? Are there ways in which you're trying to expand the shape of what a movie can be?

MS: Obviously, the experience of it—you go to the movie, you sit down, there's a beginning and an end, you get up, you leave—you can't get away from that part. But I think within the story itself, or the storytelling, there's a lot you can do. I'm sort of anti-continuity. I'm talking about the idea of continuity in film, where you're shooting and you're told you

Stills from The African Desperate, *2021.*

should get a lot of coverage—coverage being all the different angles, so when you're editing you can cut to this person, then to this person, and it all feels "continuous." I don't care about that. I'm not interested in that convention. In some cases I use it. It's not like I don't use it at all. But ideologically, I feel like it's oppressive, and it makes for one way of seeing, because the way these things get presented is how people start to frame their own experiences.

The other day I was listening to music, fake DJing in my house. It's really fun to me to put very different styles of music next to each other and find what's continuous between them. Whether it's the BPM, or the key they're being played in, or an instrument, or words, the lyrics, I like finding a connection between them that's not a genre. That's the way I edit, in general. One time I was DJing at this party, and this girl was like, "Oh, you just put anything next to anything else?"

She was kind of saying it shady, but I was like, "Yeah, look, everybody's dancing." It works; you just gotta listen to it in a different way. I feel like that's the whole beauty of editing. You literally can put any two things next to each other and you just have to figure out the way they connect. I like thinking about the cut in film as a kiss. It brings things together.

III. A NEW AGE FILMMAKER

BLVR: I just saw the writer Akil Kumarasamy give a talk, and she was saying she writes novels as though she were making a film, in the sense that there's a finite budget for locations. I thought you'd like that—treating one medium as though you're working in the conventions of another. It creates new constraints. Because fiction is so infinite, right?

MS: Fiction could be, but film's so not. People treat film like it's the same medium it was a hundred years ago. We haven't gotten very far past that. Honestly—*The Birth of a Nation*, supposedly the first Hollywood-style film? We're still making the same kind of film. In music, there've been so many styles.

BLVR: As a viewer, I love to find continuity errors in films. Part of that is a "gotcha" thing—like, Oh, they fucked this up. But part of it is also being excited about seeing the seams, seeing the materiality. You get a glimpse into what it must be like to actually make a film and how many moving pieces there are.

MS: I like that "gotcha" thing. I also like recognizing locations.

BLVR: That's so LA of you.

MS: Yeah, exactly. When I was growing up, one of my sister's friends' house was the exterior of Brenda and Brandon's house on *90210*. That was the exterior of their house, and they always had tourists in front of it taking photos. Pasadena is used as a lot of different places in movies—like in *American Pie 2*, the city hall in Pasadena is supposed to be Spain. It's very funny when you're like, That's definitely not Spain— you see the seams. A film that does that in an incredible way is Zia Anger's movie *My First Film*.

BLVR: That's a movie about a movie that was made but never finished, right?

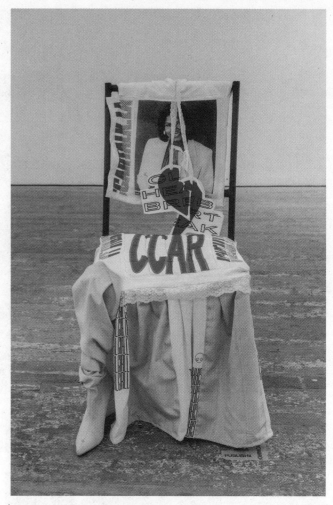

Bonnet Core. © 2021 by Martine Syms. Cotton, rhinestones, metal, paint, lace, polyester, thread. 39 ⅜ × 18 ⅛ × 25 ¾ in. Photograph by Gregory Carideo.

MS: Yeah, the original movie was an aborted project, and then, six years or something after the project was canceled, or didn't work out, Zia started doing a performance talking about it, and then *My First Film* is a fictionalized version of the performance.

BLVR: Are there any things in your own past that you'd want to revisit like that?

MS: I feel like *The African Desperate* was a revisiting in some ways, because I hadn't gone back to campus until I made that film. It was a funny way of re-creating things and revisiting memories. One of my friends I went to school with, I saw him sometime after he'd seen it, and he was like, "I felt like

Installation view of Boon *at Secession, Vienna, 2019. Photograph by Peter Mochi.*

you were in my memories." I've heard that from different people, which has kind of been fun. Capturing something true. Not exact, but true.

BLVR: Having other people say your words is a thrill, I'm sure. But having actors pantomime experiences you've drawn from your own life is like sublimating your memories through other people's bodies. What does that feel like?

MS: That's why I call it a portal. I don't know if you've ever heard of constellation work? I'm gonna call it "new age" because I've been trying to bring that phrase back.

BLVR: I didn't realize it left.

MS: Like "ambient music"—they don't say "new age music" anymore. People say, *Oh, that person's witchy*; they don't say, *They're new age.* I'm going back to *new age.* I've also been using the word *starfucker* again. We need to bring that back. *Clout-chaser* is so ugh.

Anyway, constellation work. I've done it as both the subject and the resonator [a stand-in for the subject's immediate family or ancestors]. If I'm the subject, I'm trying to work something out from my past. I tell the facilitator what it is. They don't tell the other people in the group. And then we open up "the field," which I'm very big on. Then I, as the subject, will start asking the other people, the resonators, questions. The facilitator will start to work with them, and then they act out the thing you're working through. Once

Installation view of Boon, *2019, at Secession in Vienna. Photograph by Peter Mochi.*

you open up the field, the resonators can *feel* it. It's so crazy. You're like, How did they know? The person who told me about it, Asher Hartman, is a playwright and an intuitive.

BLVR: So what you're saying is that you're a new age director.

MS: I feel like this idea of constellation work does apply to acting, because when you're working with actors, they're interpreting your words, but that's only one level of it. Something else is being accessed. They have *access* to something. That's why I love actors—it's also why they're kind of insane people: because they can access this whole range of emotions. The first time I started working with actors, I was like, Oh shit, this is a whole other level of the material. Sure, I wrote it, and there are things I'm thinking about, there's a subtext, blah, blah, but a good actor has so much more they can

bring to the words. They can bring out subtleties. I find it really incredible. I'm so into the collaboration of it. That is actually what got me into wanting to make features. I was always into it, and I've loved films since I was kid, but it wasn't my dream. I felt pretty confident that at some point I would make one, but I was very content in the work I was doing. When I started to work with actors, I was like, Oh, this is cool. It does feel like we're tapping into something. That's what is exciting to me—that and all the visual stuff you can do, obviously. I would love to be Christopher Nolan making some weird set that rotates. Doing some *Tenet* shit would be cool.

BLVR: Someday.

MS: Someday.

IV. "DON'T TRY TO ESCAPE YOUR TIME"

BLVR: How would you feel about working with other people's material? Writing an adaptation?

MS: It's a funny thing to adapt something, because in my art, obviously, there's text or things I've been referencing or thinking about, or, you know, I'm taking stuff from one medium and putting it into another, being like, *I read this book and there's this thing I was thinking about*. But that's such an abstract adaptation. It's not a true adaptation; it's just an inspiration—or an idea, or a trigger. Whereas actually *adapting* somebody else's words is more like channeling—that's gonna sound really new age. I guess that's where I'm at this morning. Some days a different me comes out: the craft me, the new age me, the business me. We're getting "deep channeler" today.

I think Charlie Kaufman's [film] *Adaptation* is one of the best adaptations ever made. Obviously it's not very faithful. But I was watching interviews with Susan Orlean about that film, and the craziest thing to her was that she *did* have stuff going on in her marriage when she was writing that book. She *was* having these other emotional things that she didn't think were present at all in the book, but that he brought up as top notes in the film. She was like, How? I was talking to another friend of mine who does a lot of adaptations—that's her specialty in screenwriting. And she was like, "Yeah, dude, you just gotta channel it." You read the book and then you have to put it away and be like, What is this *actually* about? Because there are things you can do in a novel that you can't really do in a movie, in terms of interiority. You have to visualize or make things present through interaction or dialogue—so you do have to channel it.

BLVR: I just assume you'd be good at adapting a novel, because you're always adapting your own life. You use yourself as source material so often in your work, culling from your Notes app, from your camera roll.

MS: Those are daily practices for me, but I'm actually taking a break. I used to carry a camera every day—from the time I was eleven or twelve until, like, two years ago. Recently, in the past week or two, I've been like, Just bring your camera again. If you've read *The Artist's Way*, there's a part where [the author, Julia Cameron] talks about the moment when you want to take a photo of something, but you're with people,

so you feel like, No, I'm not gonna do it, I'm being weird. So [in *The Artist's Way* twelve-week course] there's a week when you just do that thing: You hang behind so you can take the photo or jot down the note. I think that's something I started doing really young, but I got sort of annoyed with it in a way I'd never felt before, maybe because it started to feel like, I don't know—hip? *I, too, have my 35 mm camera and my old digital camera*. I started to feel very *Oh god* about having a camera on me all the time, which I'm trying to get through right now. So I've started carrying it again.

But, yeah, writing down my dreams, having a camera on me, taking photos, the Notes app, or a notebook, or a sketchbook—I'm just recording all this material, all the time. There was a long period when I very religiously journaled. I mean, I call it a diary. I really recorded my life. And there would be gaps when I wouldn't do it, but then sometime in 2021, my grandfather was like, "You forget stuff. You're gonna forget stuff. You don't think you are, but you're gonna forget all this. You're gonna forget all these people. You should just write

---

LOST ARTWORKS RECOVERED AT FLEA MARKETS

★ Pierre-Auguste Renoir's *Paysage bords de Seine*—found at a flea market in Harpers Ferry, West Virginia
★ Albrecht Dürer's *Mary Crowned by an Angel*—found at a flea market in Sarrebourg, France
★ Jon Corbino's *Palette*—found at a garage sale in Sarasota, Florida
★ Peter Carl Fabergé's Third Imperial Egg—found at a flea market somewhere in the Midwest
★ N. C. Wyeth's *Ramona*—found in a thrift store in New Hampshire
★ Ansel Adams's negatives—found at a garage sale in Fresno, California
★ First-century bust of Roman general Nero Claudius Drusus Germanicus—found at a Goodwill in Austin, Texas
★ Two panels of Willie Herrón's mural *Mi Vida y Sueños Locos*—found at an estate sale in Los Angeles

—list compiled by Hannah Langer

Steven or Act II. © 2023 by Martine Syms. Video, color, and sound in custom frame. Duration: 2 min., 52 sec. Frame: 51 ⅝ × 51 ⅝ × 12 ¼ in. Photograph by Katie Morrison.

Ate or Act III. © 2023 by Martin Syms. Video, color, and sound in custom frame. Duration: 4 min., 52 sec. Frame: 51 ⅝ × 51 ⅝ × 12 ¼ in. Photograph by Katie Morrison.

it down." He was like, "The stuff that I didn't write down, I truly don't remember." The OCD in me started to record everything that was happening. That stuff, though—I use it. I've used it in short stories, I've used it in films. I've used the dialogue, I've used so much. I do feel very attuned to people's speech patterns, the way they talk or write. I think that's something that's just a natural gift. It's something I paid attention to as a kid for no reason. I would repeat the way somebody said something, or I would hear a phrase from someone and think, Oh, I like the way that sounds. That's also why I'm into music. There's something about listening. I like to go somewhere and just hear what people are saying.

BLVR: You're so good at capturing things from life that are specific to your experience but also universal. And also things that are in between the personal and the public, that straddle the authentic and the performative—more quantum Martine stuff.

MS: It's a funny thing for me to navigate this interior-exterior thing, or public-private. The things I share in my work don't actually feel private to me. I'm just recording what stuff looks like, where I am, what people are saying around me. It's almost like a documentary. If I hear something funny, or poetic, I'll put that in my notes. That's just how I build. Yes, it's me—obviously it's *me*, listening. It's my perspective. It's what I think is funny, or what I think is a weird way of saying something. It's what stands out to me, to my eye. But it doesn't feel that personal, or *intimate*.

Even something like [my 2020 book] *Shame Space*, which is taken from my diaries, from a tough period of time—I edited it so much. It's not the whole picture. I was specifically looking for stuff I wouldn't want to share with people. Someone asked me about it, and they were like, "Did *anything* good happen to you that year?" Lots of good stuff happened, but I'm just choosing the "bad stuff," because that was what I was interested in showing—what we think of as bad or shadow material. By the time it was a book, it felt so worked.

BLVR: Do you think the way you work with that personal material has anything to do with the fact that you've also worked a lot with archives? Because I think you have an eye for what might be useful, or interesting, later—in a different context.

MS: I guess I hadn't thought about that, but it's true. l do work with a lot of archival material and with *actual* archives—like, going to an archive and finding stuff and scanning it. Because I spend a lot of time doing that kind of thing, I love that. At some point I was going through the Altadena Historical Society archives. It has a locations photos archive that's incredible, incredible. When the person was shooting those photos, they probably didn't think much of it. But it's fascinating to me now. I do probably treat my own material in the same way, where it's something I can use in service of an idea. And it tells me about the time too. I've been working on this book for an exhibition I'm gonna do at [the Paris art gallery] Lafayette Anticipations. I'm going through all my work, which has been a very weird feeling. Talk about quantum. It feels like different lifetimes.

I'm going through all the stuff from Golden Age, which was a project space, bookshop, whatever, that I ran in Chicago—recently I heard somebody refer to it as a "speakeasy," which I thought was funny. But I was going through all these photos from it, and when I was *taking* the photos, I didn't think of them as any kind of time capsule. It was much more about "Javelin's playing, Lucky Dragons is playing, let's take a photo of it so we can put on the internet." But looking through all these photos and at all the people that were in the crowd—that was the thing that was really getting me. I knew a lot of the people who came to these parties, obviously, but I didn't know everyone; there are people I've met *since* that were there. Like, a friend of mine in Paris—there's a photo of him and his now wife outside this one party. And I was like, Oh shit, that's crazy. I'm looking in the audience, and I'm like, Wait, *that* person was there? And also the way people are dressed…

BLVR: Oh my god, I know.

MS: It looks so old. It was almost twenty years ago. If I was to re-create that time, which I thought would be fun to do, this underground scene—I mean, you were very much part of it, so I don't have to describe it to you. I have had this idea that it would make a fun movie. The petty drama of it all. I had an idea of what it looked like in my head, but looking at those photos, I was like, Oh no: *that's* what it looked like.

BLVR: Somewhat related to what your grandpa said about how you don't remember anything unless you write

STRUCTURE
by Margaret Ross

Walking back I pass
a block-long dune
of rubble and the man whose job
it is to shovel it. An iron rectangle

he's nestled in debris makes
a little door he's slinging
shovelfuls of crumbled
plaster through, no reason.

Three old women from a facing
building stamped for demolition
watch. The man's toss makes it,
misses, makes it. Across

one woman's quilted vest
fans an orange blossom pattern. A ten-foot
stack of styrofoam is tied nearby.
Everyone is laughing.

---

it down—you also don't realize how much things change until you look back at those recordings you made. Art is a marker of time.

MS: It is. I've always been like, Don't try to escape your time, as much as I love to time-jump. There's a word that art historians use [*style*] to describe the qualities that are shared by work made in a certain period. And maybe this is to your point of using myself as source material, but I've always felt it would be impossible to escape that quality, even if I didn't like it. I wanted to be a Gen Xer when I was a kid. I have photos of myself at six, wearing a mechanic's shirt. I wanted to be that generation, or even older, you know? I was like, God, this is so lame, being a millennial. This just sucks. But at the same time, I can't escape it. I'm not consciously trying to make something *of* this time, but I'm not trying to get out of it, either. Something about me has always been like, That's impossible. ✮

INSID

With stable employment exceedingly difficult to come by, intellectually disabled adults have another, occasionally lucrative, way of participating in American society: they can become artists.

FONT

by **PEPPER STETLER**

DISCUSSED: *A Stack of Cardboard, The Dark Ages, Non-Direction, The Lanterman-Petris-Short Act, Mind-Expanding Impulses, Judith Heumann, Curb Cuts, The Civil Rights Movement, Creative Essence, Art-World Mantras, Roger Cardinal, A Demeaning Trifecta of Affinity, Market Expectations, Medicaid, Awkward Bureaucrats, The Gift, Two Worlds, Nomadic Wanderings, The Dignity of Work*

OPENING ILLUSTRATION BY:
Kristian Hammerstad

ART THROUGHOUT BY:
Nicole Storm

O n a Monday morning in early June, Nicole Storm arrived at the Creative Growth Art Center in downtown Oakland, California. Light poured in through broad windows that faced the street. Nicole put her jacket and lunch away in the closet and then selected a large piece of cardboard from a stack in a hallway. A staff member helped her secure the makeshift canvas to an easel and set out her paints and markers. She chatted with some fellow artists and then explained to me that she is starting a new project, after having finished a few paintings last week. Nicole refers to her artistic process as "taking notes." It is a way for her to organize the events of a day, although the results never look like a typical archive or journal. She creates bright washes of color that provide a glowing background for lines and shapes that appear like an indeterminate form of writing. Nicole records what is going on around her with marks that may initially seem impulsive and spontaneous. But they are the culmination of a well-honed practice, undeniable creativity, and decades of sustained work.

Nicole was born in 1967, during what her mother, Diane, refers to as "the tail end of the Dark Ages," when someone like Nicole, who has Down syndrome, would almost certainly have lived her entire life in an institution. At that time, Diane recalls, "I sent away for some information about Down syndrome and what I got was bleak. The life expectancy was twelve years. Fifty percent of people were dead before their fifth birthday. So I threw that stuff in the trash and decided to do it my way."

Diane and Nicole are closer than most mothers and their adult daughters. They live together, and Diane volunteers once a week at Creative Growth when Nicole is there. Nicole inherited Diane's round face and direct stare. They both speak with a great deal of confidence. Diane attributes Nicole's confidence to how she "ran with the pack" as a kid; she was thrown into the deep end of progressive schools that included her with the rest of the students. Diane's confidence developed out of her fierce advocacy for Nicole and a lifetime of fighting with bureaucratic systems that did little more than tell her what her daughter would not be able to do. I mentioned to Diane that my daughter, like Nicole, has Down syndrome. "You know how it goes then," she said. "We had no support when she was growing up, but I'm sure your daughter has a bright future."

Diane is right. My daughter is part of a generation with more opportunities to attend school with her peers, although she still faces plenty of challenges. I hope she might be able to find a job and work in a supportive community. But historically our society has expected very little of people with intellectual disabilities, which makes Nicole's success as an artist all the more remarkable.

When Nicole was in her twenties, Diane searched for a day program that Nicole could attend while she worked full-time. But they struggled to find a suitable situation that met Nicole's need for routine and predictability. She spent most of her days on public transportation. Diane recalled a time when Nicole traveled with a group to an event at a library in Berkeley, only to have to catch another bus fifteen minutes later to come back home. Eventually Nicole moved into a group home for people with disabilities, where she lived in an apartment with the help of support staff. Both Nicole and Diane believed this was the independence Nicole deserved. But after two and a half years, she wasn't thriving. Nicole wasn't developing much of a life outside her apartment, and the support staff wasn't as attentive as Diane had expected. After Nicole became seriously ill with pneumonia, they decided they had had enough. Nicole went back to living with Diane. An artist friend told them about Creative Growth, and Nicole started attending the program regularly. The new sense of routine and purpose transformed her almost overnight.

"It was the most wonderful moment," Nicole remembered.

"You're right," said Diane. "That's when the magic started to happen."

Installation view of Nicole Storm's exhibit at White Columns, New York, 2021.

There are a range of ways to describe what Creative Growth is. It is a twelve-thousand-square-foot art studio in a building that was once an auto-repair shop. It is a space where artists come to work on projects and prepare for upcoming exhibitions. It is a place of artistic pursuit, but it is also a provider through the Regional Center of the East Bay, and serves people who have historically not been given the chance to express themselves or to be part of a community. Creative Growth is a nonprofit organization and its mission is to advance the mainstream inclusion of artists with intellectual and developmental disabilities.

Most day programs for people with disabilities include crafts because it is assumed those activities are difficult to get wrong. These programs exemplify the way people with disabilities are treated like children: by comparing their work to grade school projects. This is emphatically not what Creative Growth does, and it has fought for the recognition of those who make art in its studio as serious artists. It was the first of hundreds of art studios that now serve people with disabilities in the United States, and the importance of its mission has gradually been recognized. Earlier this year, SFMOMA marked Creative Growth's

fiftieth anniversary with a major exhibition of 113 works, and paid $578,000 to bring many of the pieces into its permanent collection. It was touted as the largest acquisition of work by artists with disabilities by an American museum.

What is easily overlooked in this achievement is Creative Growth's equally remarkable but far less glitzy daily operations, which serve about 140 artists per week. Many—including Nicole—never thought of themselves as artists before they enrolled. At the time of my visit, it had a six-month waiting list for services, and there were usually about seventy artists

© Undated. Acrylic pen on paper.

there each day. But I didn't do an exact head count, and I wasn't always able to identify who was an artist enrolled in its studio program and who was there as a staff member or volunteer.

I came to Creative Growth with questions about creativity—where we think it comes from and how we find value in it. I was interested in how the art world has historically positioned artists with disabilities as "outsiders" and whether the boundary that used to separate them from "insiders" was still maintained. But my interest in creativity and value was also personal.

My daughter likes to make linocuts. She carves a design into the rubbery surface of the plate with a small tool, presses a piece of paper against the plate's inked surface, and then gives the resulting print to family and friends. As I watched artists at Creative Growth delight in the liquid gooeyness of paint, I recalled the wet sound of the ink as she rolls it into the grooves of the plate. I thought about how much my daughter would love it here—the materials, the camaraderie, the undirected time free of demands for productivity and proficiency. Eventually

I began to think, Who wouldn't want to be here? The place exuded an aura of radical acceptance and deep support. I wondered about my daughter's future as an artist and how her work would be valued, even if being an artist is not considered a normal kind of work.

When it began, in 1972, Creative Growth responded to a profound shift in public policy regarding people with disabilities. Five years earlier, then California governor Ronald Reagan signed the Lanterman-Petris-Short Act, which sought to end the indefinite and involuntary commitment of people with mental health disorders in the state. Florence Ludins-Katz, an artist and teacher, and her husband, Elias Katz, a psychologist and the chair of the Art and Disability Program at the University of California, Berkeley, founded the center in response to Reagan's plan. There was a growing consensus that community-based support was a more humane way of caring for people who had persistently been treated like outsiders than institutionalizing them. But there was no infrastructure in place for integrating people who had lived for decades in an institution back into mainstream American society. Without support, those who had been institutionalized were at risk of ending up homeless or in prison. As Nicole experienced, living options that appropriately balanced independence with support were difficult to find. In 1968 and 1970, Elias Katz published two manuals, *The Retarded Adult in the Community* and *The Retarded Adult at Home: A Guide for Parents*. The titles alone suggest

that reintroducing people to both their families and a society where they have been told they do not belong might be disastrous if not done carefully. Elias and Florence understood that those who were transitioning from a life in an institution to a community-based setting needed to find new routines that provided social interaction and a chance for self-expression, and they sought to tackle the problem in a deeply pragmatic and person-centered way. With Creative Growth, the Katzes proposed to establish this pathway through artistry.

According to Tom di Maria, Creative Growth's executive director since 2000, the Katzes were hippies influenced by the pop psychology and the mind-expanding impulses of the Bay Area counterculture. They started Creative Growth in the garage of their East Bay home when disability-rights activists in Berkeley, such as Judith Heumann and Ed Roberts, were fighting for access to basic public services like curb cuts and accessible public transportation. Heumann, Roberts, and the Katzes all drew inspiration from the larger civil rights protests of the time, but some of the leaders of those movements kept activists who were demanding disability rights at arm's length. "When I told them we were all fighting the same civil rights battle, they didn't believe me," said Roberts, a polio survivor who founded the Center for Independent Living in Berkeley. "They didn't understand our similarities. I did. Even now, many people don't realize it." The Katzes saw access to creative opportunities as a civil right, but they must have faced similar doubts about whether people with intellectual

disabilities could even claim a right to human dignity.

The Katzes' mission was to establish artistic creativity as a form of communication, and they identified the need for art studios to serve as centers of open exploration. Over the course of ten years, the Katzes opened three studios: Creative Growth Art Center, which eventually moved to its present location in Oakland; NIAD (Nurturing Independence through Artistic Development) in nearby Richmond; and Creativity Explored in San Francisco.

All three centers provide an environment where artists with intellectual disabilities could work at their own pace. Without offering any formalized classes, instruction, or therapy, staff members act as facilitators and advisers when needed. The purpose of the studio experience is not to improve the skills of the artists, but to foster their innate creative potential.

"Creative self-expression is the outward manifestation in an art form of what one feels internally," the Katzes declare in *Art and Disabilities: Establishing the Creative Art Center for People with Disabilities*, their 1990 book that reads like part disability-rights manifesto and part manual for replicating their centers throughout the country. They emphasize that a nurturing and nondirective environment promotes growth and self-confidence. "The Creative Art Center sees each person, no matter how disabled mentally, physically, or emotionally, as a potential artist." To the Katzes, creativity endures in an individual, no matter the circumstances. "Does a person who is disabled, who has been deprived, who has never had the opportunity to express

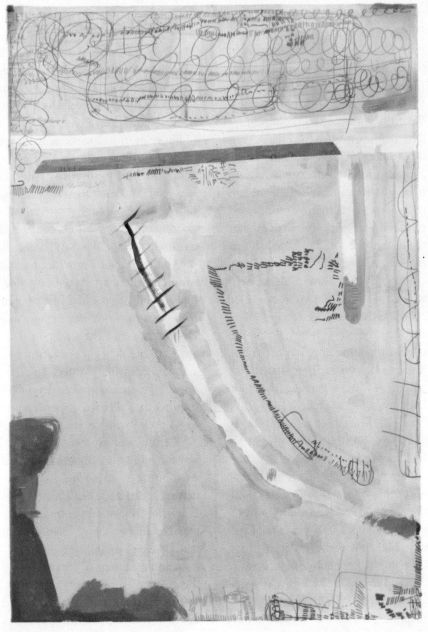

© 2020. Acrylic pen and watercolor on paper.

in a state institution. When that institution closed, George started coming to Creative Growth because there was no other community program available. "He is blind in one eye, has a large tumor in his neck, shuffles when he walks, and seems completely disconnected from the world," they write. George struggled to communicate verbally, but the Katzes describe the rapid development of his art, from a few dabs of paint to canvases with brightly colored squares and rectangles. They clearly took pride in the artists they worked with. "Recently George's work… was singled out by a gallery owner as being among the most promising," they say, celebrating the recognition of human creativity as much as George's individual efforts.

At Creative Growth I met an artist named Joe Spears who was making a collage, gluing pieces of a painting he'd made and cut up onto pieces of blue paper. A staff member helped Joe get the glue onto the paper, but she was careful not to intervene in the artwork without Joe's permission or guidance. She asked questions but avoided making any decisions for him. She told me, "Joe likes the process," an acknowledgment that the tactile stickiness and arrangement of shapes might be what draw Joe to make art. Emma, an artist who had been coming to Creative Growth for only a few weeks, liked watching Joe work. In another part of the studio, a staff member began to sing and play a ukulele.

Making art can appear to be a slow and impenetrable practice, and the time I spent at Creative Growth sitting

himself still retain the essence of creativity?" they ask. They compare the creative expression of artists in their studio to the "surge of flood water when the dam has been removed."

Art and Disabilities is a record of the Katzes' determination to expand creative opportunities for people with intellectual disabilities, but it also captures their devotion to the individuals they worked with. Their treatise is filled with firsthand accounts of artists like George, a man in his sixties who had spent most of his life

and watching often felt unproductive, like I was at a party where I was desperately trying to make friends. I hovered over one table with people I'd just met. Then I noticed a woman weaving in another part of the studio and wandered over. I watched her work a piece of thick crimson yarn back and forth through the warp, deftly coordinating the moving parts of a loom that had been jury-rigged for wheelchair users so the foot pedals could be operated by hand. After several days, I mentioned to di Maria that my time there felt undirected. "Well, that's what we do here," he replied. "We are all about non-direction."

Di Maria, a small-framed man, floated from one end of the studio to the other, checking in with artists and staff members. Over the last quarter century, he has been a tireless promoter of the artistic and commercial value of Creative Growth. But he also cultivates a studio environment that supports many other reasons for being at the center.

I tried to embrace di Maria's idea of non-direction and to let go of the idea of productivity. While many of the artists there think of themselves as ambitious, even successful, some seem less self-conscious about their practice. "Everyone defines success differently here," di Maria told me. Every artist is given the opportunity to exhibit their work, either in the center's gallery space or in national or international exhibitions. And while some of their work has sold for tens of thousands of dollars and found its way into the collections of major museums, many artists are not focused on gaining success in the gallery system at all.

The Katzes thought success depended, in part, on an artist's ability to communicate something about the human experience. They begin *Art and Disabilities* with an epigraph, a famous quote from the abstract expressionist painter Jackson Pollock: "When I am in my painting I am not aware of what I am doing. It is only after a sort of 'get acquainted' period that I see what I have been about." The quote supports the Katzes' claim that art expresses something universal about the human condition, something beyond the immediate control of the individual artist. It also demonstrates that this principle was already an accepted mantra of the art world by the time the Katzes started Creative Growth. The gestural, impulsive marks of Pollock and others had long been established as examples of creativity in its purest form. But claims to universal expression have also faced their share of skepticism. When I was a college student in the late 1990s, I learned that Pollock was an important artist even if his claims of losing conscious control over his work struck me as ridiculous. Was there really such a thing as a universal human condition? And if so, was it possible to find a satisfying way of expressing it artistically? What could Jackson Pollock's creativity have in common with the experience of Creative Growth artists? Now I wonder why the Katzes needed to invoke Pollock's lofty ambitions to legitimize the work of artists at Creative Growth, as if the mere opportunity to define their own version of success, which had been systemically denied to so many of them by our ableist world, wasn't enough to give their practice value.

The act of making art often stands apart from the efficiency, speed, and productivity that modern life demands and that people with disabilities can find challenging to navigate. But do they have privileged access to creative inspiration? The art critic Roger Cardinal, who published *Outsider Art* in 1972, believed they do. Cardinal's thesis is that human creativity is most evident when social and cultural conventions are disregarded. Creativity is "genuinely primitive," Cardinal claims. "It emerges from the chaotic realm of undifferentiation, being released at the near-instinctual or primary levels of creation." True art, according to Cardinal, is created by untrained artists "whose position in society was often obscure and humble." Cardinal devises a demeaning trifecta of affinity between art made by colonized people (mainly Africans and Indigenous Americans), art made by children, and the art of the mentally ill. To Cardinal, all three groups exemplify an untrained hand and prerational mind.

Cardinal's *Outsider Art* casts those with intellectual differences as a radical version of the troubled Romantic genius, free of all convention and cultural influence. True creativity, he believed, comes from the inner drives of people who are outsiders, uninitiated in social norms and artistic conventions. But, according to Cardinal, the artist and the outsider aren't exactly creative equals. Artists seek the spiritual meaning and mark-making that seem to come easily to those on the cultural periphery. In the history of art, it is not the outsiders that get recognition. It is the insiders—Paul Gauguin, Paul Klee, Jackson Pollock—who turn the creativity of the outsiders into a proper style.

There is a big difference between the outsider artist and how the Katzes saw the artists in their studios. The Katzes centered the creative potential of artists with disabilities and responded to their social and individual needs. Cardinal's framing of the outsider artist is more of a backhanded compliment, celebrating the mysterious depth of the art while showing little concern for the well-being and resources of those who create it. And he isn't focused only on those with intellectual disabilities or mental illnesses. An outsider artist can refer to someone who is self-taught, a folk artist, or anyone whose creativity doesn't fit the mold of MFA studio programs. These days the term *outsider artist* usually appears in exhibition catalogs and reviews in scare quotes, to acknowledge a discomfort with the cliquish boundaries the term defines, while admitting that there's still something useful and familiar about its meaning.

There is a persistent belief that art expresses a universal human experience, that art embodies an instinctual urge to make a mark, whether that mark is drawn by Pollock, a person with schizophrenia, or a three-year-old child. I have noticed certain words and phrases used repeatedly by gallerists, art dealers, and collectors to adulate the outsider art they support: *powerful, on the edge of contemporary art, mysterious, raw, impulsive.* I have asked them to clarify what they mean by these terms, but their attempts to elaborate have never really satisfied me. As an art historian, I have been trained to be skeptical of these descriptions and to recognize how they traffic in clichés of emotional subjectivity and suspect pathways to an inner self. They have always sounded lazy to me. Art that can be anything or be made by anyone isn't strong enough to create any focused meaning on its own. And how can we know what is being expressed, if it is couched in opacity, something we can never truly understand? What can a work of art tell us about our world, if the best we can do is celebrate its mystery? Although describing art as "mysterious" might give it value to insiders, it does little to address how people with disabilities have historically been treated as outsiders, or whether those conditions might change. In other words, maybe the connection between disability and creativity is easier to cultivate, while connections to other parts of the world through employment, community, or civic action are much harder to establish.

The Katzes designed Creative Growth, in part, as a way to convince the public that people with disabilities could be skilled artists with commercial potential. "To come to the Art Center," they write, "to see the seriousness and intensity of the students as they are involved in creating art is a revelation to all who visit." The Katzes believed that Creative Growth might change the public's perceptions about people with intellectual disabilities. And given the profoundly low expectations at the time, it is easy to see why they identified this purpose, even if now the goal might feel uncomfortable, as if people with disabilities are required to prove their human worth to a nondisabled audience.

The Katzes cite many reasons to have a commercial gallery space attached to their art centers. "The money is a welcome addition to the praise of a job well done," they write. "The Art Center takes pride in the recognition that the art of persons with disabilities is much sought after and has value to society." Creative Growth has benefitted from the fact that the idea of outsider art has become, paradoxically, the way in which the art of marginalized people is given commercial value. At first, the field of outsider art was driven by collectors who saw it as whimsical and intriguing. It eventually moved to galleries and art exhibitions. Today, outsider art straddles the high-end art market and grassroots community. The Outsider Art Fair has run annually in New York since 1993. Another ran in Paris from 2013 to 2022. Many Creative Growth artists have found audiences for their work in these venues. But it is often difficult to match their art with what the market expects of artists with disabilities. I've talked to gallerists about how art buyers often have specific ideas about what outsider art looks like, although artists don't necessarily feel compelled to meet those expectations. "Artists who do portraits or landscapes are easier to place in art fairs and expos," one gallerist told me. "Artists who work from Disney models are harder. There are copyright issues."

Artists at Creative Growth use a variety of artistic strategies, constantly defying the art market's expectations for expressive gestures, portraits, and landscapes. Many artists no longer depend on Outsider Art Fairs for their commercial success. Nicole Storm is ambitiously seeking out solo exhibitions and collectors for her work. When she first began making art at Creative Growth, Nicole hid away in cardboard boxes, drawing in the calm of enclosure. Now she moves about the studio space in what di Maria described to me as "nomadic wanderings." She dances and chats with other artists and sets up her painterly drawing practice at one of the many wide tables. Nicole finds her material by scavenging in the hallways and storage cabinets. Of all the artists I met at Creative Growth, she seemed the most immersed in her process, although I could not understand whether that process had a purpose or not. Her tally marks on cardboard seemed meaningful to her, but she eventually covered them up with paint, and I was left unsure whether she did this as a gesture of erasure or layering. But it was clear that Nicole sees her work as connected to her environment. She was one of the first artists to have a solo show at Creative Growth's gallery when it reopened after the pandemic in 2021. Later that year, White Columns in New York asked her to create a similar installation in its gallery. Storm filled the white walls with her fluid, glowing paintings. In one corner she placed a brightly painted cardboard box, referencing her beginnings at Creative Growth.

In *Our Sanctuary*, a piece recently exhibited at the Oakland Museum of California, Nicole arranged abstract paintings in thin washes of blue, orange, and red on brown cardboard, freestanding paper cylinders, and posterboard of varying sizes to cover an alcove from floor to ceiling. To install the piece, Nicole lay down

© Undated. Acrylic and watercolor on paper.

on her back and directed a museum staff member, who hovered above in a mechanical bucket, where to hang her work. She then painted and drew on the white walls between the pieces of cardboard to create a site-specific installation that conveyed her profound sense of comfort with the creative process. The space was a haven of glowing orange and purple tones. She created much more than just art to be displayed by a museum, or work to be paid for. She was making a place to belong.

It would be easy to see the growing prominence of the work of Creative Growth artists like Nicole as evidence that our world now values the art and the lives of people with disabilities. Some artists that Cardinal would have considered outsiders are now on the inside; their work is included in major museum collections and is priced on par with that of nondisabled artists. This is an ambitious and just achievement. But there is a limit to their insider status in a world that does not see most people with disabilities as valuable—that is, as able to contribute productively to the economy. Like many people receiving social security benefits and Medicaid, Creative Growth artists are at risk of losing health care, transportation, and other vital forms of support if they have more than two thousand dollars in assets. This restriction complicates their ability to earn money and support themselves as artists.

"Did you ever think good news could be such bad news?" Diane Storm joked, referring to the irony of the situation. The good news is that internationally renowned museums and galleries want to exhibit Nicole's work and pay her for it. The bad news is that getting paid compromises her benefits and health care. The rules of Social Security Disability Insurance permit Nicole to earn only eighteen thousand dollars per year before she would be forced to pay back some of her benefits. Nicole depends on Diane to navigate the bureaucratic red tape, as it is notoriously hard to play by the rules of the Social Security Administration.

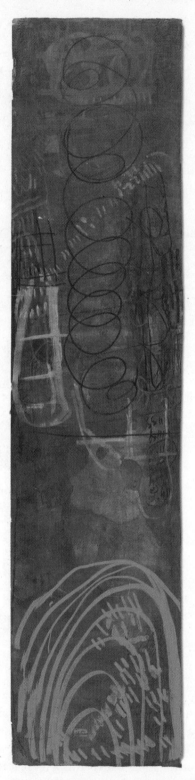

© Undated. Acrylic and watercolor on cardboard.

"The system is designed to confuse us," Diane told me. They report Nicole's earnings honestly, but it often feels like a shot in the dark. "We don't know what we're doing," she said, "but they [the SSA] don't know what they're doing either." Creative Growth takes a commission from artist sales—the art world standard of 50 percent—that goes to pay for supplies and gallery costs. But even after the commission, Nicole's income from her art and installations is beginning to reach the limit of what she can earn without the potential loss of her benefits.

The outsider artist model allows the art world to remain comfortably unaware of how our society persistently impoverishes people with disabilities by drastically limiting their income. If creativity is something intrinsic though vaguely defined, then we need not worry if people with disabilities have access to it. The reality that these artists lack social support, adequate health care, employment, and equal pay can remain conveniently outside the scope of art institutions. Creative Growth functions between these two worlds, fulfilling the needs of its artists while also depending on the financial interest of the art world. It provides a path through a bureaucratic and capitalist system that so rarely offers people with disabilities the dignity of work.

In many ways, the routine of artists at Creative Growth takes the shape of a workday. Most artists arrive around nine in the morning, take a lunch break, and leave in the late afternoon. They work side by side at tables, focused on their own projects, but also take time to socialize with others in the open space. Working at Creative Growth mimics the pace of a job, except that it isn't a job, at least not in the way our society usually conceives of one. Creative Growth gives people with disabilities routine, purpose, dignity—all benefits of the best kinds of jobs. But ultimately, those in the program are not working in response to the expectations of bosses and industry. They are making art, which defies our society's normative sense of work.

I am told that the families of some of the artists, especially the younger adults, question whether drawing, modeling clay, or painting at Creative Growth is an acceptable way to spend time. They are skeptical of the value of making art, and, like the families of so many nondisabled artists, wonder whether their loved ones would be better off trying to get real jobs. But opportunities for disabled adults to get a real job are appallingly low. Only 19 percent of adults with intellectual disabilities are employed in the United States. Our society defines disability as the inability to do work. This has created the need for places like Creative Growth. In other words, access to creativity is something we owe those who come here, because the world outside has struggled to offer them much else.

When Nicole was growing up, Diane had no expectations that her daughter would eventually find a job, but they were open to exploring opportunities. Nicole tried out a few jobs before she came to Creative Growth. She worked as a maid at a local bed-and-breakfast, but she had no structured support and there was constant pressure to fold and clean sheets and towels more quickly. She then worked at a few chain restaurants and coffee shops. But they were

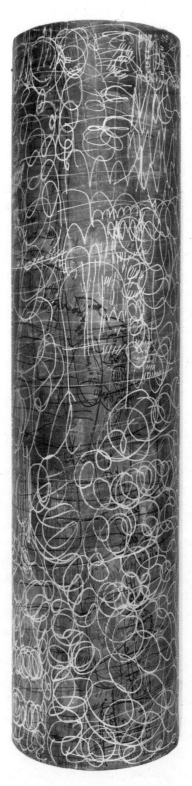

© Undated. Acrylic pen and watercolor on cardboard tube.

too fast-paced, and sometimes Nicole would get irritated with the customers. Steady work never seemed like a good fit for her. But whether this was because of a cognitive impairment or Nicole's creative spirit no longer really matters. "She is an artist," Diane told me.

Our world judges a person's value by their ability to work. Yet work isn't necessarily dignified or humane. In *The Gift: Creativity and the Artist in the Modern World*, Lewis Hyde distinguishes between work and labor. Work is what we do for money, Hyde tells us, but labor sets its own pace. It is often accompanied by idleness, or a period when one might seem to be struggling to be productive in a capitalist sense. Labor, according to Hyde, is "often urgent but… nevertheless has its own interior rhythm, something more bound up with feeling, more interior, than work." For Hyde, creativity is aligned with labor more than work. His words in *The Gift* take on a transcendent tone, exalting the preservation of creative labor in a world that constantly asks us to live for money and what we can buy with it.

In its most idealized form, creativity stands apart from work and outside economies of value and time. It maintains a kind of purity and disinterest. Monetizing or quantifying creativity, we tend to believe, corrupts it, giving it a pragmatic purpose that sullies its connection to truth and the human spirit. In this way, creativity and art are profoundly worthless. But during my visit to Creative Growth, Hyde's distinction between work and labor seemed too simplistic. To see the artists as laboring would mean to see them as outside systems of work and economic value. It would place them apart from the economy that structures our lives. And as flawed as a capitalist economy is, people with disabilities deserve the option to be fully part of it. Labor, in the way Hyde explains the term, would imply worthlessness, and so it would be a problematic term to use in the context of Creative Growth. To call the labor of these artists worthless is to come dangerously close to calling *them* worthless, to repeat the historical marginalization of the lives of people with disabilities that the Katzes originally fought against. The acknowledgment of the value of a person's creativity has social and political importance, and work and labor are intertwined in necessary ways.

It may be true that Creative Growth artists aren't totally outsiders anymore, but the studio must still navigate between the ableist tendencies of the established art world and the needs of the disabled community. Creativity and individualism are given value here, but that does not mean the art studio is untouched by the pressures of ableism and productivity that are part of our capitalist world.

A few days into my visit, Donald Mitchell, an artist who has worked at Creative Growth since the 1980s, came back after being gone for several months, due to issues with his living situation and problems securing transportation from his home to the studio. "We lost track of him," di Maria told me, "but it took him about a minute to get started this morning." He announced Mitchell's return, and I sensed some relief and lightness in his voice. The other artists and staff members broke out in applause. The moment felt like a homecoming. It was a reminder that Creative Growth is more than an art studio, but a way of keeping track of people who can fall through the cracks. Most of the artists access Medicaid with the help of California's Department of Developmental Services (DDS). The studio is a service provider through the Regional Center of the East Bay, one of about twenty private, nonprofit corporations under contract with the DDS. Most of the other service providers that are part of the Regional Center of the East Bay are residential homes and care centers. Creative Growth, Creativity Explored, and NIAD—all started by the Katzes—are among a handful of art studios that are also service providers.

When the Katzes began Creative Growth, there was very little social support for people with intellectual disabilities who wanted to live independently. Now there is more. Because they receive financial assistance through the Regional Center, most artists have an Individual Service Plan (ISP), which requires the staff to help artists develop goals for their practice, but the document might also include social or behavioral milestones, like developing strategies to create relationships or follow rules. Portfolio reviews are also part of the ISP, and each report notes which exhibitions the artists has submitted work to, the works of art completed, and the time clocked in the studio. Each staff member at Creative Growth is assigned a caseload of six to eight artists. But the staff, who are also artists themselves, make for awkward bureaucrats. Last spring, they declared their intention to unionize, reflecting the gradual pressure to evolve from the collaborative, community-based relationship between staff and artists that the Katzes established to something more formal. Even here, paperwork and other, more tedious aspects of work have their place alongside creative labor.

All this bureaucracy is at odds with Cardinal's outsider artist, and Hyde's conception of labor, both free from social and cultural constraints. Artists come to Creative Growth to create, to learn, to be together. But they are caught between two ways that insiders make sense of outsiders. On the one hand, museums and collectors still tend to understand the creativity of outsider artists as the outcome of expression and mysterious drives. On the other, the artists are subjected to documentation, in which getting what they need from the system depends on how useful and productive their time appears to those at the DDS.

I recognized the reports and goal-setting from my daughter's own assessment in school and the familiar routine of playing by the system's rules so she gets what she needs. The Individualized Education Program (IEP), a government document that develops and changes with my daughter as she moves through school, provides an agreement on goals and accommodations that is similar to the ISP submitted for many of the artists at Creative Growth. Every year my husband and I meet with a team of educators to review her educational progress. My daughter's most recent IEP included a "measurable postsecondary goal." This is intended to help prepare her for competitive integrated employment, or work among her peers for equal pay. This is a notable difference from the world Nicole and Diane faced decades ago, when not being institutionalized seemed like a remarkable step forward. But people with intellectual disabilities still struggle to find appropriate jobs. My daughter is being asked to think about what she might like to do after high school, and hopefully by the time she is ready she will be able to find fulfilling work.

By fighting for access and the recognition of their own human dignity, disability-rights activists have led the way in demanding innovations that have improved the broader world. Curb cuts began to be implemented nationally after Ed Roberts revealed the need for more accessible urban spaces in Berkeley. Disability accommodations in higher education have forced society to start to question its narrow definitions of learning and the value of achievement. For their part, the Katzes envisioned an alternative definition of work. While navigating between creativity and bureaucracy, Creative Growth shows us a way to work that is not defined by productivity but by dignity and shared responsibility.

The Katzes dreamed that eventually the establishment of art centers for people with disabilities would be unnecessary, and that in the future, "all people will be able to work together toward the highest fulfillment of each individual and of society as a whole." They imagined the full inclusion of people with disabilities in society, and their access to meaningful work. Fifty years later, we are not there yet. Reaching the Katzes' goal will require more than just the acquisition of art by people with intellectual disabilities by major museums. It will require changing our society's ideas about work and creativity. It will demand that we recognize that all humans have a right to access both.

Until we get there, Creative Growth artists continue to change the art world by contributing to it. Nicole Storm is now a successful artist with exhibitions scheduled at international museums for the next several years. Her art seems still to be a product of her nomadic wanderings, of searching for materials in hallways, and with a purpose that is clear only to her. But since Storm's work has been in greater demand, she has started to approach her art with greater urgency. "She has a tremendous work ethic," Diane told me. "When she has a deadline, she works." It's an approach that defies a more simplistic separation between work and creativity. "I want to get a paycheck," Nicole said. But there's more to it than that. And what seemed clear to me when I talked with Nicole and Diane is that they see Nicole's art as a product of their circumstances, which are deeply informed by their love for each other. On the days when she doesn't go to Creative Growth, Nicole sets up her studio in their home while Diane gets breakfast. "Nicole's art gives us a sense of focus and brings us together as a collaborative team." As a mother, I know this is one of the most gratifying experiences a caregiver can have. "I feel very lucky that she includes me in her life," Diane said. I thought about my daughter and how lucky I would be—how lucky any of us would be—to have a future like this.

I am unsure if I want my daughter to have what most people would refer to as a "real job," although I recognize that she will need to financially support herself. I hope she will choose what is best for her. Right now, she wants to be a scientist, a ballerina, and an artist, but there is no way to know if those dreams will pan out. I imagine the drudgery and monotony of the jobs that might be available to her, and my heart starts to race with panic about what her future might hold. I wish for more for her than work. I want her to find creativity and self-direction, but there are so few opportunities for a creative life in the modern world. In the daily work of Creative Growth, there is a different conception of productivity, and a different conception of human worth. It provides artists with a sense of meaning and purpose, which is a remarkable difference from a world where a life can seem to have little value if it is not profitable and productive.

According to modern parenting, I am not supposed to want my daughter to be an artist. And the broader world tells me I should be grateful if my daughter finds a job at all. But maybe employment is only part of what we should want for people with intellectual disabilities. The truth is that I want my daughter to find a supportive community that helps her cultivate her own unique contribution to the world. I want her to be an artist, and I also want her to make money and be part of an economy that respects and values her contributions to it. The problem is that these things seem rarely to coexist. My daughter will be asked to either complete oppressive work or not work at all. Art and work so rarely function together. But I have seen the possibility of an alternative future in which value is determined not by productivity, but by codependence and love. ★

THE FORGOTTEN BLACK MODELS OF WESTERN ART

1400

c.1475
THE ADORATION OF THE MAGI
Hieronymus Bosch

This popular religious art theme, which depicts three fabulously dressed kings from faraway lands offering gifts to the baby Jesus, often includes a regal African ruler. Across Europe, his presence was meant to symbolize Christianity's international reach.

c.1490–95
HUNTING ON THE LAGOON (RECTO); LETTER RACK (VERSO)
Vittore Carpaccio

As Venetian bird hunters shoot clay pellets, viewers gain a rare window into the everyday life of Black Africans in Renaissance Italy. During this time, Black boatmen were not an uncommon sight—many would have been part of ferryman guilds with their white peers.

c.1643
DON MIGUEL DE CASTRO, EMISSARY OF CONGO
Unknown

A wealthy ambassador on a diplomatic mission on behalf of the ruler of Sonho, Don Miguel arrived in the Netherlands around 1643. Portraits of Don Miguel and his two servants, Pedro Sunda and Diego Bemba, were commissioned by the Dutch West India Company.

c. 1631–50
FAMILY GROUP WITH A BLACK MAN
Willem Cornelisz Duyster

c.1640–43
MILITIA COMPANY OF DISTRICT VIII IN AMSTERDAM UNDER THE COMMAND OF CAPTAIN ROELOF BICKER
Bartholomeus van der Helst

1623
MARCHESA ELENA GRIMALDI CATTANEO
Sir Anthony van Dyck

1600

1650
JUAN DE PAREJA (CA. 1608–70)
Velázquez

Juan de Pareja was a successful Afro-Hispanic artist in seventeenth-century Spain. Until at least 1654, he was enslaved in the household of famed painter Velázquez. Remarkably, after he was freed, he began an art career in Madrid.

c.1830
IRA ALDRIDGE AS OTHELLO
Henry Perronet Briggs

In London in 1825, a teenage Ira Aldridge became the first Black man to perform in Shakespeare's *Othello* as Othello. He had recently moved from his birthplace in New York to Europe to pursue an acting career, and went on to become one of the most celebrated actors of his time.

1857
PORTRAIT OF OTTO MARSTRAND'S TWO DAUGHTERS AND THEIR WEST-INDIAN NANNY, JUSTINA ANTOINE, IN THE FREDERIKSBERG GARDENS NEAR COPENHAGEN
Wilhelm Marstrand

1859
BUST OF AN AFRICAN WOMAN
Henry Weekes

1861
FANNY EATON
Joanna Mary Wells (née Boyce)

c.1861–62
CHILDREN IN THE TUILERIES GARDENS
Édouard Manet

1868–69
BASHI-BAZOUK
Jean-Léon Gérôme

1900

c.1906
ISABELLA
Simon Maris
A portrait of a twelve-year-old girl, whose name was only recently discovered in 2020. Such an expressive and gentle rendering of a young Black girl in the early twentieth century is a rare treasure.

c.1818–19
STUDY OF THE MODEL JOSEPH
Théodore Géricault

1800

1782
CHARLES STANHOPE, THIRD EARL OF HARRINGTON AND MARCUS RICHARD FITZROY THOMAS
Sir Joshua Reynolds

c.1765
PORTRAIT OF A MAN AND AN ATTENDANT CARRYING A PORTFOLIO
John Hamilton Mortimer

1648–64
PORTRAIT OF A BLACK WOMAN WITH A PEARL NECKLACE
Cornelis van Dalen (II), after Govert Flinck
Due to booming trade in the Netherlands during the Dutch Golden Age, a significant Black community grew in Amsterdam. Artworks of real models of color, as well as imagined Black men and women, became more commonplace.

1668
MARGARETHA VAN RAEPHORST
Jan Mijtens

1700

1534–35
ALESSANDRO DE' MEDICI
Jacopo da Pontormo (Jacopo Carucci)
Young Alessandro de' Medici, the first duke of Florence, acted for only half a decade until his assassination by a cousin in 1537. His mother was an African servant, and he became the first biracial ruler in Renaissance Europe. His nickname was "Il Moro," or "The Moor."

1530–40
SUPPER AT EMMAUS
Unknown

c.1525–30
PORTRAIT OF AN AFRICAN MAN (CHRISTOPHLE LE MORE?)
Jan Jansz Mostaert
This is one of the earliest individual portraits of an African man, but his identity remains unknown. Black clothing indicates that he might have been a soldier or Christian pilgrim, but the artist's own travels suggest that the subject may have been a part of the Habsburg court of regent Margaret of Austria.

1500

c.1525
ADORATION OF THE MAGI
Joos van Cleve

In cultural institutions across the globe, from Los Angeles to Copenhagen, there live many extraordinary European artworks featuring men and women of color, yet they remain widely unknown and unexplored. Black models have long been dismissed and glossed over in the art and academic worlds in favor of a whitewashed and narrow study of the past. But if you look more closely at the works of Europe's famed artists, you will find their Black neighbors, brown faces hidden in large crowds and mythical scenes, members of royal courts, and even Venetian gondoliers. As relations between the territories, peoples, and cultures of Africa and Europe changed over time, European art inevitably reflected a wide range of views concerning individuals of African descent, from dignified portraiture, to fantastical African kings used as religious tropes, to anonymous models symbolizing the exotic and unknowable, to brown skin as a contrasting element that draws the eye. Still, even when partially obscured by an artist's prejudices, the existence of the Black subject persists as a testament to a history in which many people of color had agency, and African kingdoms were active members on the global scene. To fully understand our world as it is and as it can be, we must look back and acknowledge these omitted histories. The above timeline highlights this legacy.

—Zaria Ware

AN-MY LÊ

[PHOTOGRAPHER]

"PEOPLE EQUATE PHOTOGRAPHY WITH TRUTH.
BUT ALL PHOTOGRAPHY IS FICTION."

Benefits of using a view camera, according to An-My Lê:
It uses a larger negative
It records landscape in its minute details
It describes space in a more experiential way
You can feel the air between things

An-My Lê is a photographer whose body of work, developed across thirty years, has been focused on the various manifestations of war and conflict—not as fixed moments in history, but as deeply imagined realms through which attempts are made to reapprehend the past or, however fitfully, imagine a possible future. As MoMA curator Roxana Marcoci has noted, Lê's work highlights "intimacies that grow, paradoxically, out of conflict." Thus, seemingly disparate geographies and histories are drawn closer together, suggesting relations across time and space: the Mekong Delta and the Mississippi Delta; deserts in California and the Middle East; wars in Vietnam, Iraq, and the United States; rivers and roads demarcating and erasing borders.

    Lê's gaze, like the military personnel and reenactors she works with to make her photographs, is focused on pushing the present moment, scene, or setting toward what is not there; rehearsing and practicing the act of launching oneself

Illustration by Kristian Hammerstad; photographs throughout courtesy of the artist and Marian Goodman Gallery

into the landscape toward what is held in the mind's eye. *War and conflict—whether anticipated through training maneuvers and simulations (*29 Palms*); or approached in its aftermath as a reenactment (*Small Wars*); or limned to reveal its displacements and continuities by shifting the focus from figures to the landscape (*Viet Nam*); or considered through the lens of past and current acts, sites, and emblems of contestation (*Silent General*)—are, in Lê's photographs, fictions that belie deeper truths about human desires and frailties.*

An-My and I spoke via Zoom in June 2024, on the morning after the presidential debate between Joe Biden and Donald Trump. An-My had watched the debate; I had not—though I had glanced at the headlines prior to logging on and had absorbed that it had been a debacle for Biden, who would drop out of the race less than a month later. Though our conversation did not touch directly on the debate, the urgency of the moment—the unspoken question of What next? What now? *for the ongoing experiment of democracy—informed our conversation.*

Prior to our call, I had sent An-My this message: "I am curious about the poetics of your gaze—the juxtapositions and shifts in scale, the still and restless eye—which, even as it traces the processes and residues of anticipated or recorded rupture, does so not toward any defined end, but deeper into the mysteries of the nature of self, memory, reality, change, and impermanence."

Our conversation touched on all that and more: Elizabeth Bishop's "The Fish"; Walt Whitman's Specimen Days; *Robert Frank's* The Americans; *two iconic images from the war in Vietnam; landscape and land art and view cameras; pornography and Pompeii; notions of the monumental and the subtle and what cannot be "wrangled into the rectangle" of a photograph. Threads of peace, violence, and hope in the face of uncertainty were woven in throughout.*

—*lê thị diễm thúy*

I. FOCUS ON THE HOOKS

THE BELIEVER: Are you in Brooklyn?

AN-MY LÊ: Right now I'm in Carroll Gardens. But we're moving. Where do you live?

BLVR: I live in Western Mass.

AML: Oh, you do! I think you have a bunch of photographers living up there near you.

BLVR: In these hills?

AML: Yeah.

BLVR: You were talking about what you say to your Introduction to Photography students…

AML: Yeah, we talk about describing what you see, what the signals are. You look at events and you notice things. How do you interpret that? The photography I'm interested in is one that describes moments, facts in the real world. I always tell my students that it's so important to describe the world in as many details as possible, and to look for entities that have textures, that have possibilities for an open interpretation. And as the students get more sophisticated, they may capitalize on this possibility.

BLVR: Mm-hmm.

AML: The more you describe—the more precise you are, the more judicious you are in choosing what to describe, in choosing your point of view and the moment—the more specific your photograph can be. But at the same time, it is these descriptive, objective properties that also bring about its subjective aspect and allow us to riff beyond what is in the frame.

BLVR: So you're playing upon the viewer's subjectivity through what you choose to describe?

AML: Yes, though when you are photographing, you really shouldn't be thinking about the subjective aspect. You should be in tune with potentials, but you're there just to pay attention to how things are unfolding, to the surprises that pop up, and you try to grasp all the possibilities that happen in front of you. With more experience, you understand that certain gestures can lock the meaning into something too specific—in a way that allows only one interpretation—while there are certain other gestures that may provide an open interpretation, depending on who is reading the photograph. Photography is not exactly an equivalent, but there's

Sailors on Liberty from USS *Preble*, Bamboo 2 Bar, Da Nang, Vietnam, *from* Events Ashore. © 2011 by An-My Lê. Pigment print. 40 × 56 ½ in.

something that runs parallel to literature. You have words; you want to use your words to express your ideas; in photography, you have a world you want to describe in a vivid, factual way, not just in order to suggest the moment, but to speak about human existence.

BLVR: What did you mean by "signals" earlier? Material signals?

AML: Yes, absolutely material signals! Cues and signals, as constructs. It's sort of like that Elizabeth Bishop poem about a person going fishing. Is it called "Fishing"?

BLVR: "The Fish."

AML: "The Fish"! She describes the specificity of the fish: this humongous, vividly colored animal. But then she zeroes in on the hooks. So what? They're just hooks! But then she realizes that that fish had been caught previously, that it had traversed, already, difficulties and so much else in life. And she decides to let it go.

BLVR: Part of what you're talking about is the eye that's brought to bear upon the thing, the consciousness that's brought to bear upon the thing. That consciousness is reading, gleaning, and perceiving that the fish is a thing in time—that it has a history. And *then* there's the response. So in photography, what you're describing are these split-second, unspoken choices. You're absorbing all the signals and cues, and there's a constant re—

AML: Re-shuffling and re-shifting.

BLVR: Right, if you maintain soft eyes, a soft gaze, so as not to fix the frame.

AML: [*Laughs*] Well, at some point you have to fix.

BLVR: What is that point?

AML: We use different methods, the way one would in fiction, paying attention to the details, the gestures. For example, a man is walking, and sometimes the walk looks generic. But perhaps there's some kind of gait that is interesting, that suggests: Oh! There's an effort there, or this is something they do all the time, or they're just walking really quickly. Those differences matter because they can add up to suggest something about his personal history. Describing space is equally important. How do you draw a viewer in? How do you create tension?

BLVR: Why is tension important?

AML: It keeps everything taut. You often read a photograph from left to right. But sometimes you may be taken for a spin. It is important to be able to draw the viewer in and give him some sort of experiential, physical experience. Landscape is what I am most comfortable speaking about. Olmsted, he designed Central Park, Prospect Park, and has been very influential. I am often telling my students that they need to photographically construct a landscape similarly to the work of a landscape architect. You need to provide an entry point and lead the viewer through your photograph the way the architect may take a stroll over a bridge, through meadows, up a hill. You want someone to get lost in the image, and as they get lost in the image, they start thinking about everything they read and what it means to them.

BLVR: Associations.

AML: Associations, history, personal history. Often, artists who are not photographers think there's a lack of authorship in photography. Because you just push a button, right? It's not synthetic, the way painting is, where every [*mimes a brushstroke*] counts. But there actually is! Where you place the camera, the moment, the height. There are a lot of small things that seem not so obvious, but they do matter. And there's a consistency too. Everyone can make one or two great pictures. But how do you build up the body of work?

II. "WHAT HAS NOT BEEN ANSWERED?"

BLVR: I was able to catch your show [*Between Two Rivers/ Giữa hai giòng sông/Entre deux rivières*] at MoMA, and it was great to see the range of forms. In seeing so much of your work in one space, I really had a sense of the development over time: that movement from the early work, when you first went back to Vietnam, toward something more immersive, and the emergence of different bodies of work.

In terms of the photographs you made in Vietnam, you have talked about how you had certain expectations, and then you arrived, and it was neither what you remembered nor what you'd been told, but everything in between. Your eye initially looks toward people, but then your eye shifts to the landscape—rivers and things—which gives you a sense of continuity. Change and continuity—these seem to be recurring themes in your work: what remains, what is altered. They feel very much like explorations that are not necessarily planned but organically unfolding.

AML: I think that's very perceptive, that notion of something changing over time. But then somehow you still need to find something that reverberates, something that you can identify and carry with you, something that feels substantial. This is what's anchoring me. What has not been answered? What are the next questions? What was I not able to do? What would I like to try? That's what always leads me to the next thing. In the end there are all sorts of intermingled, unified questions that somehow connect back to one another.

BLVR: I know that Michael Heizer's work and [Robert] Smithson's work are potent for you. I was thinking about this as your "double negative": You're not a victim, and this is not about trauma. Those might be frames that others want to bring to the work or bring to you as an artist. But you're like: *That's not mine, and that's not me.* As a result, your exploration of war, the psychic aftermath of war, the anticipation of conflict, as well what it means to prepare for an imagined event—it's all so complex, the threads you're weaving. And throughout, you shrug off these two notions of the victim

Untitled, Ho Chi Minh City, Việt Nam. © 1995 by An-My Lê. Silver gelatin print. 15 ¾ × 22 ⅜ in.

and the trauma. Not that there aren't consequences of these events. But you resist those two frameworks, and that is what allows for the depth and richness and continual movement in your work.

AML: That was not always clear to me. Making the work slowly made me understand. At first, people would suggest ideas for projects and it was always, *No!* When I first went to Vietnam and I was photographing landscapes, friends would say: *Oh, you should look at the effect of Agent Orange! Or: You should go to the battlefields.* That is the direct causal effect of war, and of course it was devastating. But it was too specific, and I wanted to move to a different terrain.

How do you move beyond the specificity of your own

story? I had a teacher in graduate school who was very matter-of-fact. He said: *Nobody cares about you. They just care about what's on the wall. If you make great work, people are interested in everything. But your story itself is not that interesting. Nobody cares.* He was very blunt.

BLVR: But that's useful!

AML: It steered me on the right track.

BLVR: It's the work that remains. It's the work that is the site of exchange and interaction.

AML: The idea of the victim is also complicated. When

Infantry Platoon, Alpha Company, *from 29 Palms. © 2003–04 by An-My Lê. Gelatin silver print. 26 ½ × 38 in.*

my family came to the United States, we were showered with support. We felt saved. My father could have been in the reeducation camp for dozens of years because of his involvement in education. And we could have lost years because of the nonexistent education in Vietnam at the time. We felt so lucky. We got support, and we were able to go to good colleges. At the same time, to Americans we were reminders of the devastation—the fact that Vietnam was such a failure. They thought of the violence; they thought of the consequences on American vets. They were reminded of the student protests.

BLVR: Did you feel that—

AML: It was a burden.

BLVR: Uh-huh…

AML: When I was in college, whenever the word *Vietnam* popped up, I could feel the tension; people avoided looking at me. I remember seeing [the Oliver Stone movie] *Born on the Fourth of July* with friends, and I would be vocal about something, and they would go: "Oh, somebody's getting personal here." I felt like I was carrying the burden of that failure. We were accepted, we were embraced. But at the same time, we were proof of this awful episode in Vietnamese—in American—history. It was my goal to get past that. I am not a victim. That's why that picture of the young girl burned by the napalm bomb [Nick Ut's *The Terror of War*] is traumatic to me. The way people seized on that image—it made sense: they wanted the war

Ship Divers, USS *New Hampshire*, Arctic Seas, *from* Events Ashore. © 2011 by An-My Lê. Pigment print. 40 × 56 ½ in.

to stop, and these were iconic images that were helpful in that sense.

BLVR: *The Burning Monk* [Malcom Browne's photograph of Thich Quang Duc's self-immolation in 1963] is also iconic, but very different.

AML: Especially the pictures that were taken at the beginning, before he was completely immolated. It felt like one of the rare moments when violence and peace came together at the same time. It was an incredible act of protest and resistance.

BLVR: Returning to Heizer's and Smithson's work and the notion of monumental and massive engagements with land. Those guys are digging trenches, and the work is about what's

not there: this wedding of destruction and creation, of nature and man. We have these processes that are man-made, like war. War is something that we as a species do. We make it, and peace is something we also make. With Thich Quang Duc, it was all so intentional. Someone is willing, with their own body, to illuminate the possibility of hope. There are others who have gathered there to witness it. We wouldn't say that's an individual act. That's a collective act.

AML: It's a collective act. He was supported.

BLVR: And it was planned. It reflects back on *everything*—everything that is at stake about being alive. It is such a spectacular act, but it's also so deeply subtle where it wants to reach.

AML: It's small, in a sense, but it's so far-reaching.

BLVR: In the midst of a monumental thing like the war. These shifts in scale also come up again and again in your work.

AML: Scale is something I've definitely been concerned with, whether we're talking about landscape or even portraiture. At first, it was insurmountable, thinking about it.

BLVR: How come?

AML: To deal with something that's greater than you, that big subject of war. The big subject of conflict. Can you do that as a photographer, not using a lot of text and using simple titles? When you're not a writer, when you're not a researcher, a political scientist, a historian?

BLVR: And you're not doing reportage.

AML: Right. Trusting that the medium, in the way I'm using it, can carry the day was not always clear to me. But it's the notion of scale, yes. It's obvious to me in the landscape that there are so many opposing forces. The idea of destruction but then of renewal. Or the idea of constructing something, only for it to disappear over time. But then there will be another movement to counterbalance that. Often there's order and disorder in the way things come toward an equilibrium. Perhaps it was very naive of us to look at America and think: This is the land of opportunities. This is where we can rebuild our life and give a future to our children and grandchildren. Now democracy in America is questionable. But that's an experiment that's been going on since Walt Whitman first wrote about it. It's still an experiment. America is a very young country, so I am hopeful that things will continue to forge ahead.

BLVR: You're hopeful.

AML: I'm not brushing things under the rug. I see what is happening and it's stressful, and that's why I started photographing in the United States. But I am hopeful, yes.

III. A STITCHING OF OLD AND NEW

BLVR: It's interesting that you're pulling from Walt Whitman's book *Specimen Days* as you travel the country for your current series, *Silent General*. Whitman is attending to Confederate and Union soldiers. He sees into the moment, the wreck, the ruin. And he also maintains hope by *doing*, by dressing wounds and such.

Equilibrium is a word you keep coming back to. In your conversation with Hilton Als [first published in *Aperture* in 2005], you also talk about clarity. You're working to arrive at clarity, which is "not necessarily the truth." I found that so interesting. When something becomes clear, there's the follow-up question: And then what? The work is not prescriptive. It doesn't say, *Therefore, do this,* or *Do that.* It's almost like sounding a bell. And in that possibility of clarity, one comes closer to perceiving all the entanglements, all that is actually present and interlaced, what cannot be cut off from the other. That is what prompted my question about the poetics of your gaze, a gaze that has developed over time, and that is not separate from your intellect and your passions and concerns—it is the inflection of how you might touch the world through the camera's lens.

You've had such a long relationship with the view camera; you talk about how it's clunky, how you clamber with it. It makes you visible in the landscape. It is a signal that something is happening. What is your relationship to the camera?

AML: I started using it because I was working for this guild of craftsmen [in France] where I photographed objects and architecture. The view camera is ideal because of its ability to control perspective and focus. It uses a much larger negative, which can record a landscape in its minute details. A print from this larger negative describes space in a more experiential way. Enlargements really hold up. You can feel the air between things. But the camera is very cumbersome. It's heavy.

BLVR: How heavy is it?

AML: It's not just the camera itself. You have the film holders. Instead of using rolls of film, you have sheets of film that fit into these holders. There's only two shots per holder, and each holder is probably heavier than a paperback. I carry thirty of those—that's sixty sheets of film—for a long day of work or half a day, if it's really busy, and then I reload. Then

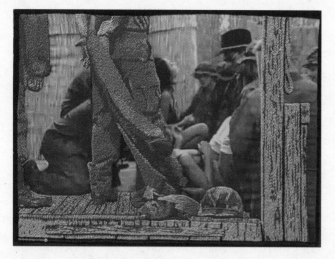 

Left: 00:04:13, Someone Else's War (Gangbang Girl #26), for Stuart Elster. © 2022–23 by An-My Lê. Cotton and embroidery floss. 11 ⅜ × 8 ½ in; *Right:* 00:03:52, Someone Else's War (Gangbang Girl #26). © 2022 by An-My Lê. Cotton and embroidery floss. 11 ⅜ × 15 ¼ in.

you have to carry all the film and the changing bag. You have to set up, you have the tripod. Then there's that disconnect of seeing the image through the ground glass upside down, and then having to close the lens—you stop seeing what it is you're photographing.

BLVR: When you stop seeing, is it kind of like a held breath? What is the sensation when you stop seeing?

AML: I always pre-visualize my frame. I try to imagine where my frame is out in the landscape, and which people are coming in and out of the frame. It's not such a self-conscious act anymore. It taught me to see the frame before I open my camera.

BLVR: In your mind's eye?

AML: Yes. I would drive around, and I would look, and I would already see the picture. The camera is often just for the minor adjustments. But sometimes I don't see it, even though I know I have to make a picture. Then it's a bit of a struggle, looking through the ground glass. There's also the fact that you can't photograph action. Sometimes you can fudge a little bit. But basically, you have to ask someone to hold still. Or you have to find ways to photograph things either before they happen or after they happen. That taught me a lot, in terms of thinking about the nineteenth-century photographers who covered the Civil War, like Timothy

H. O'Sullivan. He set things up and photographed before or after a big battle. Or I have to look for something that is not the main event. That has become my MO—figuring out something even though I am not there in time, as an event unfolds.

BLVR: What about the body of the camera in relation to your own body?

AML: You want to be subtle, but how can you be subtle when the camera itself is so commanding? Everyone pays attention to you, so you have to perform.

BLVR: What are you performing? Are you performing the photographer?

AML: When I first photographed in Vietnam, I was really self-conscious. Do I need to look like I know exactly what I'm doing? Am I asking them to move around too much? Do I look like I don't know what I'm doing? But there's something about the camera that gives you authority. I became less self-conscious about how people perceived me. Then there's the issue of working with an assistant. When I was working in Twentynine Palms [for *29 Palms*, a series in which Lê photographed Marine Corps recruits at a training camp in the Mojave Desert], you often have to pack up in two seconds, and you gotta jump in the Humvee. You're carrying all this stuff by yourself, and as a result you're exhausted by the end of the day. And then you can't work as well the next day. So I started asking students to come with me when I couldn't afford an assistant—which means you're performing not only for the people you're photographing but for whoever else is looking at you. I quickly got over that. But yes, there is something performative about knowing that everyone's looking at you.

BLVR: You're the cause of the pause!

AML: Yeah. In the same way that I don't like asking people for help, while I'm photographing, I also don't like to stop things and say, *Oh, can we do that this way.* But sometimes I question myself: Did I go far enough? Did I ask for everything I wanted? Did I stick around long enough?

BLVR: Going back to *29 Palms*, the second time you were there, after COVID, you were coming to terms with the fact that your mother was in the early stages of dementia, which was exacerbated by the isolation of COVID. You were at Coyote Perch [part of the Marine Corps Air-Ground Combat Center in Twentynine Palms, California] and looking out onto a landscape you had seen before. But then things became "unmoored"—that was the word you used. You were experiencing an overload of information and stimuli. And you arrived at this realization that you could no longer, in your words, "wrangle things into the rectangle." Instead, what was required, you noticed, was a more immersive response. I feel like this is one of those key moments in the trajectory of the body of your work, where what's happening inside you in relation to the landscape and what you're looking at comes to a head. Because "the rectangle," or the frame you're used to, is no longer sufficient. There emerges a new relationship with both your camera and your work. I am very interested in that moment—because it's bodily.

AML: Yeah, it's bodily. I didn't feel like I needed to produce something. I allowed myself to just be in the moment and experience and get emotional. I let my mind wander.
    To go back to land art: I still haven't seen *Double Negative*, and I saw Heizer's *City* very recently, long after I made *29 Palms*, but I had been thinking about visiting various land art as a way to escape photography and be more physical about dealing with the landscape—to be more ambitious, in a way, or break out of the strictures of photography. I was just tired of those strictures, and I wanted to be out of bounds. The larger scale of the prints in *29 Palms* and the projections allowed me to do this.
    Around the time I got out of grad school, photographers felt the need to make work that would hold up in an art gallery versus a photography gallery. There was always this notion that you should print your pictures as large as possible. I resisted that a bit. But maybe this was a way of not just making a huge print, but making something that is physical and experiential, something that is more of an installation. That's how the idea of the cyclorama and the circular installation of *Fourteen Views*[1] came about.

BLVR: Which is interesting because the cyclorama points back to early photography and to early moving images.

AML: It's still about tradition, yes—I sort of love that. I could have gone completely high-tech and digital. But I was more interested in showing how it could be both immersive and rudimentary at the same time, which is the way vision works. How can you connect a horizon line? How can your eyes associate two structures that are very different things? The eye allows you to connect many different things visually and intuitively.

BLVR: It's a leap, or a kind of stitching.

AML: Yeah, it's a rudimentary stitching. I wanted to retain that sense of something being simple, of things being made by hand—something that hearkens back to the nineteenth century. But at the same time, I don't fetishize old things. I'm totally excited about new technology and I use it a lot. I love this hybridization of the old and the new. This hybridization is also in the content of the work: talking about the present, perhaps suggesting the future, but also walking back through history.

---

1. *Fourteen Views* is a photographic installation referencing the painted cycloramas of nineteenth-century Europe; Lê's take on the cyclorama, a theater stage device that creates the illusion of open space, upends the notion of one unbroken and idealized view of the landscape by bringing together fourteen different sites, stretching from the Mekong River in Vietnam to sugarcane fields in Houma, Louisiana.

Fragment I: Battle of Corinth, Film Set (Free State of Jones), Bush, Louisiana, *from* Silent General. © 2015 by An-My Lê. Courtesy of STX films. Pigment print. 40 × 56 ½ in.

IV. "YOU HAVE TO MEET THE DEVIL HALFWAY"

BLVR: Let's talk about *Someone Else's War (Gang Bang Girl #26)* and *Gabinetto*.[2] There, you're going from a film, to a video, to making stills, which you're then turning into embroidery. I was curious about your interest in having these different frames.

AML: Yeah, there's a kind of layering.

---

2. The installation of *Someone Else's War (Gang Bang Girl #26)* and *Gabinetto* pairs two sets of sexual imagery: one a reworking of stills from a pornographic film depicting American GIs and Vietnamese sex workers, the other photographs of erotic sculptures and wall paintings excavated from the ruins of Pompeii. These images, separated by two thousand years, highlight the recurrence of racialized sexual performance and spectatorship in relation to war and conflict.

BLVR: A layering. And then going back, the frescoes [in Pompeii]. You're framing the pornographic.

AML: There are the larger landscapes, the establishing shots, and the more explicit ones. When we embroidered the explicit shots, my assistant and I just kind of scaled the images down to the size of a laptop, which is how people watch porn. And we were able to control the colors more.

I'd had that film [*Gang Bang Girl #26*] for so long, since 2000. It had everything I was interested in: this idea of a fake war, of people reenacting something, of landscape—because it happens in the landscape, which is really unusual. But at that point, when I first got ahold of the video, it was too intense, so I put it aside. Then at some point I realized it was something I needed to tackle. Even though you don't want to look at it, pornography is so present in society. The fact that people went to such great lengths to make this film, it must have been popular, right? Just as popular as the fetishization of nurses and doctors. You have to meet the devil halfway. I stopped thinking about the intensity of it and got to work.

BLVR: In a way, you're overwriting with embroidery thread.

AML: I'm covering it up. I'm trying to make it—what's the word?—less problematic, or less jarring, similar to how I photograph people rehearsing for war. Even though I had wanted to go to Iraq, I ended up photographing people who train for war. Maybe it's a way to not be the photojournalist who's right there as the thing happens. I think every kind of action is a removal of the real thing, turning it into something that's hopefully more revealing and more interesting.

BLVR: You're handling one of the aftereffects of the war, the continuation of one of the lines of fantasy. Like earlier, when we were talking about the cyclorama and the idea of pulling something from the past into the present. The embroidery thread pushes the image back, but also surfaces something.

AML: Right, and the image is still present underneath. Most people have watched some kind of porn, so they're familiar with the types of figures and actions. I think, with our imagination, we can fill in the disconnect very quickly, on top of the stitching. I had a bit of an issue with how beautiful the transformation was—from pornographic film to embroidery.

BLVR: Was the softening an intention?

AML: It's an intention, yes. Because that's what the medium of embroidery does—it removes some of the specificity. When you photograph, you want the specificity. But I think that's what I learned from painting: If you look closely, you can't really see what you're looking at. But as you step back, the

image comes into play. Instead of brushstrokes, we're using stitches. And over time I became more sophisticated in terms of color theory. At first, I just used real colors. Like: This is green, so I'll use green thread.

BLVR: Matching.

AML: Yeah, matching. But then eventually I completely changed the color palette and went with only pinks and reds or blues or some other totally new palette, which was fun and experimental. I stopped seeing the image itself. But I'm glad the final work still contains its origins, in that there are whiffs of this issue of disparate power—the sex labor, the vulnerability of children and women in war. So many themes are still embedded in there. I brought the pictures that I had made in Pompeii [to the installation of *Someone Else's War (Gang Bang Girl #26)* and *Gabinetto*], not just to talk about desire or eroticism, but to talk about this imbalance in power. Many of the sex workers back then were slaves. They were spoils of war. This may seem so jarring and awful, but it's always been war and sex—they have always been connected somehow.

BLVR: So what happens, say, in *Small Wars*, when you are the only woman in the woods with these guys who are doing the reenactments? I loved that in your conversation with Monique Truong and Ocean Vuong [at MoMA in March 2024], you said, "They were working out something, and I was working out something. And it was the safest war." That notion of it being the safest war was so striking to me.

AML: I have to say, those reenactments were safe physically. But emotionally and psychologically, they were not safe at all, because in my head it made me go back and think about both the war and what it means to be an object of desire. I think those guys really believed in the myth of the Vietnamese woman, the female warrior. I've had some of them come up to me with crazy comments. It was shocking at first, but then they would say: "Oh, we're just in character," or whatever.

Fragment I: General P.G.T. Beauregard, New Orleans, Louisiana, *from* Silent General. *© 2016 by An-My Lê. Pigment print. 40 × 56 ½ in.*

BLVR: You were entering into their reenactment, but you were also making the pictures. I was curious about the process of setting up the image, assuming the role, playing the role. How long did the take go for after the image was made? After you set it up, when did the reenactment pick up again without the camera?

AML: I switched between being an actor and being a director.

BLVR: It sounds like you were also conscious of a certain gendered dynamic that still exists, since you were the only Vietnamese person and the only woman there.

AML: When I wore the Vietcong black pajamas uniform, some reenactors would come up to me and say, "Oh, you're so hot." There's a picture that a friend took of me holding an AK-47, which is not in *Small Wars*. But it's one photograph in a stack of prints that I had brought back to the reenactors to thank them for posing for me. I never thought it would be so popular. I thought they would prefer the pictures of themselves. Instead, many of them wanted that photograph of me. They even offered to buy it. Something about that photo really triggered their imagination—I'm sure it's based on movies and literature about Vietnam they've read. It happened mostly when I wore the VC uniform. The North Vietnamese army uniform was not as interesting to them.

That whole issue about being an object of attention, or being hypersexualized as an Asian woman, was one of the things, among others, that led me to really push forward with the embroidery. Even though the embroidery happened many, many years later. You see something that's interesting and you don't know what to do with it. You put it in a drawer, and then it comes back later.

BLVR: It has a kind of murmuring quality. It asserts its voice at some point.

AML: Yeah, the reenactments also helped me realize that I can make something productive out of this experience and be a director and take charge. That was very empowering—that I could help us understand something; that the work is as much about Americans' popular imagination of the war in Vietnam as it is about the event itself.

V. THE ARC OF HISTORY

BLVR: How do you feel as we move further away from the time of the war and its direct aftermath?

AML: When I made that work, it was before we had invaded Iraq. I think Vietnam was still the main war that people remembered. Afterward, things shifted, but I shifted as well. As our politics became more embattled in the United States, I shifted to photographing here. I wasn't sure if I could be inspired by a subject that was nonmilitary, non-war-related. But I realized that my work is about conflict, and we are deep in a contemporary conflict in the United States.

BLVR: When was the shift?

AML: I finished *Events Ashore* [a series in which Lê traveled with the US Navy on maritime and coastal missions across nine years] in 2012 or 2013. Then I was at a bit of a loss as to what to do next. I was invited onto the set of [the 2016 historical war film] *Free State of Jones* by the director [Gary Ross], and I started photographing their setups of the trench wars, like the Battle of Corinth. I loved working on film sets—the preparation, the repetition reminded me of working with the military. I thought those pictures alone would not be enough for a project.

BLVR: But that's what generated the first fragment for the project *Silent General*. So you're stitching together these fragments…

AML: Yeah, and then other works in the South, in the beginning of the lead-up to the presidential election of 2016. When things started really unraveling in the United States, it made me consider the American road trip for the first time. As much as I love Robert Frank—I've been teaching him for a long time—I never felt implicated in it. I realized that I needed to do my own American road trip. And that's what I've been doing.

BLVR: The novel I've been working on is deeply informed by Robert Frank's *The Americans*. The notion of what "the road" is, the road as a ribbon. And this being such a big country! When you move through it, the air changes, the landscape changes, the people change, the accents are different. It's when you move through it that that you feel the density of the atmosphere, and the history. I recognize that in your work. I spent some time in Marfa, as well. Pinto Canyon and the border patrol station. It's so close to the Rio Grande. Mexico is right there. In parts of the Rio Grande you can just walk across the border.

AML: There's such a fluidity there. So the idea of a wall, per se, is not necessarily a solution.

BLVR: I have a friend who lives out there. She's married to someone whose family has had a ranch there for some time. And migrants come through the land. They have bits of carpet that they pull behind them as they walk, to hide their tracks, to avoid border control. These are the layers of what is going on on the ground.

AML: And people come to work for the day, and then go back across the border. Or people cross to have lunch with family. It's so organic.

BLVR: And medical care. It's very porous. It relates to that question of what makes America America? As you're on your road trip, what is it that you're gleaning? What is your camera picking up?

AML: This democratic experience, we struggle to realize,

is complex because of how vast and wide and wild the landscape is. I don't think we'd be who we are if we were the size of France. Size-wise, France is smaller than Texas.

Toward the end of Walt Whitman's life, after he had a stroke, he started meditating more on the landscape—what it means, and how vast and wild it is, but also how restorative it can be. It's always that push and pull. We are always focused on the current moment, but still we need to step back and look at the entire arc of history. Perhaps this moment is just a very tiny fraction of our history, and things will come around.

BLVR: Thinking about landscape, it's hard to keep your eye on the simultaneity of loss and emergence.

AML: Well, with *Spiral Jetty*, what peeks out versus what remains submerged is all dependent on the time of year.

BLVR: Time plays such a big part in what becomes visible. One thing we didn't really get into is your work in color. In *Events Ashore*, color allows you to differentiate between the sky and the sea. You were working in black and white for so long.

AML: In black and white, you pay more attention to the way things are drawn. You are removing information by removing the colors. With less information, something else happens. Maybe your imagination is forced to play a little bit more. The color in *Silent General* connects it to the unfolding of today, the contemporary world. There's an urgency there.

BLVR: You're clearly very sensitive to the texture of color, of light. You've talked a lot in interviews about being a "straight photographer," but part of what's so poetic about your work is that sensitivity.

AML: I think the details provide the physical experience to the viewer. I like to try to pack as much as possible into a photograph. Whitman was a journalist, and you can sense that descriptive quality in his work, which is poetic but still very concrete. I love that. And that's what's great

about photography—how concrete and specific it can be. But also poetic.

We haven't yet talked about truth. [*Wags her finger*]

BLVR: We didn't talk about truth!

AML: Maybe it's for another conversation.

BLVR: I love that you wagged your finger… so Vietnamese! You were like, *We didn't talk about truth*.

AML: Because that is the scandalous part of photography. People equate photography with truth. But all photography is fiction.

BLVR: Maybe photography reminds us about the construction of truth.

AML: Or the construction of a certain moment that you want to draw people into. I'm surely not interested in telling people what to think.

BLVR: You're not prescriptive. I totally get that! There's a steadfastness, but it's not a conclusion.

AML: I mean, I know what I think.

BLVR: You just don't tell me!

AML: I hate when I read or see a movie and I feel like they really tried to manipulate me. And maybe I am manipulating you a little bit by providing all these facts.

BLVR: But you're creating a world.

AML: Yeah, the way a fiction writer does.

BLVR: Yes, there's a kind of architecture.

AML: I want my world to be convincing. I want you to feel that you are experiencing something. ✭

FINDING WIN NG

by NICOLE LAVELLE

In the 1960s, a Chinese American ceramicist built one of the first widely known lifestyle brands. Why, despite the iconic status of his work, is so little known about the artist himself?

DISCUSSED: *Cartoon-Animal-Orgy Mugs, The Sexual Revolution, Spaulding Taylor, A Mysterious Uncle, Crash Pads, Chinatown's Living Room, Jade Snow Wong, The GI Bill, Dorothea Lange, The Funk Art Movement, A Kiln Fire, Goblets, Squab, Eggcraft, A Hot Wok, Tropical Houseplants, Robert Pruzan, The AIDS Epidemic, Soup Tureens, A Time Capsule*

ILLUSTRATION BY:
Kristian Hammerstad

Ten years ago in Nevada City, California, I encountered two coffee mugs in the front seat of an old Mercedes station wagon belonging to Joe Meade, an artist and collector. They immediately caught my eye: oversize and made of white porcelain, they were wrapped in charming illustrations, quirky line drawings depicting a mass of rabbits tumbling in playful, erotic entanglements. "Those are cool," I said. "What are they?" "Woah, dude, you haven't heard of Taylor and Ng?" Joe was delighted. "You're gonna love this. It's very Bay Area."

I held the cartoon-animal-orgy mugs in my lap as we drove to Grass Valley, and Joe, with his encyclopedic knowledge of California ceramics, gave me a crash course on their cultural significance and the life of their maker, the late artist Win Ng. Created for the home-goods company that Win cofounded in 1960, the mugs were subtly provocative mementos of mid-century San Francisco, evoking the sexual revolution and the gay civil rights movement. Though they joyfully depicted free love, they were sold in high-end department stores and made their way into the homes of everyday people—not just those inclined toward countercultural and queer lifestyles. In addition to running his company, Joe said, Win Ng was an exceptionally talented abstract sculptor working at a pivotal moment in California ceramics, a time when the medium was expanding beyond its siloed place as craft and into the world of fine art.

At the time of my ride-along with Joe, I was feeling like an outlier in my master's of fine arts graduate program in San Francisco. While my peers were casually discussing theory at the bar, striving for commercial gallery representation, and immersing themselves in the Art World (capital *A*, capital *W*), I was emphatically *not*. Instead, I was a graphic designer and journalism school dropout, interested in the vernacular and in hyperlocal narratives of place, especially within San Francisco, where I was born and raised. Win's story—of someone who straddled the dualities of art and design, of commerce and concept—felt like a gift, like a taste of something I was hungry for. Despite the art history classes I'd taken, and despite my attraction to homegrown Bay Area art scenes, here was a San Francisco artist I'd never heard of.

As the years went by, I continued to encounter Win's work in improbable yet familiar places. I found him on my mom's bookshelf, in a 1971 book called *Herbcraft*, published by Yerba Buena Press, an imprint of his company. Inside, on the textured, cream-colored pages, were folksy, near-psychedelic drawings of nude waifs sitting on toadstools beside enormous sprigs of mint.

I found Win in my grandmother's dank cabin in the redwoods, when I noticed, after decades of visiting, that the doorstop holding open the bunkroom door was a Taylor & Ng bacon press, a grinning cartoon pig cast in iron. There he was, peeking out of my aunt's bin of cleaning rags: a Taylor & Ng Christmas dish towel from 1983, soft and stained, featuring an ice-skating rat wearing a Santa hat. My chance meetings with these objects in my everyday life stoked the deepest sense of intrigue. To me, they represented an undercurrent of Bay Area material culture, mementos of another time, place, and energy. I was determined to learn more, so I began my process of inquiry in a place I know well: the internet.

Win Ng was born and raised in Chinatown, one of eight children. Starting in the mid-1950s, he contributed to an important movement in ceramics, as part of a loose group of West Coast artists that included Peter Voulkos and Robert Arneson, whose nonfunctional, abstract work helped shift the medium from a utilitarian, traditional craft toward a sculptural fine art rooted in expression. In 1960, just as his fine-art career was taking off—with solo shows and critical reviews—Win and his then boyfriend, artist Spaulding Taylor, began to make and sell their functional work together. Their collaboration eventually became Taylor & Ng, an early lifestyle brand that achieved mainstream commercial success. His multidisciplinary practice spanned ceramics, illustration, painting, industrial design, and creative merchandising. A critic referred to him in 1960 as "a veritable dynamo of creative energy."

Dave Weinstein of the Eichler Network and Pam Keuber of Retro Renovation contributed reporting to this story.

In 1963, Win told *Ceramics Monthly*, "I don't think of art—I just do it. It's part of living."

I dug into online newspaper archives, saving every scrap I could find to my desktop. And still, with each new fact I found, a thousand more questions unfurled before me. And what else? I wondered. Who was Win Ng? What could his life tell me about San Francisco? About my own creative practice? I quickly ran into the edges of the internet's information on Win. His Wikipedia page is anemic, and the few online artist profiles recycle the same information. He is largely absent from the art-historical record, despite his achievements and popularity. I had found a San Francisco artist's story that I couldn't easily read elsewhere, a shiny, magnetic bit of intrigue—a story that I'd have to assemble for myself.

When Win's work found me, over and over again, it spoke to me loud and clear, its personality bursting with humor and warmth. I sensed that his work and story deserved to be known. And so I called strangers, scrolled eBay, and circled the Bay Area to find the objects he made, the places he lived and worked, and the people he knew and loved. I wanted to piece together Win's story, so that others might know him too.

The first thing Ally Ng says to me when I speak to her on the phone is "My uncle has been kind of a mystery for me, too, my whole life." She invites me to come over and see Win's house, one of two mid-century modern homes built from old-growth redwood, in a family compound perched on the north side of Bernal Hill, facing the city. She grew up next door. Her father, Norman, was Win's brother.

I arrive on a Saturday and can't find my way in. All I see from the street is overgrown grass behind a low wrought-iron fence. Much mystery indeed. Ally pops out of a hidden door in the fortress of dark-stained wood siding. She's wearing a sweatshirt that says BERNAL HEIGHTS.

We walk from street level up to an enclosed hilly yard. On the south edge of the large lot is the redwood house that Win had built in the mid-1960s. The yard is overgrown in a way that is common in San Francisco: unruly, lush. Orange-tipped jade plants engulf an inoperative redwood hot tub. Yellow sour grass flowers lean over paths whose cobblestones, Ally tells me, came from the ballast of a ship. At the center is a pond, brimming with life, and from it emerge two Stonehenge-y cobblestone sculptures that Win made.

"He wasn't, like, a fun uncle who was deeply engaged," she says. She lists her memories: "He would go outside wearing a silk kimono to water his yard. He smoked Sherman cigarettes, he had a boyfriend, and he had parties." These parties often involved a yard full of nude men soaking in the hot tub and using the sauna. Ally says she grew up thinking this was typical. "You're like, OK, grown-up parties are hot tubs and naked people."

In 1959, the same year he finished his undergraduate studies, Win bought a modest, single-story Victorian house on this three-parcel lot for nine thousand dollars with a loan from the GI Bill. At the time, Bernal Heights was a working-class neighborhood, home to many families who had worked at the naval shipyard in Hunters Point. It had not yet been declared Redfin's "Hottest Neighborhood of 2014." There was no microbrewery, no e-bike shop, no pretentious food store selling Maldon Salt and Gruyère. In 1960, the *Examiner* referred to Bernal Heights as "an area that is attracting artists with its low rents and magnificent views."

Win's house is currently empty between renters, so Ally takes me through the sliding glass door into the kitchen. Though the simple, underwhelming galley kitchen doesn't match the vibey, gourmet, mid-century vision I had conjured in my mind, the rest of the house oozes with character. The living room is clad in rough-sawn redwood siding, with thirty-foot ceilings and parquet floors. Sunlight beams in through the skylights. A catwalk with a black iron railing overlooks the huge living space. All the exterior doors are sliding glass, and all the interior doors have square cast-iron pulls—there is not a single doorknob in the entire place. It feels like a Sea Ranch house, if an artist were peering over the shoulder of the architect, whispering ideas. Ally says that's pretty much what happened.

Off the carpeted upstairs hallway, each of the bedrooms has a view of the downtown skyline. Ally calls the tiny bedrooms "crash pads," where she imagines Win's friends would stay after his wild parties. Michael Hunter, an artist and queer-studies scholar who rented the house for fifteen years, told me two of the small upstairs bedrooms were labeled OFFICE and GYM in the fuse box. "It was a queer house," he said, made for entertaining and socializing. "It wasn't a family house."

According to Natalie Ng, Norman's first wife, though, it actually *was* a family house, at least initially. As soon as it was finished, Win's parents and some of his younger siblings moved in, and they all lived there together for a time. Natalie spoke of festive weekends, everyone gathering for home-cooked meals and games of mah-jongg.

I turn from the view of the city, and across the hallway I see a mural in the bathroom. Next to a normal old sink and toilet, big tonal stripes and quilted blocks of greens and blues follow the edges of the redwood boards. There's a hippo bathing and a turtle swimming in the reeds. There's an artichoke flowering above the water, a green sun, and little plants with perfect circles forming blooms along a curving stem. The mural charms me; I can feel Win's humor and intention.

I had eagerly accepted Ally's invitation to visit Win's house, hoping the place would radiate his energy in some palpable way, so I might glean inarticulable insights into his personality. The vibrancy of the mural gives me a hint of this feeling, but it also illuminates the lack I feel in the rest of the empty house. Without the trappings of his daily life—dishes in the sink, shoes by the door—I can't get the sense of Win that I had hoped to find.

I'm still thinking about the mural when Ally invites me into her mom's house next door to see a massive oil painting in the living room. It is one of Win's later works, an unfinished piece from the last decade of his life. A full golden-yellow moon sits high in a dark blue sky, with rings of light radiating from it in orange, blue, and purple. The textured landscape is layers of green jungle plants. This painting is unfinished because Win didn't paint landscapes; there are awkward empty spaces within the bushes, reeds, and sky, waiting for animals. The painting gives me the same feeling his vacant house did: that its story is waiting for me to fill in the blanks.

Win moved to Bernal Heights in his early twenties and lived there for the rest of his life. Aside from an army stint in France, the only other place he called home was Chinatown.

His childhood home on Washington Street looked out over Portsmouth Square, a place that has been called Chinatown's living room. His parents, immigrants from Guangdong Province, raised a family of ten in two two-room flats, where they warmed bathwater on the stove and used a shared bathroom down the hall.

Starting when he was fourteen, Win worked for two years sweeping up in the studio of celebrated Chinese American ceramics and enamel artist Jade Snow Wong. Though she denied being a mentor to Win, his exposure to the craft and the materials in her workspace stuck with him. As a teenager, Win began working with enamel, crafting cuff links and selling them to Italian businessmen in North Beach. By age sixteen, he had rented a storefront on Hyde Street for his budding business.

In 1954, at age eighteen, Win was drafted into the army and spent two years in France. Because of his night blindness as well as his inability to drive, he spent those years working as a draftsman and designing posters. He did not waver in his dedication to his art practice, even while serving in the army; Spaulding said Win made custom drawings on the helmets of his peers. He managed to have two solo exhibitions of his graphic work while in France.

His youngest sister, Mimi, recalled Win returning home from service to the family's apartment—by then they lived on Green Street, at the border of Chinatown and North Beach. She was eight or nine years old. "My very first memory of Win is a Saturday morning. I was sitting up watching cartoons and the doorbell rang. The door had a glass window and a curtain. I looked through the curtain and saw Win. The others were still in bed. I saw his face! I ran through the house saying, 'Win is home! Win is home!'" For a while, he slept in the living room on a pull-out couch, and later transformed a rat-infested room in the basement into his studio. He had three small kilns down there, Mimi recalled, and he employed Norman and their mother as a production assembly line, turning out small works in enamel.

I think of Win's family walking these streets, as I walk four blocks from Portsmouth Square to the historic redbrick YWCA designed by architect Julia Morgan. Today, the Chinese Historical Society of America occupies the building and hosts an extensive archive and a gallery for cultural and art exhibits. In 2004, curator Allen Hicks—Mimi's husband—organized a retrospective of Win's work, focusing on his fine-arts ceramic sculptures. Allen published a comprehensive catalog with a detailed biography. He sends me a copy in the mail, and I read it in one sitting. For a moment I doubt whether I should even write this profile—it's all here, thoughtfully assembled in *The Art of Win Ng: A Retrospective*—but I press on, convinced that Win's life and work are due for another look. Despite Taylor & Ng's success and ubiquity, and despite Win's role at a pivotal moment in the American history of ceramics, few of my peers—even those who are artists and designers—have heard of Win Ng.

Though their business wasn't officially incorporated until 1964, the seeds of Win Ng and Spaulding Taylor's creative partnership had emerged in 1959, when the two met through friends at the California School of Fine Arts (CSFA), which was later renamed the San Francisco Art Institute (SFAI).

The Bay Area in the 1950s and '60s was a potent place for the arts. Energetically, the postwar period brought a sea change of attitudes and ideas. Practically, there was an influx of men returning from military service, ready to attend school on the GI Bill. CSFA's faculty of this period—among them Richard Diebenkorn, Ansel Adams, and Dorothea Lange—included visiting instructors who brought influences from Japan, Germany, and creative centers of experimentation like Black Mountain College in North Carolina.

When Win returned from the army in 1956, he enrolled in classes at City College, San Francisco State, and eventually CSFA, which he attended for two semesters before graduating with a bachelor of fine arts degree in spring 1959. Spaulding enrolled at CSFA later that year, after his own army stint ended. Win had already begun his graduate studies at Mills College, but they connected in part because both lived in Bernal Heights.

Wok display inside a Taylor & Ng retail space, from its autumn 1980 catalog. Courtesy of Spaulding Taylor and Taylor & Ng.

At this moment in the California ceramics scene, artists like Peter Voulkos were making sculptures on a monumental scale: pinching, pushing, squishing, etching, and stacking clay. The Funk art movement was percolating at UC Davis, with Robert Arneson's humorous, figurative work reimagining ceramics as fine art. According to Joe Meade, ceramics "had always been craft, until this moment and these makers." As postwar consumers turned toward factory-produced goods, these artists were freed from the constraints of creating functional objects, and eschewed utility to experiment with abstract forms, new building techniques, and surface treatments. Ceramics, once seen as a lesser medium, was now front and center in fine art. "During this period grew the first radical movement to totally revolutionize the whole approach to ceramics," wrote *Artforum* cofounder John Coplans in 1966.

At this important juncture, Win was working right in the middle of the swirl. "He was among the first American artists to approach clay in a nonfunctional sculptural manner," writes Lee Nordness in his 1970 book *Objects: USA*. In a 1955 oral history for the Smithsonian Archives of American Art, Win's CSFA classmate Carlos Villa said, "He was like the star potter of the ceramic [studio]... the pot shop, we called it.... He could do virtually *anything* with clay.... He did these large slabs and gorgeous—utterly gorgeous—sculpture." In 1963, Win told *Ceramics Monthly*, "I don't care what's behind me or to the side of me or in

from WHEN THE ARAB APOCALYPSE COMES TO AMERICA

by George Abraham

Shall I condemn myself a little
for you to forgive yourself

—Fady Joudah, *[…]*

I condemn the blooded river that became a sea
we cannot crawl out of. I condemn the bulldozers
That, as if silkworms, shoveled our corpses into the sea.
I condemn the caterpillar of gears, the puma of sweat
shops, the hijacking of stars & bucks, & never the fall
of entities from such withholdings. I condemn the poets
that slur activists, the poetry identifying as activism, as if
any artist of empire knew what it meant to shred fences,
to hijack, to put one's own body on the line for their people.
I condemn those who say our morals have come at the expense
of our dreaming. I condemn that the pearly-gated hijacking of Yaffa
in which I walked was once the dream of illiterate men. I condemn
their entire imagination, the need to make, of nature's lines & expanses,
a border, less capacious dreaming. Terror has a name and it is boundless we—
The world at stake is just more Palestine to free—
I condemn the river, I condemn the sea.

---

front of me. I have a goal in mind and I'm working for that."

As I read art history books and watch YouTube seminars about twentieth-century Bay Area art, I note only a few minor mentions of Win, despite his accolades, awards, and significant exhibitions. Was he left out because he was Chinese American? Because he was gay? Because he detoured away from the gallery and into business for himself? Perhaps it was because of the perplexing contradiction that he was said to have influenced a critical pivot in ceramics from utility to expression, yet quickly returned to functional ceramics when he started Taylor & Ng.

I crave personal, colorful details about the scene Win inhabited at CSFA, a center of San Francisco art, at a dynamic moment in the institution's history. Who were his teachers? His classmates? Who influenced his work, and whom did he influence? Hoping for these answers, I take myself to the basement of a brick building on Hawthorne Street, just across from SFMOMA, where the school's archives are now housed.

The SFAI Legacy Foundation + Archive's folder on Win Ng is thin, and contains just a few exhibition flyers. Archivist Becky Alexander has pulled records from 1958 and 1959—yellowing booklets and binders with handwritten attendance records and grades inked onto the columned pages. I browse them, seeing Win's grades in courses like Ceramics Studio, Drawing, and Western Culture (A, A, C–, respectively). In 2004, artist William T. Wiley told Allen Hicks that Win was an understated jokester: "We would sit in… design class, and [the teacher] would be calling roll. 'Win Ng!' she would ring out. And each day Win would respond, muttering under his breath, *Who the hell is Win Ng?*" Allen wrote in the catalog, "It wasn't an identity crisis, but a jest on labels, a way to keep in check all the egos of his yet-to-become-famous classmates, himself included. It would crack Wiley up each time."

I am thrilled by the granular detail I encounter in the record books. I see that Wayne Thiebaud and Arthur Okamura taught summer courses right before Win enrolled. In the summer of 1959, just after Win graduated, Wally Hedrick—the esteemed multimedia artist, referred to as "the godfather of Funk" (art), and a founding member of Six Gallery, where Allen Ginsberg's seminal "Howl" reading took place—taught a precollege summer painting class on Saturday mornings. In attendance? A young, delinquent Jerry Garcia, who ultimately took an incomplete in the course.

I vibrate with each new connection to a storied Bay Area artist. I imagine Win meeting them at parties, passing them in hallways, sharing kiln space with them. I browse a decade of *The*

Tower, a mimeographed student publication bursting with voices and humor and headlines rendered in sloppy bubble letters. I feel nostalgic for something I've never experienced.

I leave the building disoriented, with Friday-evening traffic in a raging crawl all around me. Mentally, I'm still in 1959. As I cross the street toward the towering rear facade of SFMOMA and try to remember where I parked, I realize suddenly that I am at the corner of Hawthorne and Howard Streets, and that the SFAI Archive is located next door to 651 Howard, the site of the first Taylor & Ng retail shop, which opened in 1967.

Though Taylor & Ng's first shop was certainly a landmark for the business, it's hard to pinpoint exactly where the true company headquarters were, because they had studios, warehouses, and retail stores all around San Francisco—and later throughout the Bay Area, from Brisbane to Berkeley to Fairfield.

Spaulding and Win were studiomates first, working together in Win's basement and backyard in Bernal Heights. Spaulding lived a few blocks away. After working alongside each other for a while, they became boyfriends.

In the summer of 1960, Spaulding was in Quebec when he learned that a serious fire had destroyed their ceramics shed. Win had fired their new backyard kiln before a proper hood and ventilation system were installed, and the resulting fire burned his feet badly; he used a wheelchair for weeks. The accident pushed them to rent a studio on Folsom Street beside the Central Freeway, at the border of the Mission District and SoMa. With rent to pay, they expanded their production of salable ceramics—plates, bowls, goblets, slab-built candle towers that looked like buildings—to fund their fine-arts practices. And thus a business was born. From the beginning, the sign above their door read TAYLOR & NG. Though they later incorporated as Environmental Ceramics, and sometimes used this mark on their early products, they always did business as Taylor & Ng.

At the new studio, they had the space to welcome people for visits and sales. They were known for their hospitality, counter to the popular conception of the lone artist, locked in his studio, waiting for inspiration to strike. "Pottery must be born in the city," Win said in a 1966 *Examiner* article. "We get ideas from people… We gauge the pulse." Their sales boasted a party atmosphere. At one, they roasted 120 whole chickens inside their kiln at seven hundred degrees, nestled into Taylor & Ng casserole dishes, which people purchased and took home, dinner and all.

In another often-told story, they invited people to a Christmas party by delivering to each guest a pigeon in a cage. The recipient was to remove from the bird's leg either an "accepts" or a "regrets" tag, and release the pigeon to return their RSVP. "They weren't really carrier pigeons, but people thought they were," Spaulding said. Most just flew away after being released, but when notable columnist Herb Caen tried to return the pigeon he received, it just flew back into his home. It was a prank devised with the help of Win's brother Ed, a falconer who kept birds in the yard at the Bernal Hill family compound. The mischievous publicity stunt worked: they made it into Caen's weekly column, a uniquely San Francisco achievement. Caen wrote, "This is to inform Taylor & Ng that I won't be there and please pick up your bird." Spaulding told me with a grin that they served squab at the event.

Their successful studio sales encouraged them to ramp up production and expand their product line. Win's younger brother Herman was brought on to run the studio; he weighed balls of clay and fired the kiln. During this time, Spaulding and Win attended art fairs with their signature spirited booth setups; at gift shows, they refused the folding tables and white satin table skirts provided by the venue in favor of wood and chicken wire, metal grid systems for shelving and display, and sheets of galvanized steel, assembled by Herman. Norman and Natalie began helping with trade shows, and later became partners in the business.

Taylor & Ng popped up in retail spaces, such as a show in 1966 at Dohrmann's, a boutique glassware shop in Union Square that was later absorbed by Macy's. The advertisement promised "bottles, jugs, pitchers, vases, bowls, weed pots, frogs, owls, rocks, rills, and other whimsies." The verbose ad copy continues: "We asked Spaulding Taylor and Win Ng, two of San Francisco's brilliant artist ceramists… what was meant by their phrase 'Environmental Ceramics.' They answered: 'Briefly, it is another term for functional… ceramics to be used in enjoying everyday living… cooking, serving, entertaining, garden and sky-watching, animating the scene around the house.'"

During this early, experimental era, the company's first successful piece of

HERBCRAFT

A COMPENDIUM OF MYTHS, ROMANCE AND COMMONSENSE

Cover of Herbcraft: A Compendium of Myths, Romance and Commonsense *by Violet Schafer, with illustrations by Win Ng. Yerba Buena Press, 1971.*

environmental ceramics emerged: a chicken cooker. Spaulding designed it and Win refined the first version in 1962; it was a casserole dish hand-built from rough stoneware, with a rounded bottom and a textured, chicken-shaped lid, with the beak and tail glazed a shiny brown. As Spaulding remembered it, a friend who was a buyer at the burgeoning San Francisco discount import retailer Cost Plus asked if they could make a ceramic cooker. Natalie said that stories from her childhood in China inspired the quirky avian twist: she had shared with Win and Spaulding that the poorest people—those with no dishware or kitchen—would cover a chicken in wet mud and then build a fire on top to cook it. In 1979, Win told the *Examiner*, "The idea of a bullet-shaped ceramic cooker bored us. We began to put heads and tails and feathers in our designs."

In the beginning, they drove the unfired chickens north to St. Helena in Napa County, where their friend Richard Steltzner had a bigger kiln than they did. By 1966, they were factory-producing a third generation of slip-cast chicken cookers in Japan, made of the highest-quality porcelain. Other cookers quickly followed: a quail, and later a fish.

This leap to outsourcing production was a critical moment in their growth, and the story of the chicken cooker became a loose formula for Spaulding and Win's future successes: They would accept a suggestion from someone in the know, put their own peculiar twist on it, and then ride the energy of positive reception, iterating toward a final version for mass production. Starting with the chicken cooker, they became masters of the unexpected, offering their customers both surprise and delight.

Taylor & Ng's first retail shop opened on Howard Street in 1967, kick-starting nearly two decades of steady business growth and expansion of their offerings. The Halloween-week opening party featured an array of goods from local craftspeople and a sidewalk calliope played by Anton LaVey, founder of the Church of Satan. The brick building—originally an industrial dye shop—had an office upstairs, a warehouse below, and a large street-level space, where Win and Spaulding expanded their artistic vision into curation and retail. They imported handmade objects and sold goods made by local craftspeople. "Taylor & Ng selects fine design… for the aware individual," a 1969 advertisement read. "An eclectic collection of unusual objects is presented for your daily use and continuing pleasure." Alongside peacock feathers and baskets from Poland, the ad featured a four-foot-tall redwood lion carving by Robert Kingsbury, who later became the first art director of *Rolling Stone*. The saucy copy concluded, "Come in and satisfy your other self."

Their creative and entrepreneurial approaches were similarly frenetic. There was no strategy, just experimentation and iteration. Things moved so fast in what Natalie called the "young, adventurous years" that the company had to take things as they came. Mimi told of big, boisterous brainstorming dinners with the retail staff and the art department. "We all really bonded," she said. "It was just a very carefree time." She noted that art director Allen Wood could barely take notes fast enough to catch all the ideas flying around.

In 1971, with the publication of *Herbcraft* by Violet Schafer, Taylor & Ng launched its publishing imprint, Yerba Buena Press, which would go on to release fifteen titles over the next eleven years. The books—including *Eggcraft*, *Breadcraft*, and *Ricecraft*—were catch-all, scrapbook-style gift books, boasting recipes, history, folklore, and photographs. Many featured Win's illustrations. The authors—chefs like Rhoda Yee and Margaret Gin, and food historians like Violet and Charles Schafer—were Win and Spaulding's friends, whom they invited to realize passion projects that would also support the company's product line. The series was intended to make Taylor & Ng's gourmet kitchenware more approachable and ultimately more appealing, as part of a creative lifestyle punctuated by functional, beautiful things.

Plantcraft, published in 1973, celebrated the joy of caring for houseplants. It came with a 33 rpm vinyl record with music by composer Ken Ziegenfuss, a friend of the book's author, Janet Cox, who was the food editor at *The San Francisco Chronicle*. Win's illustrations depicted brick apartment buildings with a domestic jungle spilling out the windows, a nude guy doing yoga with a terra-cotta pot in one hand, and, to illustrate the "Propagation" section, a group of frolicking rabbits that was later adapted into a popular line of coffee mugs.

The Wild Wild Kingdom series of coffee mugs—eventually renamed Animates, and generally referred to as "the animal orgy mugs"—emerged around 1979. These mugs are arguably the company's most recognizable objects and are many people's first encounter with Taylor & Ng's work (as they were for me). At first glance, the animals appear to be wrestling, hugging, and dancing. The reality of the orgy might take a few cups of coffee to recognize, which is the genius of its subtle subversion.

Taylor & Ng released twenty distinct series of mugs. Another line, simply called Tall Mugs, featured unique bulbous shapes and monochromatic, folksy drawings of nude men with horses, nude women with birds, and cats with fishing poles. Win's illustrations were provocative and, over time, brought marginalized perspectives—queer, Chinese American, sexually revolutionized—into the mainstream via people's bookshelves and kitchen tables. Joe Meade told me the large size and offbeat personality of the Taylor & Ng mugs were perfectly timed to the rise in popularity of herbal tea in the 1970s. "They were savvy, not just in terms of design, but in knowing what people wanted," Joe said.

Their wok was another well-timed product release. In 1972, just as President Nixon's visit to China reopened trade and travel after a twenty-two-year embargo, the company's wok hit the market, with a wooden handle and a unique domed lid. The wok and its accessories—a steamer basket, tongs, and a spatula—were tidily packaged in a brightly colored cardboard box with *Wokcraft*, a how-to book of recipes by the Schafers, promising to demystify wok cooking and maintenance. While the individual components of the set weren't hard to find in Chinatown kitchen supply stores, the kits in their charming boxes made it easy and appealing for the American consumer to get into wok cooking, especially once they were wholesaled to major department stores. At one point, the company's Far East Housewares Collection—including woks, cleavers, teapots, a calligraphy set, and a tempura kit—brought in 50 percent of the company's revenue. The wok, of course, had been around for centuries—Taylor & Ng didn't introduce anything new, but it was part of a wave of retailers and chefs in the 1970s who were popularizing Chinese cooking with mainstream, Western audiences. Its peers included the Wok Shop, which opened in San Francisco's Chinatown in 1969 and still sells American-made woks from its original location; and Joyce Chen, a Cambridge, Massachusetts–based chef with a popular cooking show who patented a flat-bottomed wok to better fit contemporary electric stovetops.

In 1973, Taylor & Ng opened a second, larger retail location directly across the street from the original Howard Street store. Between 1974 and 1979, Taylor & Ng closed the Howard Street stores to open three others in more prime locations: in Palo Alto, California; on Market Street in San Francisco's Castro neighborhood; and in a little kiosk at Macy's in New York City.

In 1979, they opened a three-level, eight-thousand-square-foot flagship location in the Embarcadero Center, in the heart of San Francisco's financial district. They had arrived.

Even as the business grew, Win continued his hyper-productive dedication to the fine arts. His art star had risen early; he had received notable awards for his work in ceramics as a high school student. In his twenties, he had shown his work at prestigious arts institutions throughout the US and Europe, and had solo shows in New York and San Francisco. Gallerist Ruth Braunstein referred to him as "the hot star." His tenacious work ethic and media-agnostic, intuitive process propelled a dynamic art practice. "Work is a pleasure," the twenty-five-year-old Win Ng told the *Examiner* in 1960.

Though it's common today to be a potter-poet, a painter-builder, or a writer-musician with a day job, the art-world establishment at the time didn't quite know what to do with Win's multi-hyphenate approach to creative work, especially when he turned toward commercial mass production. Many artists must find additional sources of income to pay the bills, but this reality is rarely discussed, celebrated, or included in a holistic rendering of the artist as a complex human being living under capitalism. Win's siblings said he was always entrepreneurial, and had sought opportunities to make a living through his art since he was a teenager.

The few existing artist profiles about Win describe his "departure" from fine art or his "pivot" into business, but it was really more of an expansion: he continued to make and show sculptural ceramics and later experimented with large-scale public commissions, even as the plates and bowls rolled off the production line. Carlos Villa recalled, "He was maybe the richest guy in the school, because people were either buying his work as fine art or buying it because they needed a perfectly matching set of plates and wares." His first solo show, at age twenty-five, was in 1961 at the Mi Chou Gallery on Madison Avenue in New York, only one year after he started Taylor & Ng. The show flyer boasted of Win's "honest, humorous, ambitious, and energetic" works that "reflect the artist's true self." In 1964, as the chicken cooker production was moving to Japan, Win's show of ceramic sculptures at Braunstein's Quay Gallery in Tiburon, California, received a write-up in *Artforum*—an achievement that remains a benchmark for "making it" in the art world today. He was wildly productive, agnostic of medium or context.

In 1968, shortly after the opening of Taylor & Ng's first retail shop, Win began a period of public art commissions, his first being a colorful ceramic tile mural for the front of the Maxine Hall Health Center in San Francisco's Western Addition neighborhood. During a recent renovation, the mural was preserved and expanded onto a new face of the building. Spaulding assisted Win with works for several public parks in Sunnyvale, down the peninsula, including a chunky, concrete, *Flintstones*-esque playground structure with rounded edges, a large pond, a sculptural steel water feature, and a fountain pavilion of little concrete mountains that later became known as Fish Banks, a popular skateboarding spot in the 1980s. Spaulding had no recollection of how Win got the public art commissions. "I don't know that he was applying for them, but he was getting them," he said. In 1971 in Orinda, a wealthy suburb of Oakland, Win painted a mural at the new BART station. Today, his supergraphics-like mural of bold, geometric orange, black, and white stripes is chipping, peeling, and scuffed. Jennifer Easton, the current art program manager at BART, said she hopes to restore the piece in the next year.

Win explored mediums, context, and scale, following his intuition and seizing opportunities as they arose. Spaulding didn't think Win ever considered there to be a division between fine art and commerce. Mimi said, "He saw the opportunity to make money, and that was a draw," considering the circumstances of his upbringing. She added, "He probably felt he would get back to it." As Allen wrote, "It is well to note that it is a Western, not Eastern, point of view that denigrates utility and makes the distinction between 'craft' and 'fine art.'"

What began as Win and Spaulding's side hustle to fund their fine-arts practices exploded into a wild success, and became their focus for decades. As the two approached their business with a sense of whimsy, and worked together to create a rich, layered, nuanced brand identity, it's clear Win considered the company to be simply another opportunity for artistic expression.

The Taylor & Ng retail stores were an experiment in experience, offering the consumer an immersive, aesthetic encounter. "We looked at retailing from the artist and craft type of approach," Win said in a 1979 *Examiner* article. "We were never satisfied with the environment in which our merchandise was placed—just our own quirk." They arranged products like art in a gallery or museum. Mimi, who worked at a number of the retail stores, said, "He was quite particular. He would always be there, ditzing around." International crafts imports intermingled with studio ceramics on bespoke shelves designed by Win and built by Herman. Bright screen-printed boxes were stacked into large floor displays. Spaulding loaded the top shelves with houseplants, at first to fill empty shelves after they had sold out of inventory, and later just because he liked the way they made the space feel.

Taylor & Ng served chrysanthemum tea at its stores. It sponsored an egg-decorating contest each Easter, with prizes for adults and children. Its weekly newspaper ads offered giveaways and "This week only!" deals. It hosted wok demonstrations—some hosted by the young, then unknown chef Martin Yan—at high-end department stores like Macy's and Gump's to help people visualize cooking with a wok at home. This type of integrated marketing may sound rote in today's post-retail landscape of internet shopping, where social media floods our attention with advertisements disguised as "content" for one lifestyle brand after another. But at the time, consumer culture was still young, with fledgling postwar shoppers just beginning to associate their consumption with their identities. Mainstream television and magazine advertisements pitched products, not lifestyles. Taylor & Ng was selling the whole package: taste, objects, function, the feeling of a dinner party, and the idea of being a worldly collector without going farther than the shop down the street. "We're not here to set a style," Win said in an

Third-generation porcelain chicken cooker by Taylor & Ng. Photograph by Allen Hicks. Courtesy of Win Ng Trust.

Examiner article. "We're here to offer basic things, a mix, a range, so that the homeowner can create his own space."

Taylor & Ng also fit into a growing gourmet kitchen zeitgeist, alongside enterprises like Williams Sonoma, which opened its first San Francisco shop in 1958, selling French cookware. Crate & Barrel started up in Chicago, dealing in imported kitchen goods. Julia Child's cooking show *The French Chef* first aired on public access television in 1962, bringing a new kind of gourmet into homes across America. These folks all met and mingled at the same trade shows. As Win's family and Spaulding told it, they were leading the way in innovative product design and merchandising, and a lot of companies flattered through mimicry. Herman remembered seeing the interior of a Williams Sonoma store in San

Francisco and thinking that its wooden shelving looked familiar. Though the fern bar aesthetic later became widespread, Spaulding says he was the first retailer he knew to create lush jungles of tropical-houseplant interiors. With the rise in popularity of *Plantcraft*, Taylor & Ng began to propagate houseplants offsite at a greenhouse-roofed building on Harrison Street.

Taylor & Ng did not operate in a vacuum, nor was it the most successful home-goods business in the long term: Williams Sonoma went public in 1983 and today operates over five hundred stores between its many subbrands, which include Pottery Barn and Rejuvenation. But the company's unique offering was the alchemical union of Win's and Spaulding's creative sensibilities, drawn from their cultural context as gay artists in postwar San Francisco.

At the Gay, Lesbian, Bisexual, Transgender Historical Society's archives in San Francisco, there is a manila folder labeled "Party at Win Ng's House, 1985." Within are images taken by Robert Pruzan, a photographer and mime who diligently documented the city's gay scene in the 1970s and 1980s. I browse the contact sheets with gloved hands, encountering a puzzling dichotomy that seems to be entirely appropriate for a party at Win's. In the first images, elderly Chinese party guests are seated cozily around a sparsely decorated living room. In later images, two hunky dudes pose nude in a round redwood hot tub.

Win was known for keeping his personal life private. Despite San Francisco being a queer mecca, the gay civil rights movement didn't fully blossom until the very end of the 1960s, and before that, gayness was somewhat of a liability in public life. Win's sexuality was a bit of a public secret: known to most, but not officially acknowledged.

WORKS OF ART THAT SANK WITH THE *TITANIC*

✶ *La circassienne au Bain* by Merry-Joseph Blondel

✶ A bejeweled version of *Rubáiyát of Omar Khayyám*

✶ *Plymouth Harbor* by Norman Wilkinson

✶ A 1598 copy of Francis Bacon's *Essays*

✶ A handwritten short story by Joseph Conrad

—*list compiled by Hannah Langer*

Allen Hicks, in the retrospective catalog, wrote that Win "chose not to 'come out.'" On the other hand, Spaulding's husband, Tony Manglicmot, said, "I mean, everyone was out. Everyone knew about everyone else being gay." Win and Spaulding were referred to as "partners" in the press, but always vaguely or in relation to their business. He skillfully evaded reporters' questions about his personal life, saying work was his priority. Spaulding told me they were gay and that was that. "It was a matter of fact," he said.

Both Win's family and Spaulding said he never participated in gay rights activism. Michael Hunter, the queer studies scholar and tenant from Win's house, suggested that, perhaps due to Win's age and tendency toward privacy, he wasn't interested in activism; he was forty in 1976, older than many of the young men flocking to the Castro, the city's gay center. "Merce Cunningham and John Cage were very similar," Hunter told me. "They weren't interested in identity being part of their work."

Win was diagnosed with HIV in 1982. According to Allen Hicks, he was one of the first people in San Francisco to receive a diagnosis; the AIDS crisis had begun just a year before, in 1981. Each person I speak to about Win's illness bemoans the fact that it wasn't until many years after his diagnosis that the FDA approved lifesaving antiretroviral drugs, which today remain the only way to treat AIDS. Win was characteristically private about his diagnosis, and many of his family members were unaware of it until he began showing symptoms, in the late 1980s.

San Francisco was an early center of the AIDS epidemic in the US and for many years had the highest per capita rate of cases. Then mayor Art Agnos described it as "the biggest human tragedy in the modern history of this city." The hollowing-out of San Francisco's gay community by the AIDS epidemic had a palpable impact on the city's culture, and Spaulding and Tony told me this time of massive change also caused a major shift in the character of the company. "I think a lot of that… youthful energy that was part of Taylor & Ng kind of got lost during that period," Tony said. "Selling the lifestyle ended when the designers were no longer there." He told me that many of the designers for the company ultimately died of AIDS.

In 1983, just four years after opening its downtown flagship store, Taylor & Ng closed its retail locations and turned its focus to wholesale. The same year, Win left the day-to-day operations to return to his studio art practice; Spaulding had left the business in 1980. Natalie and Norman divorced, she left as well, and Norman took the helm. Win contributed the occasional illustration—for a holiday mug or tea towel—but focused in earnest on the creation of works for the gallery.

With time to spare, Win reactivated his half of the Belcher Street warehouse he co-owned with Spaulding, renting studio space there to other artists. In 1985, he presented a solo exhibition of ceramic sculptures, returning to show with Ruth Braunstein. The works were slab-built combinations of circles and squares, bright jewel-tone glazes applied in a quilt-like pattern. The exhibition's press release suggests that the works "exemplify the serenity and the maturity of time."

Win had the support and care of his family in his final years, something

Illustration by Win Ng for Taylor & Ng's "1.2.3 Stoneware" set. 1976. Courtesy of Taylor & Ng.

many other gay men dying of AIDS did not have. Norman handled the business operations, and Herman drove Win around for errands. Mimi visited him in the hospital often. "We were there all the way to the end," Herman said.

Win died in 1991 from AIDS-related complications, after living with the illness for nearly a decade. He was fifty-five years old. As he became weaker toward the end of his life, he abandoned ceramics in favor of painting, working in acrylic and oil on different series that diverged aesthetically and materially from his previous work.

One piece from his late-life experimentation with oil painting hangs in the Crocker Art Museum in Sacramento. Natalie commissioned Win to paint

Natalie's Jungle in 1989, and donated it to the museum in 2022. It is part of the same series as the unfinished jungle painting that hangs in Alice's house, though this one is brimming with life, each animal turned to look right at you with its eyes wide open. I stand before the sixteen-foot-tall painting in a chilly museum on a 105-degree summer day, looking for the weird little creatures hidden within it: a cat-fish with tabby markings, a hippo with a snail as its eye, a flamingo standing on a turtle, a monkey with a tiny banana. I wish this painting had a ladder alongside it, so I could look more closely at the phoenix, floating in the air at the top of the canvas: a mythical bird that can be born again after death.

I've spoken with Win's family, and I have plenty of facts. I have dates, and addresses, and the oft-repeated narrative of his rise to success. Each person tells me he was funny, and worked hard, and was generous. I ask for more: What was it like when he walked into a room? What was it like to collaborate with him? I hear similar stories repeated from different angles: Win was a terrible driver. He liked to make lists. He usually had a long, dark cigarette dangling from his lips. He had a dry wit, they said. I have encountered this challenge within my own family: It is difficult to speak about someone you've lost, especially decades later. And not just because it's painful, but because memory is strange and things fade. A person can become enshrined in lore. The stories that are repeated are the ones that stick around.

Ally said she has a fantasy of an alternative world in which her uncle is alive, they are friends, and she works alongside him at Taylor & Ng. I, too, have a fantasy of what it would be like if Win were still alive: I'd be sitting in his living room right now, my socked feet on the parquet floors, asking him questions, through a cloud of smoke, about his life and decades of work. Since I can't call Win, I call Spaulding Taylor, and hope he will invite me over. He does.

Spaulding and Tony live north of San Francisco in Sonoma, on a lush one-acre compound they designed and built. They left San Francisco tentatively after Win's death, thinking they'd split their time, but over the years their center shifted.

We sit at a large wooden table in their kitchen—which is not in their small home but in the massive adjacent studio building—with its large doors open to the sunny courtyard, a glittering pool at the center. Paintings cover the walls. I see a kiln in the corner, and an open bag of clay sitting on a worktable. Spaulding tells me he is losing his sight, so he works in clay more and paints less. His recent pieces rest on a homemade plywood shelf on wheels: raku-fired bowls of all sizes dressed in drippy, glimmering hues.

They walk around, pulling things to show me from drawers and shelves. Spaulding holds an original Win drawing, ink rendered in the smallest brushstrokes on rice paper, careful and delicate. I ask if they have any of the earliest studio ceramics. Tony exclaims, "The plates!" and rushes over to a cupboard to pull out a stack of stoneware plates from the Folsom Street studio days. They feature Win's freestyle illustrations, painted in earthy glaze: a topless woman with voluminous hair, a lion, a cat fishing. I'm relieved to see these objects, because Spaulding and Win were not precious about maintaining an archive. In 1979, they told the *Examiner* that they had few of their early works. "I didn't save any of them," Spaulding says, "but we found some in other people's garages." Win adds: "I found one of my early ashtrays at the Salvation Army."

We speak for hours, and they tell me what they remember. The general arc is clear, but some of the details are fuzzy; it's been more than forty years since Spaulding left Taylor & Ng, and more than thirty since Win died. "It's a very strange thing," Tony says, about losing friends during the AIDS epidemic, "especially now that Spaulding is ninety and I'm seventy-one. It's like a time capsule: all of these people got put in, and they're all stuck in this time period, while we've moved on."

Though he may be enshrined in the memories of his loved ones, and though his work lives in many households, Win Ng is far from a household name. He is mostly missing from the history books that survey Bay Area art. While his

---

ART-RELATED BOOKS AND MAGAZINES
BANNED IN STATE PRISONS, PART I

✸ *Comic Art Now* by Dez Skinn (North Carolina)

✸ *Tokyolife: Art and Design* by Ian Luna et al. (North Carolina)

✸ *Color for Painters: A Guide to Traditions and Practice* by Al Gury (California)

✸ *The Great Golden Age Book: Dutch Paintings* by Jeroen Giltaij (California)

✸ *Frida Kahlo: The Paintings* by Hayden Herrera (California)

✸ *Impressionist Painting in the Louvre* by Germain Bazin (California)

✸ *Art Galleries of the World* by Langdon Helen (Texas)

✸ *The Art of the LP: Classic Album Covers 1955–1995* by Johnny Morgan (Texas)

✸ *Art: From Cave Painting to Street Art, 40,000 Years of Creativity* by Stephen Farthing (Texas)

✸ *Louvre: The 300 Masterpieces* by Frédéric Morvan (Texas)

✸ *Vatican Museums: 100 Works Not to Be Missed* by James F. Quigley (Texas)

✸ *Life Drawing for Artists: Understanding Figure Drawing Through Poses, Postures, and Lighting* by Chris Legaspi (Washington)

✸ *If It's Not Funny It's Art* by Demetri Martin (Arizona)

✸ *W* magazine, the Art Issue (Arizona)

✸ *1001 Art Masterpieces You Must See Before You Die* by Stephen Farthing (Arizona)

✸ *The American Poetry Anthology* (Arizona and Louisiana)

✸ *ARTnews*: The New Shape of Street Art, January 2011 (South Carolina)

—list compiled by Juliana Luna and Megan Posco

early work is in museum collections, he hasn't had a large, solo retrospective show at any major institution, nor has his distinctly creative retail merchandising, curatorial importing, or product design work with Taylor & Ng been recognized or showcased. Many of the details on his Wikipedia page are incorrect.

In the same vein as most written history, the art-historical canon is largely oriented toward white male artists, and skims over everyone else. I was stunned to learn that even the Asian Art Museum did not present a solo exhibition of an Asian American artist's work until 2014. In the last ten years, it has presented retrospectives featuring Carlos Villa, a Filipino American visual artist, and Bernice Bing, a Chinese American lesbian painter—both former classmates of Win's at CSFA. I wrote to the museum to inquire about any potential plans for a Win Ng retrospective, but didn't receive a reply.

Today, Taylor & Ng is owned by Ally's other uncle, her mother's brother Victor Moye. In 1994, Norman got sick and couldn't keep the business afloat. By 1997, Taylor & Ng had filed for chapter 11 bankruptcy. Victor attended the auction and outbid two others. At the time, the company had no inventory warehouse, so he purchased the brand, its relationships with manufacturers, and its intellectual property. Today, its website sells woks, reproductions of some mugs, and miscellaneous imports.

Just inside the front door of Win's house, there's a redwood door to the garage. Ally and I peek inside. On one of the shelves, printed on the side of a box containing a set of deadstock tableware, I see Win's familiar illustration style: a 1976 drawing depicting a lively multigenerational gathering in a living room with an enormous window overlooking trees outside. Each smiling person holds a plate of food, a spoon, or a stack of dishes in their hands. One man pushes a rolling cart loaded with a Taylor & Ng feast: a roast pheasant, a soup tureen, a teapot, and goblets for wine. Cats, dogs, and pet bunnies lie about. A glimpse into the kitchen reveals pots hanging from a rack and a wok and a ceramic chicken cooker on the counter. Houseplants are all around; there are paintings on the walls; it's a joyful living tableau. The environment is filled with ceramics, "animating the scene around the house."

It's a scene I can imagine taking place upstairs, in Win's living room: any number of his seven siblings, serving themselves hot food cooked by their parents on the six-burner stove. Partners, nieces, nephews, and pets. Spaulding arrives to drop Win off and stays for dinner. The chatter of a close family—siblings, business partners, neighbors, housemates—rises into a cacophony mixed with the clink and clatter of forks on plates, the hiss of steam from beneath the wok lid. ✷

ART-RELATED BOOKS AND MAGAZINES BANNED IN STATE PRISONS, PART II

✷ *Leonardo: The Artist and the Man* by Serge Bramly (Virginia)
✷ *The Humanities Through the Arts* by Lee Jacobus and F. David Martin (Virginia)
✷ *USA Today: New American Art from the Saatchi Gallery* by Meghan Dailey and Norman Rosenthal (Wisconsin)
✷ *Rembrandt: Britain's Discovery of the Master* by Christian Tico Seifert et al. (Louisiana)
✷ *Defining Contemporary Art: 25 Years in 200 Pivotal Artworks* by Daniel Birnbaum et al. (Connecticut)
✷ *Art Nouveau: An Anthology of Design and Illustration from the Studio* by Edmund V. Gillon Jr. (Florida)
✷ *The Art of Drawing: Understanding Human Form and Structure* by Giovanni Civardi (Florida)
✷ *Artforum*, several issues (Florida)
✷ *How to Sell Your Art Online: Live a Successful Creative Life on Your Own Terms* by Cory Huff (Florida)
✷ *The Chinese Art Book* by Keith Pratt et al. (Iowa)
✷ *An Atlas of Anatomy for Artists: 189 Plates* by Fritz Schider (Michigan)
✷ *Street World: Urban Art and Culture from Five Continents* by Roger Gastman et al. (Michigan)
✷ *Art Attack: A Vision of Struggle* by Kevin "Rashid" Johnson, edited by Anthony Rayson (Ohio and Florida)

—*list compiled by Juliana Luna and Megan Posco*

MICHAEL SMITH

[ARTIST]

"AT SOME POINT YOU SEE SOMEBODY DO A LOT OF THE SAME THING AND CALL THEM A HACK. AND THEN I THOUGHT, HOW DO YOU BECOME A HACK? AT LEAST HACKS MAKE A LIVING."

Things Michael Smith's persona Mike has wondered:
Whether or not he has the aptitude for photography
If someone will buy his loft
Which way to the Fountain of Youth?

Over a year ago, a mutual friend let the artist Michael Smith know I was interested in doing an interview with him. The friend showed Smith the previous piece I'd published, an interview with someone also named Michael. Smith's only response, as far as I know, was "Which Mike is he going to interview next?"

Before long, Smith invited me and the friend to sit in his living room, which had an armchair and a television and several small paintings resting on a shelf he'd installed near the ceiling. Smith talked about the walnuts he'd been putting in his oatmeal and asked what the protocol was for throwing away old batteries. He talked about studying painting when he was young—before the performance work, the videos, the installations, the drawings; before the character of Mike or Baby Ikki ever stood onstage in front of an audience—and about how the head of the Whitney Independent Study Program let him stay for an extra semester because he was so tidy. He liked to sweep, he said. And from what I could tell, this was still true. His house was very tidy.

Illustration by Kristian Hammerstad

Michael Smith was born in Chicago in 1951, and after he lost interest in painting, he started going to an open mic at a hamburger restaurant. Notes he took there were the germ of his early Chicago performances, like Comedy Routine, *where he walks the outline of a stage, empties shaving cream into a tin, and pies himself in the face. "What are you doing, Mike?" asks a voice on tape, and it's a good question. Smith explored it through early, prop-heavy performances, and in the '80s he fleshed out the character of Mike in gem after gem of collaborative video. There's* It Starts at Home, *in which Mike gets his own reality show; and* Secret Horror, *in which unexpected ghosts show up for a come-as-you-are party after Mike wakes in terror one night to the sudden appearance of an ugly new drop ceiling in his home.*

Mike isn't Michael Smith; or, put another way, Smith is the artist, and Mike, the art. He's the protagonist of many of Smith's videos and performances, an everyman with a lineage in the work of Buster Keaton and Jacques Tati. Sitting in his living room that night, I couldn't help but feel like I was sitting among objects charged with potential. The space had the energy of a set. Everything was ready to use. There was the kitchen table where he ate, the broom, a window. At some point I got up to use the toilet.

Smith gave me an eight-DVD survey of his work and said that the record label Drag City, in collaboration with the publisher ARTPIX, planned to release a box set next year on Jim O'Rourke's imprint, Moikai. The more of the DVDs I watched, the more my memories of that night began to blur with the work. The patterned armchair where I'd sat—wasn't it like the one where Mike sat in his first video, Down in the Rec Room? *And when I flushed the toilet: that was familiar. When Smith took me to MoMA to see his installation* Government Approved Home Fallout Shelter Snack Bar, *a sculptural display that perfectly recapitulated the set from his '80s video of the same name, there was a moment when I saw Michael Smith standing by the shelter's bar, while, on the television in front of us, Mike, wearing a shirt with his name stitched on the collar, poured himself a cup of coffee. "Coffee," he said. "A meal in itself." I'd heard this before, hadn't I? On an arcade console nearby, a pixelated Mike blinked on and off. "I hope he's drinking decaf," said a woman on the television. "That's a lot of coffee," said another. I'd argue it's this repetition of and estrangement*

from an intentional, small vocabulary of objects—which came out of an early, insistent interest in minimalism— that begins the growth of something crucial connecting all of Michael Smith's art. A whole world.

The work on the DVDs ranges from the earliest performances of Baby Ikki—or the Baby, as Smith will call Ikki in conversation—to puppet shows with Doug Skinner and collaborations with William Wegman, Seth Price, Mike Kelley, Joshua White, and many others. There is documentation from shows he exhibited at the New Museum of Contemporary Art, the Whitney Museum of American Art, and Museo Jumex. This interview took place in Smith's studio in Williamsburg, Brooklyn, about eighteen months after we first met. We sat together at a metal table, drinking coffee.
—Hayden Bennett

I. THE COFFEE

MICHAEL SMITH: Thanks so much for the coffee.

THE BELIEVER: Have you ever been to Qahwah House, this place?

MS: That Yemeni place around the corner? I have. It's so popular.

BLVR: Yeah.

MS: Somebody who visited, they picked up a coffee from the same place. And then I picked one up. It's quite strong, which I appreciate.

BLVR: Can you talk a bit about the genesis of Mike? The character.

MS: I would always refer to myself as Mike because most people call me Michael. Mike just sounded funny. My brother would say, "Hey, Mike." It was this kind of diminutive way of talking to myself. I don't know about belittling; it was just, different—familiar or something.

BLVR: Estrangement through that familiarity, maybe. Do you remember when Mike started asking himself, "I wonder what I'm going to do today?" It's a question that often drives his narrative.

MS: A lot of the character came from the voice [*speaking slowly*], "Hmm, I wonder what I'll do." And then it's pretty flat-footed. He checks his list. Or he makes his list. Maybe it gives a sense that he's got some free time.

BLVR: Yeah, every morning there is a new to-do list. There's more coffee. It got me thinking a lot about repetition. Repetition with Mike never really gets old. It's hopeful, like something's coming.

MS: I think that has to do with my process. I sit down; I wonder, What am I going to write about today?

BLVR: There's no real anxiety for him.

MS: No, that's the thing I have respect for about Mike. He doesn't get anxious like me. I mean, he gets baffled. Flummoxed and stuff. Maybe the Baby expresses more of that.

BLVR: Oh, totally. You're very nice to Mike, how you set him up.

MS: Probably indirectly, it's me being nice to myself, which is good to see. Sometimes I don't know how to do that.

BLVR: There's an openness, too, that got me wondering whether the Quaker meetings you used to go to had a lasting influence.

MS: At the time they did. I was really young.

BLVR: How old?

MS: I went to college when I was seventeen, and then I started going to meetings. A friend of mine, a professor—we became friendly. He went to Quaker meetings. It was also a way to establish a stance against the war. I actually went to them in New York.

BLVR: Conscientious objection for Vietnam, yeah. The way Mike is—it feels like there's something about Friends meetings and the idea of presence with one another.

MS: I appreciate that connection. But I never emptied my head, really. I never thought about it. It's possible there was a connection, because I was more open then, but I wasn't a very spiritual guy. Neither is Mike.

BLVR: Receptiveness is what's crucial to him; that's what I'm thinking about.

MS: I mean, he is kind of a sponge—he takes in and there's not much he gives out. Unfortunately, I think I'm finding that the overlap between me and him is getting more and more apparent.

BLVR: What is?

MS: Oh, the distance between us is really tightening up as I get older. I'm slowing down. We're meeting together, and physically, I feel very close to him. A lot of his themes now relate to my own physical aging. That's becoming the subject matter.

BLVR: It used to feel like there was a gap?

MS: Yeah. Before, I had a sense of Mike as a younger person who was invisible. That's what it is. I'm an older person now and I understand this idea of invisibility, which happens as you get older. Mike was kind of invisible before I was. We're catching up to each other.

BLVR: In the early performances, after you stopped painting, you were thinking about Nixon's silent majority and a character who was as bland as possible—Blandman.

MS: I wrote to ask a lot of people who Blandman was. It was mostly foods that I got back—doughy, bland foods.

BLVR: Blandman sort of became Mike, right? You said that before your first video, *Down in the Rec Room*, Mike was basically a hat rack for props.

MS: Yeah, he was a plinth to hold stuff. I was trying to flesh out his character with props.

BLVR: What changed?

MS: I had a place for him. With *Rec Room* I came upon a beginning and an ending. Like, Oh, he's gonna have a party? Oh, the party is not happening? I was trying to deal with an arc that gets deflated completely. Even though the set was very minimal—it's a really impoverished set—it suggested a certain place in society, a standing. That's how I figured out Mike. I was approximating him, and the more I worked with him, the more certain themes presented themselves and it made sense for him to go up against those themes.

BLVR: There is a funny permanence to what's on the set—the armchair, the mailbox, the television. They all get used, and more than once. I'm thinking about how often Mike goes up against an external voice, telling him what to do. The tape machine, the television. There's often a voice that's almost goading him.

MS: Richard Foreman was a big influence.

BLVR: Is he funny?

MS: Some people may not find his stuff funny, but when I first saw him, I found it hilarious.

BLVR: That voice on the tape evolves into characters who call the shots for Mike, at least in the '80s videos. One of my favorites is this little hairpiece in *It Starts at Home*. He's a producer who gets Mike onto TV, something like a reality show before there was such a thing. He's an authoritative hairpiece in a chair, surrounded by cigar smoke. Proto-Steinbrenner from *Seinfeld*.

MS: That was very strange. That was something my mother made for her cat.

BLVR: I didn't know that. Oh my god.

MS: Yeah, no, she made that little mink thing. I think it was something she had left over from a coat or something. And it was a little toy. She was a seamstress. And she said, "You can have it."

BLVR: That's so funny. Eric Bogosian did the voice?

Michael Smith as Baby Ikki in Portrait of the Artist as a Young Man. © C. mid 1980s. Unique color Polaroid. 20 × 24 in. Courtesy of the artist.

MS: Eric did a really good voice for him. There was some very good dialogue written. I mean, there were many more people working on it than me.

BLVR: It was a nice thing about getting to watch the DVDs—seeing names and thinking, Oh yeah, they were all hanging out. Did Bogosian write the dialogue?

MS: No, a lot of it was written by Dike Blair and Barbara Kruger.

BLVR: I remember one name surprised me.

MS: Maybe Randy Cohen? He was the original ethicist. He was part of my group of friends. A bunch of my friends got together and did that. Eric Fischl, Barbara Bloom, Carole Ann Klonarides.

Smith as Mike in Secret Horror. *© 1980. Production still. Photograph by Kevin Noble. Courtesy of the artist.*

BLVR: Your friend group was generative for Mike.

MS: I'm very happy you were able to watch the DVDs.

BLVR: It's rare to have such an accessible record of performance art—there's a whole world in there.

MS: Yeah. I learned from the people I worked with. Especially in terms of making or inhabiting a set. For *It Starts at Home*, I worked with the painter Power Boothe. For the *Fallout Shelter* installation at MoMA, I worked with the artist, now poet, Alan Herman. He was a total pro. He had done Super Bowl commercials. I picked up a certain sensibility. Mike is always missing it a little. That also relates to me. I'm constantly a little behind.

BLVR: I mean, there can be a sadness when Mike fully accomplishes a task, or fills out the to-do list. I'm thinking of *Portal Excursion*, when he learns two words out of the dictionary every day. After he's learned the words, there's this sense of exhaustion.

MS: I take it to the absurd, but that was a true story about my uncle. He told me to pick two words every day from the dictionary.

BLVR: Did you?

MS: No.

BLVR: [*Laughs*] The way Mike describes the project, there's real wonder in it. *Two new words.*

MS: He takes pleasure in those small things. Excuse me, may I use the restroom? I'm asking your permission.

II. MIKE THE WIPE

BLVR: Did you have a lot of free time when you were making those videos?

MS: I did have free time. I always lived very frugally, and I had a little money, so I was here, working, doing my work. Performing.

BLVR: You were working other jobs?

MS: I was. Let's see now: I helped somebody do a little paste-up for a couple days. I became a professional house cleaner for several people: Mike the Wipe.

BLVR: [*Laughing*] That's what you went by?

MS: Just jokingly. I worked a couple days a week. I had a storefront. I paid $175 a month in rent, and I could afford it. It was on Spring Street and Elizabeth. I had that studio for, I don't know, fifteen or seventeen years, and then they moved me next door.

I remember going by after I left. They were renovating, and they took down the walls, the outside walls. I walked by and I looked. I said, "Huh, there's my toilet."

BLVR: Was there ever a question of whether you'd leave the art world?

MS: When I was doing those variety shows, those talent shows—I didn't leave it, but I was more focused on that commercial world. Now I'm uninterested in both. [*Laughter*]

BLVR: You started the talent shows in the mid-'80s?

MS: Yeah, in the East Village. This fellow Steve Paul—he saw a show and got very interested in working with me. He was sort of an impresario. He had a very well-known club in the late '60s called the Scene. Steve Paul's the Scene. He managed the Winter Brothers, David Johansen, Tiny Tim. His boyfriend was an artist, and we were both peripherally in this circle of people. Steve had his own label called Blue Sky. He approached me and said, "I'd like to manage you." We became coproducers of the Talent Show. He had access to people like Fran Lebowitz. I got really caught up with that for about four years.

BLVR: You were trying to pitch the show to networks.

MS: He was doing that, yeah. I had a manager, and then I got an agent from a big comedy agency. I remember being welcomed into the fold by this one guy named Roger Vorce. He was the personal agent for Liberace. I got to see Lee's last show at Radio City.

BLVR: Did you ever go to Hollywood?

MS: I did go to LA, and at one point, after the talent show didn't get picked up, I remember trying to do a kiddie show. That was, like, after Pee-wee, you know, trying to piggyback on Pee-wee.

BLVR: Was he an influence?

MS: I remember going to his stage show in the late '80s at Carolines. And then I started doing a regular show there. For a while it was kind of exciting. I was dealing with all these comics. It's amazing who went through my show. Kids in the Hall's first live act.

BLVR: Did that grow into your HBO Special [that aired on Cinemax]?

MS: Yeah, it was really funny. They saw the show and said, "You need a famous cohost." We spent a year going for a visual discrepancy—we approached Schwarzenegger, Danny DeVito, Cyndi Lauper. Different people. Most of them came back with "Who's Mike?"

BLVR: Did you talk to any of them?

MS: My partner, Steve—he was more in that world than I was.

BLVR: The executives liked you?

MS: Yeah, the executive who was curious, who said, "Go ahead and find a famous cohost" before seeing the show. And then they came to the Bottom Line in the Village, saw a show, and said, "Oh, Mike's OK. We like Mike. Deliver this in six weeks." Then we had to do it.

BLVR: Did you enjoy doing the talent shows?

MS: They were so much work. I was a producer. I was a stage manager, schlepping that shit all over the place. I did enjoy it. But I didn't make any money.

BLVR: You weren't living off it.

MS: Living off it? Oh no. I lived off grants for many years. Fellowships and grants. I think it was around '92 when I realized the '80s were over and I was broke. That's when I started to do manual labor, working for friends, house painting.

BLVR: The '80s do seem like a different time as far as fellowships and grants and anything where federal funding's concerned.

MS: I sort of deceived myself then, thinking I was busy. I just kept going forward. I lived modestly.

BLVR: Did you like the odd jobs you were doing?

MS: Not at all.

BLVR: How'd you find them?

MS: I put an ad in the *Times* to clean and to cook for people.

BLVR: That was Mike the Wipe?

MS: No, that was Mr. Smith.

BLVR: Do you still have the ad? I guess the *Times* probably archived it.

MS: I mean, it'd be very tiny. I just said, "Will clean or clean and cook." I'm not a bad cook. But I said, Oh, I'll try this. I think I got one call. It was this person saying, in a breathy voice, "Do you do windows?" And I said, "Yeah, if they're dirty I'll do them." And she said, "Do you need rubber gloves?" I said, "Well, I don't really use rubber gloves." And she said, "Will you do ovens?" And I said, "You know, yeah, if you—" and she said, "Do you need rubber gloves?" Everything was about rubber gloves. [*Laughter*]

They finally gave me the address, and I went. There was no one there. A total waste of my time.

BLVR: A prank?

MS: A prank, or just getting off on talking to me. Mostly I cleaned for people. Some of them gave me their keys. I cleaned for this guy who had a torture chamber in his house. That was interesting. Another person—this guy in the West Village—had all these things in capsules. They looked like those packets to preserve foodstuff or something. They were poppers. I would pull them together and put them in a dish. He thought that was so cute. I didn't know. I didn't do poppers.

BLVR: Did you cook for anyone?

MS: No, no one wanted me. They just wanted my cleaning. I basically have no skills. So it was hard.

BLVR: Organizing's a skill.

MS: Yeah, but I can't even do that. For others, I couldn't do that.

III. MILK IT

BLVR: There's this one early interview you did about Baby Ikki. You've since expressed that you were pushing back because you hadn't really analyzed the Baby.

MS: That was in one of the first issues of *BOMB*, I believe.

BLVR: Yeah, yeah. I was wondering if being closed off about the Baby served you. Or if not talking about Baby Ikki was an advantage.

MS: Right, well, I wasn't really keeping up with the readings everybody was doing. I had done therapy, but I wasn't going that deep with the Baby. People would mention infantilism and stuff like that and I would kind of go, "Huh." I'm a repressed guy. I didn't even want to acknowledge that until I collaborated

with Seth Price. We looked at infantilism sites to get certain ideas. When I started out, they were having adult babies on these talk shows and stuff. Now there is this thing with Trump supporters wearing—what is that with the diapers?

BLVR: I don't know.

MS: Yeah, there are some people in diapers supporting Trump. I have to look into that. It's always odd for me when people go, "Oh, you're the Baby guy." I do it well, but you know, it's an odd thing.

BLVR: I can see how it's purposefully not verbal.

MS: I don't do a lot of thinking for the Baby. There's really no conceptual approach.

BLVR: You can't really see in those sunglasses, can you?

MS: I can see.

BLVR: OK, you can see.

MS: I mean, the sunglasses are great because they cut me off in a way. They're a little ridiculous and undersized for my head. They really press up against my eyes and it sort of completes the mask and creates a space for me. I have to look forward in them—they're like blinders—and I'm not so aware of peripheral stuff. Babies get distracted really easily.

BLVR: Distracted by what?

MS: What's in front of me, usually. A noise or, I don't know, a child. Something shiny. If I sense a certain kind of, like, discomfort or vulnerability, I'll go to that person. I'll just push it a little, you know, but I'll never purposely make someone totally uncomfortable. I'll go close to that.

BLVR: The Baby's also got a sense of wonder.

MS: He gets preoccupied with nothing. There's times when he's just playing with a feather. Or a little speck on his finger. He'll spend a minute looking at it and nothing's happening except the sharp focus. People are wondering what I'm looking at—or they see what I'm looking at and it's, you know, a feather. It's very dumb.

BLVR: What's it like to embody him?

MS: It's a very physical experience. Because I get double-jointed. [*He demonstrates with his hands.*] Stiffness. Some people who knew me found it really uncomfortable. I remember going out with some people and I'd be doing the Baby and they were just...

BLVR: People you were dating?

MS: Yeah. My sister was very uncomfortable. She was an occupational therapist, but it made her uncomfortable. That's where the sunglasses come in handy.

BLVR: It's hard to separate somebody from their character sometimes.

MS: Yeah, when people don't know you. When people do know me and see the Baby, they just wonder, Why?

BLVR: What was it like coming up with him?

MS: I remember I had invited people to my studio. I just had this idea. I had no idea what the Baby would do, or how it would move. I got onto the floor and started moving.

BLVR: That's the first one, the performance on the DVD. It felt like he wanted to understand why he was there, asking, "Why do people have babies?" Writing his name on the blackboard, "Ikki."

MS: That's the process I went through when I was coming up with the character. All these friends of mine were really deeply involved with feminism and support groups. And I thought, Hmm, "gender."

BLVR: The baby doesn't often go in for excess. I guess there's that part of *The Dirty Show* when [the performance artist] Brian Routh comes onstage and pours food into his mouth. People have expressed that Ikki can make them feel a real motherly concern, and when Routh pours the mashed-up food into your mouth, that was a moment when I really thought, Oh god, don't do that to a baby.

MS: That was so uncomfortable for me. I don't usually bring the Baby to such dark places. And also, he was talking about Nazis and stuff. That was really uncomfortable for me, being Jewish. It was just weird. But I like it in relationship to the other stuff.

BLVR: Well, he tied you up. You couldn't speak.

MS: There was a certain sadism. It was kind of curious. He was married to Karen Finley. I could hear her cackling in the background.

BLVR: I know Mike Kelley also wanted to go the darker route when you brought Baby Ikki to Burning Man.

MS: He was interested in seeing something a little more abject. There was that one woman who whispered in my ear. "I feel like I'm lactating," or something like that. I followed her into her tent. I had no idea what I was doing. I have a feeling she was wondering what I was doing. The Baby checks in and checks out immediately. He sort of tests the water and then leaves. I sort of posit this possibility but don't really let it develop that much, I guess.

BLVR: I think there's an innocence to the Baby. There's a relationship to Mike in that.

MS: The Baby's very forward, and Mike's fairly passive.

BLVR: And they've both got your eyebrows. That's a feature you know how to milk.

MS: Ad nauseam.

BLVR: That's kind of my question: How do you know when to stop? It's very tight in the videos.

MS: That's where editing comes in. Our shooting ratio was so out of control. I got good at that. Also, when you're not talking, you know. Mark Fischer focused on it. We noticed it.

BLVR: When you have a shtick that works, how do you stop it from running into the ground?

MS: It's touchy. When you identify a shtick, you kind of back away: Oh boy, is he stale. Boy, is that stale. At one point you see somebody do a lot of the same thing and call them a hack. And then I thought, How do you become a hack? At least hacks make a living.

IV. STRIKE A CLAIM

BLVR: There's that interview you did with Mike Kelley that ends with him mentioning how your work is ahead of the culture sometimes, like with *Beavis and Butt-Head* or *The Truman Show*. At the end of that interview he was like, "Why not claim it? Everybody else does."

MS: What did I say?

BLVR: The interview ends.

MS: I don't want to be held accountable. Things are in the air. Maybe I felt that I did what I did, and I carved out a little place for myself. And I'm between the cracks, you know?

BLVR: The idea of "claiming" something is just odd. Some artists, that's what they're really interested in, it feels like. Where their focus is.

MS: I have an ego. I mean, if the writer wants to do that, fine. But I don't find that very modest, you know, claiming your turf or whatever?

BLVR: It's not modest, no. It's a false idea of what working creatively is, right?

MS: I think also, as my father would say, "That and $2.75 will get me on the bus." [*Laughter*]

BLVR: It's not an ego thing, really, but where did the MIKE belt buckle come from? It is his name...

MS: Canal Street. I walked by Canal Street, I saw it, and I thought, Oh, yeah, maybe I should get that.

BLVR: And people gave you MIKE clothing.

MS: People did eventually, yeah. Little things. Now people don't give me that stuff. I don't gravitate toward this MIKE stuff. It actually makes me a little uncomfortable. I have a few things. I belonged to this club called Mikes of America.[1] But now I'm all about rainbows.

BLVR: When did that start?

MS: I lived in this incredibly depressing place. It was like a converted garage, like a shack. One friend of mine who stayed there, he called it the Unabomber's Cabin. It was when I was going back and forth to Texas to teach, and I didn't do a lot of decorating, let's say. I had a bed and a table and then a kitchen. I mean, it was minimal. I had a chair that I sat in.

At one point, I thought, It's a little depressing in here, and I was at a thrift store—because I did a lot of my propping at thrift stores—and I saw this very kitschy rainbow. I mean, a really stupid, poofy one. I thought, kind of ironically, I need a little color in my life. So I bought it, and I put it up. And then I bought another one. And then I thought, Yeah, I need a little color, maybe a little hope. Next thing you know, people started giving them to me.

BLVR: The selective accumulation is interesting. It makes me think of some other projects you've done: drawing credit cards, collecting bags from hospital visits. You were drawing open zippers for a while.

MS: The rainbows and unicorns, I think they're going to yield something. I don't know when, but I think they'll yield something.

BLVR: I was thinking that cataloging is maybe like tidying. You do like a tidy space.

MS: I do, yeah. The studio is even kind of messy now, but my house is, yeah, tidier. You've been.

BLVR: It was striking how it felt—not like Mike's house, exactly, but it had that energy to it. Like a set.

---

1. According to its website, Mikes of America is the biggest name-based organization in the world, "reaching out to all Michaels for a show of unity by focusing on what we all have in common rather than the things that divide us."

MS: I like to sweep. I even have a good vacuum, but I prefer sweeping.

BLVR: Watching the DVDs in order, it's really interesting to see Mike go from being in the home, getting the mail, figuring out what errands to do, to dealing with colonialism and other globalized systems.

MS: It's probably me responding to a particular social thrust or a certain context. You know, I'm presented with a context, and I respond to it.

BLVR: Your idea for the International Trade and Enrichment Association came about that way, right? You're responding to these global systems—Mike as the colonizer. It came out of reading *Heart of Darkness* for a group show, right?

MS: Yeah, I read it for that. Dense. Really dense. I was expecting, Oh, this is going to be, you know, a breeze. It was like reading *Ulysses* or something.

BLVR: You put Mike in the new context.

MS: That's probably when my life influenced Mike more. That came out of a period, in '94 or '95, when I could not get fucking arrested. I started to respond to this business of art. The hyping up of the professionalism of art or something.

BLVR: *Interstitial*, a collaboration you did with Joshua White, is similar. I really have no idea what any of the artists Mike is interviewing are saying. Even the premise: "The place between two places where ideas and dialogue and opinions come together, intersect, or overlap"—I mean, I guess it means something. The editing is kind of jaw-dropping. I love *Interstitial*. Riffing off public access stylistically like that really picked up later, but how directly influential *Interstitial* was to comedy, I don't know. It feels very ahead of its time.

MS: I don't know how many people saw it, yeah. I think it's that deadpan humor. It was sort of in the air. I mean, you know, I come from Chicago; there was Bob Newhart, and then there was that stuff in the in the '70s that was purposely flat, Andy Kaufman and Steve Martin. Jackie Vernon's delivery was very influential for me.

BLVR: *Doug and Mike's Adult Entertainment* also has some perfect art-world satire. There's this puppet gallery show in the basement of a Blimpie. I think about it all the time. The cheese log.

MS: Thank you for mentioning the cheese log.

BLVR: They had a show called *Reconsidering Context*?

MS: Yeah, I made that up.

BLVR: I ask because I kept thinking—both that and *interstitial*, they're sort of nothing puff words, but they have a real relationship to your work. You do recontextualize the to-do list, the rec room.

MS: Oh, *Reconsidering Context* was for Hans Ulrich Obrist's *Museum in Progress*. The *DO IT* piece *How to Curate Your Own Group Exhibition*. That was a little prescient in terms of, you know—I think I recently heard somebody talking about being a content provider. I had that line in that piece: "Artists are content providers of the future."

BLVR: Do you feel like artists are the content providers of now?

MS: I don't know. I don't give a shit. [*Laughter*] Whatever. They do add to it.

V. "IN MY EAR AND OUT MY EAR"

BLVR: I can see where any one culture can get to feel small—especially when it's so professionalized. The first novel that I wrote was an art-world satire.

Notes came back from editors that were just like, "People don't care about the New York art world."

MS: You didn't have enough drugs in it?

BLVR: Not really. It was what I found funny. At the time I figured everybody was interested in Donald Judd's son.

MS: [*Laughter*] Flavin?

BLVR: His name did a lot for me.

MS: Have you been to Marfa?

BLVR: I haven't, no.

MS: Judd's time-out room stuck in my head. He had a room with a window, a small room. A lot of books in there, where he would go not to be bothered. You could see him. I think you could see the back of his head. It was a small room, near his library. I remember I thought, It's really odd.

I remember walking through the courtyard with these high walls around it separating it from the town. And I was there with Dan Graham, and out of nowhere he starts talking about the Branch Davidians. I thought that was so perfect. David Koresh. That was very funny.

BLVR: I've been to Judd's house in New York.

MS: I used to pass that a lot because I lived down the block on Spring Street. One of those bad galleries was across the street, you know, with flowers and things like that. Because it was so bright at night, it would reflect onto Judd's windows. You could see these shitty paintings in his windows.

BLVR: For whatever reason, his art really mystified me as a kid. Art in general— my parents took me to museums and we'd never really talk about it. You've mentioned a similar experience with your parents: seeing theater and not talking about it.

MS: Or my mother, her comment would be "That was interesting."

BLVR: Right. My mom said that too: "That was weird."

MS: They took me to some curious productions.

BLVR: Genet, right?

MS: Yeah, was it *The Maids*? *The Blacks*, maybe? Wasn't there one called *The Maids*?

BLVR: There's both, yeah.

MS: They took me to *The Maids*. And some Living Theatre productions. *The Brig*. That was so interesting.

BLVR: How old were you?

MS: Probably twelve or thirteen. That really stuck in my head. That was totally real life. In fact, I show my students that video.

BLVR: There's a lot of screaming.

MS: I was just, like, struck by it, baffled by it. I mean, not a lot happened, but it was an assault, you know? I didn't know where to put it.

BLVR: What TV do you like?

MS: Well, I think TV informed my thinking. I don't necessarily like it now. I mean, I just go into a stupor when I watch this stuff. The algorithm, you know: *You like this shit. How about this shit?*

BLVR: What about *Storage Wars*?

MS: I binge-watched it. I was intrigued. Then they started to develop these different characters and I lost interest. And then they would do it in different places, almost like these chef shows or something. I don't give a shit.

Still from It Starts at Home, *1982. Courtesy of the artist.*

BLVR: You were in it for the lockers?

MS: They were opening up these lockers just filled with shit. They don't address the fact that, a lot of the time, these are people's lives. Why they left them there, they don't even address that. It's all about the ridiculousness, the way the price adds up. I know about that stuff. It's worth shit, most of it.

BLVR: Yeah, every time they see an instrument case: "I hope this is a Stradivarius."

MS: Right, right, right. I used to look at garbage sometimes. At one point, uptown, I found some really good stuff. I found a small gay porn collection—I must have made a good five thousand dollars from it. This was many years ago. I kept one piece. Probably it's worth a lot more now.

BLVR: In the past, you've talked about the freedom you feel with the drawings you do, right? A lot of them are plans for performances. And then those performances can become videos, and those can become sculptural installations. An idea occurs. You make it work.

MS: I should follow those more. Trust myself a little bit more sometimes with those drawings.

BLVR: Yeah, I guess I have the advantage of seeing the work once it's done—and all at once. When I look at the drawings together, their logic makes sense to me. That's what I was talking about, something in the interstices. The

movement between forms feels significant. Where the freedom's concerned, you feel like you're stopping yourself?

MS: Oh yeah. Do I trust myself? No.

BLVR: Thinking too much will make you stop?

MS: Yeah: Does this make any sense? This is dumb. Or: I'm insecure.

BLVR: How do you push past the insecurities?

MS: A lot of times I forget. Or I distract myself with something else. Deadlines help too. I don't know if I get insecure now; I just need to move on. By sort of daydreaming. You write—you're familiar.

BLVR: The appealing thing is the daydreaming.

MS: God, I can do that. I'm so good at that.

BLVR: I guess there's a reason Proust wanted to be in a cork-lined room, in bed.

MS: When you started talking about those Friends meetings before: maybe that's what I've noticed. More and more I'm just looking out with my coffee, listening to the radio, but it's kind of going in my ear and out my ear.

BLVR: What station?

MS: I've got one of those radios that NPR gives you. It's fixed on one station, but I've never gotten it to work. Maybe because I've never had fresh batteries in it. It comes on strong and then it shuts down. I'm just looking at it. It becomes an object to look at. And then I turn it on again and it goes on for, like, twenty seconds, and then it goes off again. A lot of times with podcasts, I'll be listening and the next thing I know, I don't remember anything. I have to rewind it. It's mostly an activity of rewinding.

BLVR: I'm remembering it now, in your kitchen. It's a WNYC radio?

MS: Yeah, yeah. I've got to get some new batteries. I'm going to do that tomorrow. ✭

THE FOURTEEN BEST EXHIBITIONS OF 2024 (ACCORDING TO US)

OUR FAR-FLUNG CORRESPONDENTS REPORT ON THE BEST ART SHOWS THEY SAW THIS YEAR

Clockwise from top left: Angisa: a language of living *at Andrew Reed Gallery;* Into the Brightness: Artists from Creativity Explored, Creative Growth and NIAD *at Oakland Museum of California;* MiCasa *at Darryl's UWS;* Being There *at Corbett vs. Dempsey.*

FUN-A-DAY

ARTISTS: *Various*
GALLERY: *Fourteenfifteen/Alpaca*
CITY: *Albuquerque, NM*

Fun-A-Day, now in its tenth year, is a celebration of the art of daily practice and of community. Participating artists create art every day for the month of January, and the resulting body of work is shared in a large group exhibition. Forty-three artists participated in 2024, and their work was thoughtfully curated in two modest exhibition spaces in the Barelas neighborhood of Albuquerque.

The exhibition creates space for experimentation and serves as a call for artists to reconnect with the intention surrounding their practice by asking, simply: Why do we do what we do?
—*Amanda Dannáe Romero*

I TASI: CONNECTIONS IN BETWEEN

ARTIST: *Connie Ann*
GALLERY: *Kaleidoscope Studio*
CITY: *Las Vegas, NV*

Tasi, which means "ocean" in Chamorro, was everywhere in Connie Ann's June 2024 show at Kaleidoscope Studio in Las Vegas. Connie is a local photographer and artist, with roots in

Guam. She specializes in cyanotypes, some as dark as ultramarine pigment, others faded, like a sliver of Las Vegas sky. On one wall of the exhibit hung a large cyanotype printed on fabric. A human figure with long flowing hair left their mark in the center of the fabric, surrounded by objects. Their outlines were crisp. On a bench next to the piece were vases, shells, flowers—all featured in the cyanotype.

On the far wall was a collection of smaller cyanotypes, hung with clothespins from netting. There were portraits of Connie's loved ones and bits and pieces from Connie's travels in Guam. The prints resembled hazy memories, and made me wonder what it would be like to yearn for an ocean home while living in this desert city. They were a form of recollection, a step against erasure.

—*Lille Allen*

A BERRY, A BOOT, A BUILDING, A BLUE DOOR

ARTIST: *Mike Young*
GALLERY: *Elbow Room*
CITY: *Portland, OR*

A Berry, a Boot, a Building, a Blue Door featured many of Mike Young's colored-pencil drawings on white paper—arrangements of bottles, animals, furniture, fruit—often outlined in ink with dimensions that leaned and tipped unexpectedly. The exhibition was guest-curated by Kristan Kennedy, artistic director and curator of visual art at the Portland Institute for Contemporary Art, and was held at Elbow Room, an art studio and gallery in Southeast Portland

that provides "material support, mentorship, and meaningful exhibition and collaboration opportunities for artists with intellectual and developmental disabilities." As I peered closely at the pages, Young's dancing shapes began to evoke an illusion of motion, becoming a kind of visual stim. I felt I had entered a realm of sensory intrigue, a place to be curious about Young's arrangements and his ineffable sense of how things fit together and belong.

—*Hannah Krafcik*

PETRICHOR

ARTIST: *Lisa Waud*
GALLERY: *Boyer Campbell Building, Detroit Design District*
CITY: *Detroit, MI*

I often assert that artists aren't wizards who conjure art out of thin air, but Lisa Waud's ability to make entire realities wink in and out of existence over the course of a long weekend verges on the uncanny. I visited her series of three installations during her residency at the Detroit Design District's Boyer Campbell Building in the summer of 2024, and I confess I'm still not sure how she laid down a carpet of sixteen thousand square feet of living sod for *petrichor*, then made it all disappear.

She might be a wizard after all. Detroit is given to entropic spaces—houses and businesses that have been reclaimed by the churning biomass—but the pairing of tidy monoculture and industrial abandon made a new alien place: *The Stepford Wives* meets Ford Motor Company. One could play croquet, or observe the decay, or sit and smell the humidity hanging in the air. There's more than one way to touch grass.

—*Sarah Rose Sharp*

AS FOR ME, I'M JUST PASSING THROUGH THIS PLANET

ARTISTS: *Jacob Jackmauh, Caitlin McCann, and Benjamin Stallings*
GALLERY: *Bad Water*
CITY: *Knoxville, TN*

The title, a quote from perpetually tapped-in Southerner Howard Finster, describes how I felt as I stumbled into this exhibit—and into Knoxville. A newcomer here, I was led to the outbuilding of a house where the director of Bad Water gallery, curator Kelsie Conley, once lived. This nimble shed-gallery is at the confluence of professionalism and DIY. The walls were gallery-white, yet barn-like. The floor I can describe only as "clean dirt."

Right: That Land Where Joy Will Never End (Folk Song Machine IV). © 2024 by Caitlin McCann

Jacob Jackmauh's haunted fiberglass readymades spoke first. The lichen-marked fragments of discarded hollow animals sprouted from Bad Water's inherent in-betweenness. Meanwhile, Caitlin McCann's improvised audio contraptions—a wire-stuffed briefcase, a see-through telephone—interposed some stilted, faraway folk tunes. A chapbook by Benjamin Stallings evoked the region's omnipresent kudzu as both affective and arterial. The fact that the first two artists live in New York, as I had just finished doing, was meaningless in the tangle of vines. Next door, some dogs barked.

—Bucky Miller

DECOMPOSING FEM
ARTISTS: *Gwendy Smith and Fyre Wood*
GALLERY: *Icebox Project Space*
CITY: *Philadelphia, PA*

In spring 2024, I attended a haunting and captivating performance, *Decomposing Fem*, at Icebox Project Space in the South Kensington neighborhood of Philadelphia. This evening-length piece was choreographed and performed by Gwendy Smith and Fyre Wood; Kat Nzingha crafted the sound score.

Gwendy and Fyre spent three years creating this piece, their first

performance together, which centered, highlighted, and generated opportunities for queer, trans, and gender-nonconforming people. It showcased a radical environment crafted to hold shifting and morphing bodies during a time when their safety and existence are threatened. The performers invited the audience to feel a spectrum of emotions, ranging from love, fear, and power to pain and infatuation.

—Andrea Barnes

INTO THE BRIGHTNESS: ARTISTS FROM CREATIVITY EXPLORED, CREATIVE GROWTH AND NIAD and CREATIVE GROWTH: THE HOUSE THAT ART BUILT
ARTISTS: *Various*
MUSEUMS: *Oakland Museum of California and SFMOMA*
CITIES: *Oakland and San Francisco, CA*

Just in time to celebrate Creative Growth's fiftieth anniversary, two museums, in Oakland and San Francisco, celebrated an essential and often-overlooked group of artists from Creative Growth, NIAD (Nurturing Independence Through Artistic Development) Art Center, and Creativity Explored in back-to-back exhibitions in 2023 and 2024. These three organizations, which support the vision—and now the careers—of artists with developmental disabilities, are critical to the political and social ethos of the Bay Area arts community. How novel it was to feel excited and refreshed in a museum, and to be reminded that some of

the most important art in the world is being made locally. Work by fan favorites Camille Holvoet and John Patrick McKenzie carved out some of my favorite comedic moments in the exhibitions, and William Scott's extraordinary mural *Praise Frisco: Peace and Love in the City* projected a contagiously optimistic energy for a future that's right around the corner—if we want it.

—Lindsey White

ANGISA: A LANGUAGE OF LIVING
ARTIST: *Cornelius Tulloch*
GALLERY: *Andrew Reed Gallery*
CITY: *Miami, FL*

Since meeting Cornelius Tulloch three years ago, I've watched the twenty-seven-year-old multidisciplinary artist's career soar, from Miami to New York to Paris to Venice. But no matter where his art takes him, he always makes it back home. *Angisa* is the paragon of Tulloch's signature style and work ethic. Inspired by Tulloch's residency in Suriname, he and gallerist Andrew Reed transformed the gallery, in Miami's Allapattah neighborhood, with mustard-colored walls and elaborate wood carvings. Tulloch painted jewel-toned portraits and serene landscapes that captured Suriname's beauty and serenity. For years, Tulloch has worked hard, taking little time for himself in between ambitious exhibitions and prestigious residencies. The Suriname residency was "the first time I've ever really slowed down in my life," he said. The result was a collection of works that show

Photograph of Decomposing Fem by Vaughn Cummings

off Tulloch's diverse skills and distinctly South Floridan point of view. As a native Miamian, I've found it hard to put into words the essence and aesthetics of this larger-than-life Caribbean American city. But I don't have to. I can point you to Tulloch's work instead.

—Amanda Rosa

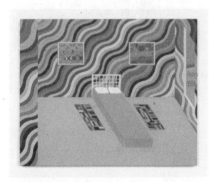

BEING THERE

ARTIST: *Rebecca Shore*
GALLERY: *Corbett vs. Dempsey*
CITY: *Chicago, IL*

This show featured Rebecca Shore's geometric paintings of domestic architecture, the clinical rigor of which belies their strange poignancy.

Beds—solitary and in pairs—appeared in plain gray rooms, empty of inhabitants and free from conventional pictorial perspective. Barren trees and empty trellises were paired with new shoots in garden planters. Beaded curtains, doors left slightly ajar, and stairways leading nowhere were recurrent motifs that suggested a space beyond that was unavailable or murky.

Mountain landscapes appeared as paintings within paintings, juxtaposed

with "real" scenes of rolling hills and pastures seen through windows. The moon was a fugitive motif, hiding out in the paintings' "real" and "fictitious" landscapes, illustrating the thrilling and alienating quality of all representational art: the idea that what is depicted is not really there.

—Tom Bolin

"MOMENTARY LAPSE OF REASON" and TIME SNAIL ROMAN

ARTISTS: *Rigo Alberto Zamarrón and Eva Claycomb*
GALLERIES: *galerie ego and Do Right Hall*
CITY: *Marfa, TX*

Rigo Alberto Zamarrón showed at galerie ego, which is in the laundry room of a private home. Lighting was supplied by clamp lamps affixed to an upside-down ironing board. One person or two intimates could view the show at once. Rigo's paintings are smallish, about thirty inches across and twenty inches vertical. The energy is circular, one wanders o'er the whole of the painting swiftly, and abstract shapes fade in and out. I think of Amy Sillman and Carrie Moyer as kin but Rigo has a swoop.

Eva Claycomb at Do Right Hall makes illusionistic work. Her small and slightly larger squares of muted colors and natural tones could be architectural details, cornices. They have the authority of stone but close up you see that it's indented cardboard that feels emblematic and strong. There was a lizardy lime green and a blue gray that could form an entire city. The sexiness

of these squares is linguistic and tart. She thinks big and delivers small parts of a built world she winkingly knows.

—Eileen Myles

AZALEAS

ARTIST: *Lotus L. Kang*
GALLERY: *Commonwealth and Council*
CITY: *Los Angeles, CA*

It has been impossible for me to forget Lotus L. Kang's show *Azaleas*, in which photographic and sculptural materials make up ephemeral installations. In the first room, curtain-like sheets of unprocessed large-format film were draped over one another, developing moment by moment, as they displayed the impermanent colors of a dry mountainside. The installation's infrastructure included cast flora, such as lotus roots and seaweed, along with tender details like the red plastic netting that holds pieces of imported fruit together. The second room was particularly magical: a tremendous apparatus, a spool twirling filmstrips, hypnotically rotated forward and back. A set of lights behind the machine illuminated images from the filmstrips in a nearsighted blur throughout most of the room but maintaining sharp focus on one small patch. Using temporality to explore a sensory relationship to loss, longing, and separation, Kang highlights a recurring experience of psychic melancholia seemingly inseparable from a postwar Korean identity. She translates the delicate process of working through one's sense of severance, rediscovering what was lost, only to lose it again.

—Estelle Araya

WOVEN

ARTIST: *Jeremy Frey*
MUSEUM: *Portland Museum of Art*
CITY: *Portland, ME*

This summer, in a darkened corner of the Portland Museum of Art in Maine, I was captivated by a video of Passamaquoddy basket weaver Jeremy Frey single-handedly felling and breaking down an ash tree. Frey comes from a family of basket weavers, and he follows their centuries-old style of gathering materials, but his results diverge from tradition.

The works featured his innovative techniques, like nested baskets whose interiors were patterned differently from the exteriors. The effect was heightened by his use of synthetic dyes: saturated colors lent a surreal quality to urn-like shapes woven into purple- and red-checkerboard or teal stripes, while squat "point" baskets, whose spiky exterior was meant to resemble the spines of a sea urchin, looked downright mad, armored in fluorescent orange.

At the end of the video, which was titled *Ash*, Frey set on fire the basket he had labored over for many days. It was a startling image that revealed an anxiety about the legacy of this work: In the future, will the knowledge of this craft and the materials it requires still exist?

—*Erin Wylie*

MICASA

ARTISTS: *Various*
GALLERY: *Darryl's UWS*
CITY: *New York, NY*

Among this year's many apartment shows, *MiCasa* was a standout. Its site-specific installations were a necessary and invigorating counterpoint to the antiseptic domains of white-cube galleries. Curators Amalia Ulman and Nick Irvin hosted this group show in their newly purchased, unrenovated Housing Development Fund Corporation apartment on the Upper West Side, in New York City, formerly home to a pair of brothers—both Gen X gamers with otaku inclinations—and one of the brothers' two daughters. The show unspools around the signs of life left behind by the tenants. Children's crayon doodles, scrawled across peeling, cerulean walls, skirt the edges of featured works like Magnus Peterson Horner's moon-eyed portrait of a little boy, and Louis Osmosis's delightfully off-kilter sculpture.

In one room, which had been used as a "game dungeon," Alex Mackin Dolan's metaphysical reinterpretation of a retro Sega video game interface shares a wall with computer monitor mounts left over from the brothers' elaborate gaming rigs. More subtle interventions, like Whitney Claflin's sinister soot message smudged onto the apartment's kitchen ceiling, blur the line between what is being introduced and what has been left behind. Within these constructed intimacies, the works serve as a connective tissue, reanimating the apartment's past lives. Part homage, part bizarro open house, *MiCasa* straddles the public and the private, the real and the imagined. The show offers a thoughtful exercise in what preservation and memory might look like in a city that always seems to be changing.

—*Isabel Ling*

MATERIAL MEMORY

ARTIST: *Kelly Taylor Mitchell and Sergio Suárez*
GALLERY: *Swan Coach House Gallery*
CITY: *Atlanta, GA*

This two-person exhibition, curated by TK Smith, included ceramics, textiles, drawings, and homemade paper, and incorporated found and natural materials like bricks, sand, and leaf fronds. Mitchell's work—dynamic, abstract shapes tethered by beaded string—hung vertically, while Suárez's sinewy, spiky ceramics were gathered on painted circular platforms on the floor. The exhibition description and the handmade objects both alluded to the theme of spirituality, but I found this most evident in the physical interplay between the artists' domains. Magic occurred when the skyward-reaching forms dared to nearly touch the earthly vessels. Two-person shows can be tricky: often the included works can feel either oppositional or too similar. Yet these artists were graciously responsive to each other in both grand and small ways.

—*Courtney McClellan*

HIGHEST-SELLING ARTWORKS

The fifty most expensive art-market deals of 2023 Christie's auctions

COMPILED BY INDIA CLAUDY

1. $74,010,000

Le bassin aux nymphéa
(The Waterlily Pond),
1917–19
by Claude Monet

2. $67,110,000

El gran espectaculo (The Nile)
(The Great Show), 1983
by Jean-Michel Basquiat

3. $52,160,000

Figure in Movement, 1976
by Francis Bacon

4. $46,410,000

Recollections of a Visit to
Leningrad, 1965
by Richard Diebenkorn

5. $46,410,000

Untitled (Yellow, Orange,
Yellow, Light Orange), 1955
by Mark Rothko

6. $43,535,000

Les flamants (The Flamingos),
1910
by Henri Rousseau

7. $42,960,000

Femme endormie
(Sleeping Woman), 1934
by Pablo Picasso

8. $41,810,000

Nature morte à la fenêtre
(Still Life at the Window),
1932
by Pablo Picasso

9. $38,935,000

Fruits et pot de gingembre
(Fruits and Ginger Pot), 1890–93
by Paul Cézanne

10. $34,910,000

L'empire des lumières (Empire
of Light), 1949
by René Magritte

11. $34,622,500

Self-Portrait, 1969
by Francis Bacon

12. $30,885,000

Orestes, 1947
by Willem de Kooning

13. $29,160,000

Untitled, 1959
by Joan Mitchell

14. $25,940,000

Sixteen Jackies, 1964
by Andy Warhol

15. $24,560,000

L'arlésienne (Lee Miller)
(The Arlesian), 1937
by Pablo Picasso

16. $24,107,000

Femme nue sur un tapis
(Nude on Tapestry), 1929
by Sanyu (Chang Yu)

17. $23,410,000

Charred Beloved I, 1946
by Arshile Gorky

18. $22,588,000

Femme dans un rocking-chair
(Jacqueline) (Woman in a
Rocking Chair), 1956
by Pablo Picasso

19. $22,260,000

Burning Gas Station, 1966–69
by Ed Ruscha

20. $21,110,000

Black Iris VI, 1936
by Georgia O'Keeffe

21. $20,477,000

Rhinocrétaire I
(Rhinocretary I), 1964
by François-Xavier Lalanne

22. $19,960,000

Untitled (Bacchus 1st Version II),
2004
by Cy Twombly

23. $19,960,000

Untitled (Bolsena), 1969
by Cy Twombly

24. $19,385,000

Early Blossom, Woldgate,
2009
by David Hockney

25. $16,420,000

Portrait of Doña María Vicenta
Barruso Valdés, seated on
a sofa with a lap-dog; and
Portrait of her mother Doña
Leonora Antonia Valdés de
Barruso, seated on a chair
holding a fan, 1805
by Francisco José de Goya y Lucientes

26. $15,360,000

Rouen Cathedral, Set IV, 1969
by Roy Lichtenstein

27. $14,785,000

Fillette en rose (Little Girl
in Pink), 1928–30
by Tamara de Lempicka

28. $14,670,000

The Gate, 2000
by David Hockney

29. $13,635,000

Nu couché (Reclining Nude), 1968
by Pablo Picasso

30. $13,347,000

L'île au trésor
(Treasure Island), 1945
by René Magritte

31. $13,060,000

White Calico Rose, 1930
by Georgia O'Keeffe

32. $11,910,000

Le square de la trinité,
1878–79
by Pierre-Auguste Renoir

33. $11,910,000

Untitled, 1981
by Jean-Michel Basquiat

34. $11,565,000

The Family of Man Ancestor II,
1974
by Barbara Hepworth

35. $11,335,000

Spoleto, 1984
by Gerhard Richter

36. $11,335,000

Cafetière, tasse et pipe
(Coffeemaker, Cup and Pipe),
1911
by Pablo Picasso

37. $10,990,000

Ich liebe Gegensätze
(I Love Opposites), 1912
by Egon Schiele

38. $10,775,000

La quiétude (Quietude), 1918
by Kees van Dongen

39. $10,760,000

Decoy, 1971
by Jasper Johns

40. $10,760,000

Felled Trees, 2008
by David Hockney

41. $10,430,000

Future Sciences Versus
the Man, 1982
by Jean-Michel Basquiat

42. $10,415,000

Quatre pommes et un couteau
(Four Apples and a Knife), 1885
by Paul Cézanne

43. $10,070,000

Untitled, 1993
by Christopher Wool

44. $9,840,000

Belle's Turquoise, 2020–21
by Brice Marden

45. $9,610,000

Badende (Bathers), 1967
by Gerhard Richter

46. $9,610,000

Chair, 1976
by Philip Guston

47. $9,574,000

L'aqueduc du canal de Verdon au
nord d'Aix (The Verdon Canal
Aqueduct North of Aix), 1882–83
by Paul Cézanne

48. $9,380,000

Dessert Table, 1996
by Wayne Thiebaud

49. $9,035,000

Mademoiselle Matisse
en manteau écossais
(Mademoiselle Matisse in a
Tartan Coat), 1918
by Henri Matisse

50. $8,690,000

Untitled, 1959–60
by Lee Bontecou

THE PUZZLE OF INCREDIBLY WIDE AND DEEP KNOWLEDGE

IF YOU COMPLETE THIS PUZZLE, YOU ARE A GENERALIST OF BROAD SKILL AND GREAT RENOWN

by Wyna Liu; edited by Benjamin Tausig

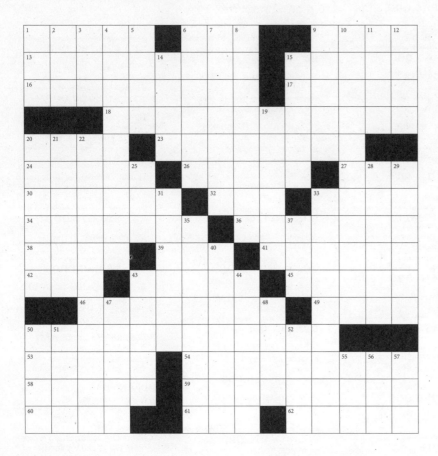

ACROSS

1. Only sign represented by an inanimate object
6. Judge's stat, notably?
9. Exasperated cry
13. "Sure, food sounds OK now"
15. "With any luck!"
16. Calls from behind?
17. Big name in lotion
18. Swedish mystic and pioneer of abstract painting
20. Word before Bravo or Romeo
23. Allow, as a bit of rule-breaking
24. Rib playfully
26. "Brooklyn" star
27. "The More You Know" spot, e.g.
30. Where to make a tie-dye shirt or friendship bracelet
32. ____ June Paik, whose technology-based sculptures were the first to show abstract forms on a TV
33. Makes like a dove
34. Subject of an iconic bronze statue in the Capitoline Museums (called Lupa Capitolina in Italian)
36. Horse seen in heraldry
38. "Bye-eee!"
39. "___: Fear Eats the Soul" (1974 Fassbinder movie)
41. Philosopher who wrote on Giacometti and Calder
42. Class focused on developing reading and writing skills, for short
43. Bacteria type, familiarly
45. Welcome in
46. Accept defeat
49. Zigs instead of zags, say
50. One studying the contexts in which works were made
53. Imitated a cow
54. Lazy river need
58. Elements of elements
59. Oils that show water
60. Trueheart of comics
61. QVC alternative
62. Array on a zoetrope

DOWN

1. Ad ___
2. Hosp. section
3. What a CAPTCHA proves you're not
4. Sculptor whose woven wire works were commemorated in a series of postage stamps in 2020
5. Supermarket chain from Germany
6. Tool used for finishing holes
7. Largest lake in central Europe
8. "Piece of cake!"
9. "Madonna and ___" (icon title)
10. The one for "The Exorcist" was inspired by Magritte's "Empire of Light"
11. Request from a dentist
12. Bar specification
14. Ingredient in gravlax
15. Color, as a comic
19. Oilers' rivals
20. One small bite
21. "___ Weapon"
22. Pictures on a mug?
25. Post-hardcore offshoot
28. Like pink grapefruit vis-à-vis red grapefruit
29. Selling points
31. Images in a photography book
33. Budget offering?
35. Like soda that's been left out for a short while
37. Bit of slapstick
40. Pocket staples since 2007
43. Slides sideways, say
44. Miami-based painter Bas
47. Passive-aggressive attention getters
48. What omissions might amount to
50. Latin 101 word
51. Boring means of learning
52. "Multiplication of the ___" (1954 Yves Tanguy painting)
55. Longtime news inits.
56. Pot builder
57. Letter in a dollar sign

(answers on page 132)

PAINTING CAPTCHA

CAN YOU IDENTIFY THESE NINE WORKS OF ART?

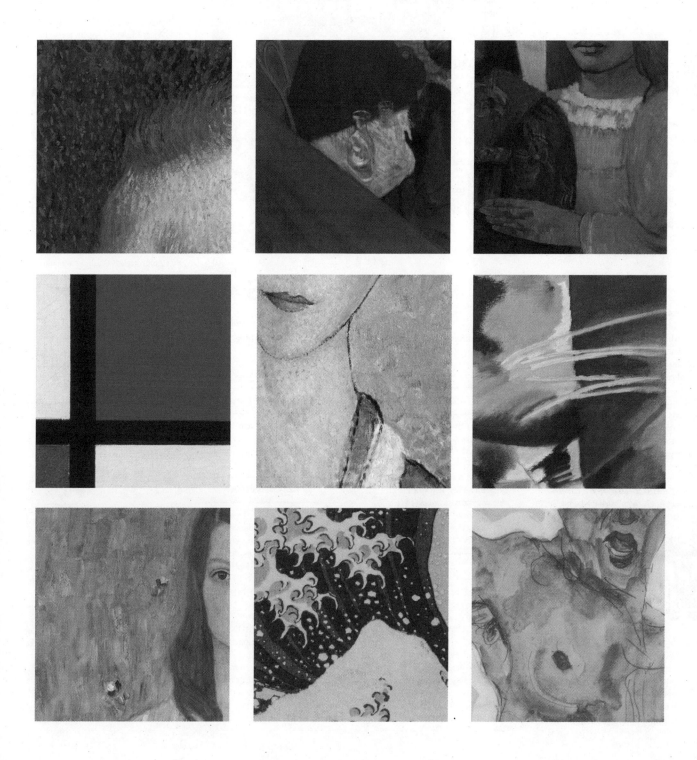

FOR SALE

FORTUNES TO DISCOVER— Find luck, love, lore @ https://kendra.studio/.

BACK ISSUES of *Believer* available (2007–2015)— Destinationbooks.net https://bit.ly/4aJaWL7

<3   J AND C ARTS   <3 cups and bowls and teeshirts / artbooks, posters and prints / records, tapes and cds / unique AND mass produced / by Johanna Jackson and Chris Johanson / JandCarts.com.

MISSED CONNECTIONS

DO YOU WORK AT A DINER on Dundas? You made me a blueberry mojito and stumbled over your words. I ordered the curry of the day. If I sit at the bar on 1/13/25, will you please say something?

FRANK ZAPPA LOOKALIKE— To the tall, Frank Zappa-looking fellow singing Patsy Cline alone at the karaoke bar on a Tuesday night—you made me feel like I was in a David Lynch film. I'd like to grab a cup of coffee with you and discuss '60s music, art film, and the dark side of the surreal. If I don't see you next Tuesday, I'll chalk it up to a lucid dream.

LISTEN UP

IT'S ONLY MONDAY NIGHT— Let Annie Siegel's debut album strum your heart strings and stroke your eardrums with shades of Joni Mitchell and Adrianne Lenker. Out on all streaming platforms.

I WISH I WAS A RAT—Spiral XP's new album *I Wish I Was a Rat* captures the often aimless or misdirected wistfulness of the shoegaze genre—in its title as well as its tracklist. If you harbor a formless yet unshakeable desire for loud guitars over whispered vocals, tape-saturated tones, and tasteful guitarmony, your wish is granted on all major streaming platforms.

CLASSIFIEDS

Believer Classifieds cost $2 per word. They can be placed by emailing classifieds@thebeliever.net. All submissions subject to editorial approval. No results guaranteed.

SERVICES

TEXT YOUR ADDRESS, I'll mail a postcard. 917-412-6791. Brian McMullen.

TEXT ME A PHOTO of whatever Brian McMullen sent you and I'll sing you the postcard over live piano. 917-848-7006. —Minna Choi (host of *Just Add Music* podcast)

APOLOGIES

TO THE CARD THIEF— Kyle, I'm no longer mad at you for stealing my holographic Raichu Pokémon card in 2nd grade. That whole incident left a bad taste in my mouth, and the hit your reputation took was unfair. Hope you're well, pal, and that you haven't dwelled on this as much as I have.

ACTUALLY FREE

LONELY INSTAGRAM COLLAGES seeking curious viewers: instagram.com/adamgreen666. Adam Green.

FELICITATIONS

FINALLY OF AGE! At long last, you've turned 21. Like the rest of America's spirited youth, I know you've dreamed of this day for years… the day you can finally (and legally!) get a birthday shout-out in *The Believer.* So, without further ado, Happy Birthday Sam!

CONGRATULATIONS to Alex and Jen, whose nuptials spur us to celebrate the "hierarchy of soup" in our family's traditional way: with bird's nest soup, baby! We'll spring for the good stuff—soft, nubbly on the tongue, the fewer feathers the better.

NEW & RECOMMENDED

HOW WE GOT HERE by David Shields is a provocative, accessible, persuasive, and addictive new release, in which Shields argues that Melville plus Nietzsche divided by the square root of (Allan) Bloom times Zizek (squared) equals Bannon. Kellyanne Conway, Donald Trump, Rudy Giuliani, Q-Anon, Fox News, etc., etc., etc. have kidnapped the last century of intellectual thought and philosophical investigation: poststructuralism, quantum physics, deconstruction, the current "crisis" in "nonfiction"-journalism-media-"truthiness." If the perceiver, by his very presence, alters what's perceived, Steve Bannon, Vladimir Putin, Vladislav Surkov (performance-artist-turned-Putin-strategist), et al., have quite consciously created—are all still quite consciously creating on a day-by-day basis—a universe in which nothing is true and therefore public discourse is, in effect, over. God is dead, so everything is permitted. Or is it? See for yourself by purchasing the book here: https://tinyurl.com/4xe6ks96

SUBMISSIONS

PENCILHOUSE—We read WIPs and write feedback on 'em, simple as that. FREE submissions monthly, capacity-capped; $6/mo for submit-whenever, cap-free subs. ALWAYS SEEKING VOLUNTEER CRITICS. pencilhouse.org (http://pencilhouse.org/)

DEAREST EMERGING AND WELL-ESTABLISHED WRITERS—*Southeast Review* wants your fiction, creative nonfiction, poetry, book reviews, interviews, for our biannual issue. Be weird, be fun, be electric at southeastreview.org.

SEEKING ARTIST PHONE NUMBERS—Submit your phone number to be included in a new publication from Bathers Library Press "500 Artist Phone Numbers" (and get a free copy of the book once it's complete). Text 415-250-5527 to be part of it (no names, phone numbers only).

Illustrations by Tomi Um

NOTES ON OUR CONTRIBUTORS

George Abraham is a Palestinian American poet, performance artist, and writer from Jacksonville, Florida. Their debut collection, *Birthright* (Button Poetry, 2020), won the Arab American Book Award and the Big Other Award in Poetry. They are a writer in residence at Amherst College.

Lille Allen is a Latinx designer and writer based in Las Vegas. She is currently a designer at *Eater*.

Hilton Als is a staff writer at *The New Yorker* magazine. He teaches at UC Berkeley.

Estelle Araya is an artist and writer based in Los Angeles. She earned her MFA from the Milton Avery Graduate School of the Arts at Bard College in 2020. Initially trained as a photographer and sculptor, Araya has brought her studio inquiries into writing. Araya has published her work in the *Los Angeles Review of Books*, *Artillery* magazine, and *The Brooklyn Rail*.

Andrea Barnes is a curator and founder of Salmon Run Gallery, an online art gallery based in Philadelphia. She graduated from the Maryland Institute College of Art with a BFA in fibers and a concentration in experimental fashion. Andrea has worked for various arts organizations, including the Fabric Workshop and Museum, and with artists such as Alex Da Corte.

Hayden Bennett currently lives in New England. (480) 768-7931.

Tom Bolin is a painter living in Chicago.

Trina Calderón is an author, journalist, and TV-filmmaker from Los Angeles. Her most recent book is the short story collection *Once Upon a Time on Grateful Dead Tour*. She is devoted to stories with social impact and diverse participants.

Monica Datta's novel *Thieving Sun* was published last spring by Astra Publishing House.

Claire L. Evans is a writer and musician exploring biology, technology, and culture. She is the singer in the Grammy-nominated pop group Yacht; cofounder of *Vice* magazine's imprint for speculative fiction, Terraform; and coeditor, with Brian Merchant, of the anthology *Terraform: Watch/Worlds/Burn*. Her 2018 history of women in computing, *Broad Band: The Untold Story of the Women Who Made the Internet*, was named one of the Greatest Tech Books of All Time by *The Verge* in 2023. She lives in Los Angeles.

Benjamin Garcia's first collection, *Thrown in the Throat* (Milkweed Editions, 2020), was selected for the National Poetry Series by Kazim Ali. This collection won the Eugene Paul Nassar Poetry Prize and was a finalist for the Kate Tufts Discovery Award. His poems and essays have recently appeared or are forthcoming in *AGNI*, *American Poetry Review*, *The Kenyon Review*, and the *New England Review*.

Hannah Krafcik is a Portland, Oregon–based transdisciplinary neuroqueer artist. Throughout all their making, they rely on their proclivity for pattern recognition to locate connections, cultivate language, and build relationships. Their ever-growing list of practices includes performance, photography, new media, and arts journalism.

Nicole Lavelle is a writer, artist, and designer living in the San Francisco Bay Area.

Isabel Ling is a New York City–based writer and editor. She is the editor of *MOLD* magazine. Her writing on art, design, and ecology can be found in outlets such as *e-flux Journal*, *Frieze*, *Spike* magazine, and *The Cut*.

Courtney McClellan is an artist and writer living in Atlanta. Her work has been shown in museums and exhibition spaces like SculptureCenter in Long Island City, New York (2018); the University of Michigan Museum of Art in Ann Arbor (2020); and the Museum of Contemporary Art of Georgia in Atlanta (2021). She is the editor of *Burnaway*, an online magazine that celebrates art in the South and the Caribbean.

Bucky Miller is an artist and writer from Arizona who currently teaches in Knoxville, Tennessee. He is a recipient of the Aaron Siskind Foundation Individual Photographer's Fellowship and is one-third of the Brooklyn, New York–based collective Wraymour and Flanigan. His Substack is called *Cookietown*, and his forthcoming book of photographs is called *Onions*.

Eileen Myles (they/them, b. 1949) is a poet, novelist, and art journalist whose practice of vernacular first-person writing has made them one of the most recognized writers of their generation. Their most recent books are *Pathetic Literature*, an anthology; and a *"Working Life,"* poems. They live in New York and in Marfa, Texas.

Amanda Dannáe Romero is a nuevomexicanx experimental artist and musician based in Albuquerque, New Mexico. Her work incorporates sound, coding, colcha embroidery, tinsmithing, video, and performance. She has exhibited both nationally and internationally at spaces such as SITE Santa Fe and Castellar de la Frontera.

Amanda Rosa is the arts reporter at *The Miami Herald*. Originally from Miami, Rosa covers exhibitions, performing arts, galleries, and issues facing local artists. She graduated from the University of Florida and previously worked at *The New York Times* as a metro fellow.

Margaret Ross is the author of *Saturday* (The Song Cave, 2024) and *A Timeshare* (Omnidawn, 2015). Her poems and translations have appeared in *Granta*, *Harper's Magazine*, *The Paris Review*, and *Poetry*.

Sarah Rose Sharp is a writer and multimedia artist. Sarah was a 2015 Kresge Literary Arts Fellow for Art Criticism and is a 2018 winner of the Rabkin Foundation Prize. She was a spring 2024 resident at Surf Point in York, Maine, and most recently mounted a comprehensive survey of more than seventy southeast Michigan fiber artists as part of Detroit's fourteenth annual Month of Design.

Ross Simonini is an interdisciplinary artist, writer, and musician living in Altadena, California. His first novel is *The Book of Formation*.

Pepper Stetler is the author of *A Measure of Intelligence: One Mother's Reckoning with the IQ Test*. Her work on issues facing people with disabilities and their caregivers has appeared in *The New York Times*, *The Wall Street Journal*, *Slate*, and *The Progressive*, among other outlets. She is a professor of art history at Miami University in Oxford, Ohio.

lê thị diễm thúy is the author of *The Gangster We Are All Looking For*.

Zaria Ware is a writer and independent curator based in the US. Her debut art book, *BLK ART*, was nominated in spring 2024 for an NAACP Image Award for Outstanding Literary Work in Nonfiction. She is developing the first digital database dedicated to models of color in Western art. For updates on future projects, visit her website, zariaware.com.

Lindsey White is an artist based in San Francisco. Her new book, *What? Is? Art?*, is available now from Colpa Press.

Carmen Winant is an artist and the Roy Lichtenstein Chair of Studio Art at the Ohio State University. Her work utilizes archival and authored photographs to examine feminist care networks, with particular emphasis on intergenerational, multiracial, and sometimes transnational coalition building. She is also a community organizer, prison educator, and mother to Carlo and Rafa, shared with her partner, Luke Stettner.

Chelsea Ryoko Wong (b. 1986, Seattle) is a painter and muralist. She was awarded the 2023 Harker Fund Residency at the Oakland Museum of California and was a 2022 finalist for SFMOMA's esteemed SECA Art Award. She has participated in recent group exhibitions at the de Young Museum, Yerba Buena Center for the Arts, and Creativity Explored, among other places. Wong lives and works in the Mission District of San Francisco. She is represented by Jessica Silverman, San Francisco.

Erin Wylie is a writer based in Oakland, California. She is the cocreator of the newsletter *Blackbird Spyplane*.

IN THE NEXT ISSUE

Not all contents are guaranteed; replacements will be satisfying

Sisyphus in the Capital . . . . ESKOR DAVID JOHNSON
For a brief period of time in 1990, the government of Trinidad and Tobago was overthrown. What was the effect on the national psyche when the violent insurrectionists were allowed to walk free?

Adventures in Jesusland . . . . DAVID MORRIS
Confessions from a former member of Campus Crusade for Christ, the most powerful evangelical group you've never heard of.

The Magic Well . . . . KRISTIN KEANE
After becoming transfixed by an uninterrupted web-stream of a family of cheetahs, one writer began to wonder what it is we see, exactly, when we watch the lives of animals play out through our screens.

SOLUTIONS TO THIS ISSUE'S GAMES AND PUZZLES

CROSSWORD
(Page 128)

L	I	B	R	A	■	R	B	I	■	C	M	O	N
I	C	O	U	L	D	E	A	T	■	I	H	O	P	E
B	U	T	T	D	I	A	L	S	■	N	I	V	E	A
■	■	H	I	L	M	A	A	F	K	L	I	N	T	■
A	L	F	A	■	L	E	T	S	L	I	D	E	■
T	E	A	S	E	■	R	O	N	A	N	■	P	S	A
A	T	C	A	M	P	■	N	A	M	■	C	O	O	S
S	H	E	W	O	L	F	■	P	E	G	A	S	U	S
T	A	T	A	■	A	L	I	■	S	A	R	T	R	E
E	L	A	■	S	T	A	P	H	■	G	R	E	E	T
■	■	T	A	K	E	T	H	E	L	■	E	R	R	S
A	R	T	H	I	S	T	O	R	I	A	N	■
M	O	O	E	D	■	I	N	N	E	R	T	U	B	E
A	T	O	M	S	■	S	E	A	S	C	A	P	E	S
T	E	S	S	■	■	H	S	N	■	S	L	I	T	S

PAINTING CAPTCHA
(Page 129)

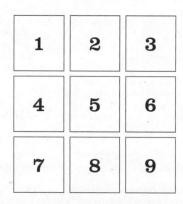

1. *Self-Portrait*, 1887, by Vincent van Gogh
2. *At the Moulin Rouge*, 1892–95, by Henri de Toulouse-Lautrec
3. *Two Women*, 1901 or 1902, by Paul Gauguin
4. *Composition II in Red, Blue, and Yellow*, 1930, by Piet Mondrian
5. *Girl in a Sailor's Blouse*, 1918, by Amedeo Modigliani
6. *Painting with Green Center*, 1913, by Wassily Kandinsky
7. *Mäda Primavesi*, 1912–13, by Gustav Klimt
8. *Under the Wave off Kanagawa (Kanagawa oki nami ura)*, 1830–32, by Katsushika Hokusai
9. *Self-Portrait*, 1911, by Egon Schiele

2024 ARTIST GIFT GUIDE

43 ARTISTS RECOMMEND GIFTS FOR OTHER ARTISTS; IN ABC ORDER, THEY ARE:

1. **AISTÉ STANCIKAITÉ** 10
Faber-Castell Polychromos Artists' Middle Purple Pink Pencil

2. **AKS MISYUTA** 2
Igia Theraheat Infrared Pain Relief Lamp

3. **AN-MY LÊ** 6
Colorful Clairefontaine Notebooks with Subject Tabs

4. **ANNA SEW HOY** 11
#2 Pencils (with a Sharp Point)

5. **BRAD PHILLIPS** 10
Soucolor Acrylic Paintbrush Set

6. **BRENDAN MONROE** 14
FrogTape Delicate Surface Painter's Tape

7. **BRIANNA ROSE BROOKS** 9, 15
Giant Microbes Plush Heart Organ;
Diptyque L'eau Papier Perfume

8. **BRUCE LaBRUCE** 7
Holy Wafer

9. **CARSON ELLIS** 5, 11
Trader Joe's Daily Facial Sunscreen;
Muji 0.38 mm. Gel Ink Cap Type Ballpoint Pen

10. **CLAIRE BOYLE** 14
Folding Table Caster Wheels

11. **CLARE ROJAS** 12
Reebok Step

12. **CLAUDIA KEEP** 8
Burt's Bees Beeswax Lip Balm

13. **DAISY SHEFF** 14
Colored Sand, Flocking, or Pom-Poms

14. **DAMIEN HOAR DE GALVAN** 3
Grizzly G0555 14 in. 1 hp Bandsaw

15. **DAVID WILSON** 2
Uncle Bill's Original Sliver Grippers

16. **ELIZABETH HAZAN** 6
Bounty Select-a-Size Mega Roll Paper Towels

17. **FRITZ HAEG** 15
2025 Hurrah Today Calendar

18. **HADI FALAPISHI** 12
Silver Duct Tape

19. **IAN L.C. SWORDY** 11
Gerber Exchange-a-Blade Pocket Knife;
Fisher Antimicrobial Raw Brass Bullet Space Pen

20. **JOHANNA JACKSON** 2
RefrigiWear Insulated Softshell Bib Overalls

21. **JONATHAN RYAN** 8, 12
Exo Terra Riverbed Sand; Bonne Maman Preserves Jars

22. **KATY STUBBS** 3
Nabertherm 5-Sided Chamber Pottery Kiln;
Popcake Commercial Automatic Pancake Maker

23. **KENDRA YEE** 4
Carhartt Men's Utility Double-Knee Work Pant

24. **KRISTIN FARR** 15
Instant Audience

25. **LAURA FIGA** 13
Aged Paper

26. **LEANNE SHAPTON** 9
Pee Funnel

27. **LÉONIE GUYER** 10
MONO Zero Eraser

28. **MADELINE DONAHUE** 5
Fiskars Scissors

29. **MARCEL DZAMA** 4
Homebrew Root Beer Extract

30. **MARTINE SYMS** 15
Custom Matchbooks

31. **MATT FURIE** 14
24 in. Toshiba TV/DVD/VCR Combination

32. **MICAH LEXIER** 5, 16
Cutco Super Shears; Pina Zangaro Machina Presentation Box

33. **NATHANIEL RUSSELL** 7
Two Identical Coffee Cups

34. **RAY FENWICK** 13
Doug's Brother's Fostex X-26 4-Track Recorder

35. **REBECCA MORGAN** 16
Wallace Berrie Figurines

36. **SAM KELLER** 4
Pantone Imaging Spectrocolorimeter

37. **SHAWN HARRIS** 15
Hobby Blades

38. **SOPHY HOLLINGTON** 11
Blackwing Natural Pencils

39. **TADÁSKÍA** 16
Ladybugs

40. **TAMARA SHOPSIN** 2
Merco Hand-Held Tape Dispenser

41. **THENJIWE NIKI NKOSI** 8
Essential New York Typist Chair

42. **WALTER ROBINSON** 13
Poly Sheeting

43. **ZAK KITNICK** 6, 9
Capovilla Grappa Wine; Fresh Pistachios in Dark Chocolate

AKS MISYUTA'S
IGIA THERAHEAT INFRARED
PAIN RELIEF LAMP
target.com

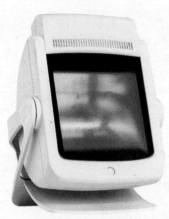

$62.82

"Bask in the glory tomorrow; bask in the warmth of
an infrared lamp today. Relaxed face and painless
painting—the ultimate gift for an artist."

DAVID WILSON'S
UNCLE BILL'S
ORIGINAL
SLIVER GRIPPERS
slivergripper.net

$9.55

"These are tweezers that lock into a key
chain. I get a lot of splinters while making
frames for drawings or just being in the
woods painting, so it's handy to keep 'the
tweezers with pin-point precision' close."

JOHANNA JACKSON'S
REFRIGIWEAR
INSULATED SOFTSHELL
BIB OVERALLS
refrigiwear.com

**STAY WARM
DOWN TO –20°F**

TAMARA SHOPSIN'S
MERCO HAND-HELD TAPE DISPENSER
kioskkiosk.com

ALL-METAL!

$36

"No parts to lose, a thing of beauty, and a pure joy
to use. Lasts forever—had mine for fifteen years."

$130.40

"A RefrigiWear one-piece for working in cold studios
and for its slight thunder-coat powers."

DAMIEN HOAR DE GALVAN'S
GRIZZLY G0555 14 in. 1 HP BANDSAW
grizzly.com

$695

"This is similar to the bandsaw I use. I'm not sure if it's the exact model but it is a Grizzly. I had a less expensive saw before this, so it was a big deal when I got a more professional one. I've been happy using mine."

KATY STUBBS'S
NABERTHERM 5-SIDED CHAMBER POTTERY KILN: N2200
hot-clay.com

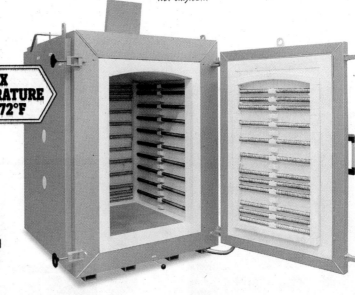

MAX TEMPERATURE OF 2,372°F

$42,953

"This kiln is absolutely huge and you could definitely put your boyfriend in it."

KATY STUBBS'S
POPCAKE COMMERCIAL AUTOMATIC PANCAKE MAKER
popcake.com

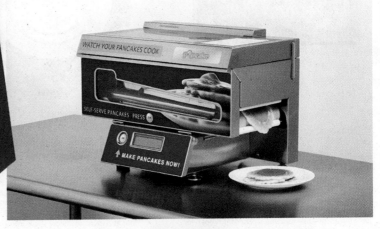

$3,700

"I once saw this in an airport and I have never felt anything like how I felt seeing my pancake being cooked by this machine. I would like to feel that again."

MARCEL DZAMA'S
HOMEBREW ROOT BEER EXTRACT
hobbyhomebrew.com

SAM KELLER'S
PANTONE IMAGING SPECTROCOLORIMETER
pantone.com

KENDRA YEE'S
CARHARTT MEN'S UTILITY DOUBLE-KNEE WORK PANT
carhartt.com

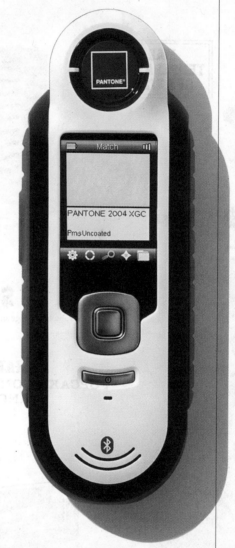

DOUBLE-LAYER KNEES WITH OPENINGS FOR ADDING KNEEPADS

$2,740

$8 (2 fl. oz.)

"I am a big fan of this root beer base. It's great to paint with. It gives a very nice brown, and the smell is so beautiful—like someone opened up a root beer factory nearby. The brown lasts quite a while. I did some archival tests with it and it won't fade, even under a window with sun, for about five years or more. You can find these wherever do-it-yourself beer kits are sold."

"As a neo-pop-art-making tool, a Spectrocolorimeter is a tool to copy or appropriate colors from real life into Pantone color formulas. For example: the paint counter at Home Depot uses one of these to mix custom colors from customers' samples. In my own art-making practice, I've brought American cheese slices into Home Depot for paint color matching (the counter person thought it was hilarious). On another occasion, I needed a quart of Oreo blue, for which I took a sleeve of Oreos from the checkout over to the paint counter. A real-life version of Photoshop's eyedropper tool."

$69.99

"A staple item in my wardrobe is my 'studio pants.' From neon-colored paint, wild clay, and perhaps even a few tears, every medium has soaked into the pockets. These pants were designed for hard work, and they act as an archive of my practice by preserving the stains of each project."

MICAH LEXIER'S
CUTCO SUPER SHEARS
cutco.com

CUT SIMPLE HERBS OR COPPER PENNIES

$141

"They are the kitchen scissors you never knew you needed. And they come apart super easy, so they are super easy to clean. I bought a pair decades ago to help out a friend's kid who had a job selling Cutco items, but the joke was on me as they turned out to be amazing. I have since bought dozens more to give out as housewarming gifts. Best gift ever."

CARSON ELLIS'S
TRADER JOE'S DAILY
FACIAL SUNSCREEN
traderjoes.com

EXP : 01/2026

TRADER JOE'S®
DAILY
FACIAL
SUNSCREEN
BROAD SPECTRUM
SPF 40

OIL FREE
INVISIBLE GEL FORMULA
FRAGRANCE FREE
WATER + SWEAT RESISTANT
(40 MINUTES)
NET 1.7 FL OZ
(50 mL)

$8.99
(1.7 fl. oz.)

"I'm a fair-skinned red-head who hates sunscreen. I recently visited LA from Oregon and 'forgot' to bring any. My sister-in-law gave me this stuff from Trader Joe's and it's really nice. It doesn't smell or feel like anything and it goes a long way."

MADELINE DONAHUE'S
FISKARS SCISSORS
joann.com

$10–$25

"My absolute favorite tool is a pair of scissors. I am passionate about scissors. I've been collecting scissors for decades and use them in every way in my studio and home life (we cut pizza with scissors). My favorite brand is Fiskars, especially the decorative pairs and the five-inch Micro-Tip scissors. When my grandmother died and her belongings were up for grabs, I took all the scissors. I found she was like me and owned at least thirty pairs. She taught me how to sew and now I have all her different sewing shears. There are rules about which scissors can be used for different materials—you're supposed to only use one pair for paper, one for hair, one for fabric. I prefer to have them all over the studio, in every drawer and always within reach. I have a visual hierarchy for which pairs are still sharp, and when a pair dulls down I put it in my ceramics tool kit for cutting plastic and clay. As a gift, buy a bouquet of different scissors—all sizes and styles. Then write love notes on the scissors with Sharpie or paint marker so the user is haunted by your presence when they use the scissors in the studio. Better yet, write your name on the scissors and accuse the person you gift the scissors to of stealing *your* scissors."

ELIZABETH HAZAN'S
BOUNTY SELECT-A-SIZE MEGA ROLL PAPER TOWELS

target.com

CUSTOM-SIZED SHEETS FOR CUSTOM-SIZED SPILLS

$34.99 (12 rolls)   "No painter can have enough of these."

AN-MY LÊ'S
COLORFUL CLAIREFONTAINE NOTEBOOKS WITH SUBJECT TABS

classicofficeproducts.com

$8.55 (pack of 4)

"I have used one for thirty years on my work trips. It's the perfect size (4 ¼ × 6 ¾ in.) to carry in my fanny pack, along with camera accessories. I use it to take notes on people, locations I photograph, and other miscellaneous useful information. It has subject tabs, which allows me to organize into categories. I have tried without success to replace them with my phone notes app."

ZAK KITNICK'S
CAPOVILLA GRAPPA WINE

astorwines.com

$50–$100 (700 ml. bottle)

"If you are buying grappa for yourself, the cheapest is best. I once conducted a taste test for myself that included twenty bottles of grappa ranging from $30 to $150. The cheapest was the best. For a gift, the most expensive bottle you can find is the best, just because. Capovilla, Marolo, and Poli are all excellent options. But all grappa is good because it's made from the pomace: the grape stalks, seeds, and leftovers from wine-making. Not in an annoying upcycling way, or a snout-to-tail way, but just because."

BRUCE LaBRUCE'S
HOLY WAFER
el-angel.com

$20 (pack of medium-sized wafers)

"The 'hostia,' the holy wafer, adds a spiritual and symbolic significance to any photo. This photo is from the 'Obscenity' series in my new photo book, *The Revolution Is My Boyfriend*, from Baron Books."

NATHANIEL RUSSELL'S
TWO IDENTICAL
COFFEE CUPS
ebay.com

$1–$5

"One contains coffee (or tea) and the other will be water for your paintbrush—and you won't know which one until you drink it. Great for the immune system! Makes brushes last longer! You will definitely drink paint! The best ones are available at thrift stores and garage sales and have good graphics and slogans such as 1993 HOMECOMING CELEBRATION, WORLD'S GREATEST GRANDMA, or a drawing of a horse."

JONATHAN RYAN'S
EXO TERRA RIVERBED SAND
exo-terra.com

THENJIWE NIKI NKOSI'S
ESSENTIAL NEW YORK TYPIST CHAIR
makro.co.za

$56.40

"These are from Makro, a warehouse store in Johannesburg, the city where I live and work. These chairs can take you across an entire studio in one push. They lean back really far and have good cushioning. They also contract down to the exact height of my couch so that I can sit at eye level with visitors. I always have at least two of them nearby. My daughter finds them excellent to spin on."

CLAUDIA KEEP'S
BURT'S BEES BEESWAX LIP BALM
burtsbees.com

$3.99

"I feel safest when I have a tube in every jacket and bag I wear. It's the best chapstick I've ever tried. I think I'm physically addicted to it at this point. You can find it at any pharmacy and many grocery stores."

$15
(10 lb. bag)

"This gift is particular to my practice: very fine, specialty sand (either purchased or found in the natural environment). I work with different types of sand in my paintings. I buy the larger-grit, more pebbly sand at the hardware store. It's very cheap and comes in large bags. However, the superfine sand isn't as easy to find, or as cheap. You can find it at craft stores and pet-supply stores (for aquariums), but it's way more expensive since it's not a bulk building material. I'd love it if someone dropped off a huge bag of this stuff, so I didn't have to worry about resupplying for a while."

ZAK KITNICK'S
FRESH PISTACHIOS IN DARK CHOCOLATE
laderach.com

$33 (0.551 lbs.)

"Stock up with a couple pounds of fresh pistachios in dark chocolate."

LEANNE SHAPTON'S
PEE FUNNEL
go-girl.com

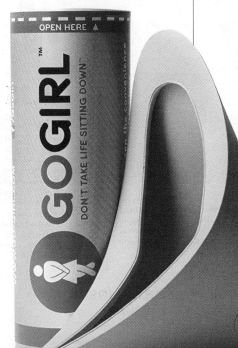

BRIANNA ROSE BROOKS'S
GIANT MICROBES PLUSH HEART ORGAN
giantmicrobes.com

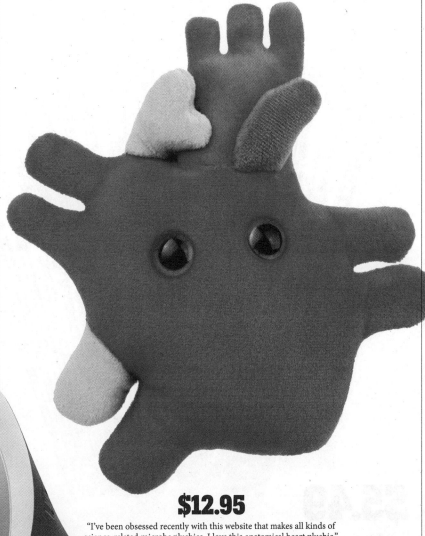

$12.95

"I've been obsessed recently with this website that makes all kinds of science-related microbe plushies. I love this anatomical heart plushie."

REUSABLE!

$14.99

"It's a great hostess gift or road trip gift. While this isn't exactly a straightforward art supply, it can be used by anyone with a vagina for painting 'en plein air.' I brought one to the Arctic when I went in 2015 and it was very handy."

BRAD PHILLIPS'S
SOUCOLOR ACRYLIC PAINTBRUSH SET
amazon.com

LÉONIE GUYER'S
MONO ZERO ERASER
tombowusa.com

WILL NOT DAMAGE PAPER

$5.49
(20 brushes)

"I've been making paintings for almost thirty years. Photorealistic paintings and simple graphic paintings. Other painters use expensive brushes made of rare animal hairs. Sometimes they cost fifty dollars. Maybe they know something I don't. I use these very cheap brushes instead, made of something aggressively synthetic. Twenty brushes for five dollars. Hard to beat that price. They don't last as long as brushes made of sable, but I don't care. I just buy new ones. I'm pretty sure my paintings look just as good as paintings painted with the finest brushes made with the rarest of materials."

$5.25

"For people who love to draw and consider erasure an essential part of their process—the Tombow MONO Zero Eraser. A must-have in my studio. I work on old and delicate papers and this is the best tool I've found for precisely erasing tiny marks without damage. I recommended it to an artist friend who said it was 'life-changing!' Note: when it's time to refill, take care to buy the correct size and shape—they make a few different eraser types."

AISTĖ STANCIKAITĖ'S FABER-CASTELL POLYCHROMOS
ARTISTS' COLOR MIDDLE PURPLE PINK PENCIL
fabercastell.com

Made in Germany   Polychromos   FABER-CASTELL

$3.35

"The best pink-purple color in a pencil I've ever come across."

CARSON ELLIS'S MUJI 0.38 MM. GEL INK CAP TYPE BALLPOINT PEN

muji.us

$1.90

"These pens are cheap, plentiful, and excellent. They have a very fine point and make a nice smooth line. I always have one with me."

IAN L.C. SWORDY'S GERBER EXCHANGE-A-BLADE POCKET KNIFE

gerbergear.com

$18

HANDLE DOUBLES AS MONEY CLIP

FISHER ANTIMICROBIAL RAW BRASS BULLET SPACE PEN

spacepen.com

$34

"Many people have a 'phone, wallet, keys' check before they leave the house. I recommend adding two items to this list for artists: the two essentials are knife and pen. These are my daily carries."

ANNA SEW HOY'S #2 PENCILS (WITH A SHARP POINT)

amazon.com

$16.82 (pack of 150)

"I love having sharp pencils around so that everyone in the house is able to write down a thought or a dream, a reminder of something to do, or a quick sketch. These are thinking tools, and we need to externalize our thoughts so we know what they are. Sharp points are key for clarity. I recommend buying a box of pink cap erasers—the pencil eraser always gets used up before the pencil! Also, I love the simple, sustainable nature of these tools."

SOPHY HOLLINGTON'S BLACKWING NATURAL PENCILS

blackwing602.com

$30 (box of 12)

"Expensive but actually worth the money if you're very invested in your pencils. The perfect point for editioning and signing prints."

HADI FALAPISHI'S
SILVER DUCT TAPE
acehardware.com

$9.99

"This year, like in previous years, I'm gifting my loved ones the most magical, practical object ever produced: yes, I'm talking about the ever-silver duct tape. This simple object has come in handy in ways that are hard to believe for a simple mind. To name a few: hair removal, opening the window of a car, a blister bandage, splinting a broken leg, keeping the tent closed, marking a trail, making a hat on a sunny day, mending shoes, repairing glasses, a handcuff alternative, leaving a note, a belt, patching a hole in a canoe, catching flies, opening a jar, a temporary hem, and literally the list goes on and on forever. The only thing I haven't been able to use duct tape for is toilet paper. Somehow it doesn't work—but that's not a big deal. And this year there is a big plus: I have insider information that Balenciaga is releasing a new $3,300 duct-tape bracelet in February of 2025. Bingo!"

JONATHAN RYAN'S
BONNE MAMAN PRESERVES JARS
amazon.com

$32.24 (pack of 6)

"The gift is geared toward painters (but it's probably useful for artists working with other mediums as well). The gift is reusable containers. Think: tuna tins, yogurt cups, jam jars with wide openings, etc.—all washed, of course. Bonus points if there is a lid. It may seem silly, but I go through so many of these. I can't get enough. They're great for mixed paint, mineral spirits, or any other liquids that I might use in the studio. Small- and medium-sized jam jars (particularly from the Bonne Maman brand) are the most useful because they are glass and have a wide mouth. You are better off buying a six-pack—then you get two gifts in one."

CLARE ROJAS'S
REEBOK STEP
reebokfitness.info

ADJUSTABLE HEIGHT

$129.99

"It's sturdy. You can stand on either end. It's not as high as a ladder, it's shorter than a stool, but not exactly on the floor, nor is it heavy. You can sit on it, and even stand on it with one foot. Paint like a flamingo. Facing forward, not twisted like on a ladder."

LAURA FIGA'S
AGED PAPER
thrift stores, public library sales

$0–$1

"There's no color like aged paper."

RAY FENWICK'S
DOUG'S BROTHER'S FOSTEX X-26 4-TRACK RECORDER
ebay.com

$300? $3,000?

"I borrowed it from Doug, but he doesn't know you and I really don't want to give it back. Please don't ask him if you can buy it. I think he forgot I had it?"

WALTER ROBINSON'S
POLY SHEETING
homedepot.com

COVERS UP TO 900 SQUARE FEET

$46.56 (per roll)

"I once gave a whole roll of Mylar (for wrapping paintings) to a guy and he gave me a box of brushes that I still use. That's definitely potlatch. Along with heavy-duty packing tape (with dispenser) and 48 × 96 in. single-wall sheets of corrugated cardboard, four-millimeter high-clarity poly sheeting is what every artist needs to pack paintings professionally for pickup."

CLAIRE BOYLE'S
FOLDING TABLE CASTER WHEELS
amazon.com

300-POUND CAPACITY PER CASTER

$59 (set of 4)

"These casters pop onto the legs of any old folding table and suddenly your palette table can follow you around the studio wherever you go. They also raise the average folding table up to a nice belly-button height. Be sure to get the ones with a locking mechanism. You can buy them through industrial kitchen supply stores."

MATT FURIE'S
24 IN. TOSHIBA TV/DVD/VCR COMBINATION
ebay.com

$100–$1,000

"A 1990s-era CRT (cathode-ray tube) TV set is the perfect gift for the creative type in your life. Artists love obsolete technology, and a bulky twenty-four-inch-screen TV from this era takes at least two people to move anywhere. Turn it on and watch the charming fuzz dance to the relaxing hum of distortion. Feel the sensation as the hairs on the back of your neck stick up to the static. This gift used to be found on the side of the road or at any thrift store but now runs between one hundred and one thousand dollars on eBay and it will be destroyed during shipping."

DAISY SHEFF'S
COLORED SAND, FLOCKING, OR POM-POMS
thrift stores, art-supply reuse stores

$1–$10

"I'm often inspired by the color combos they come in. It's great to build up texture. Sand has a satisfying bleed when you paint on it. Sometimes I let their inherent colors come through. I also use all these things on my dog sculptures as fur."

BRENDAN MONROE'S
FROGTAPE DELICATE SURFACE PAINTER'S TAPE
homedepot.com

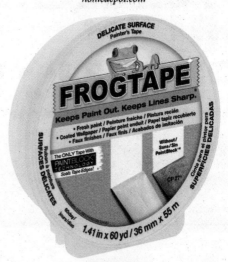

$9.48

"I love this tape for masking anything. Bit pricey, but it's worth the upgrade. It peels off gently and leaves a beautifully clean edge. A thin layer of base coat will prevent bleeding, but it's usually not even needed."

BRIANNA ROSE BROOKS'S
DIPTYQUE L'EAU PAPIER PERFUME
diptyqueparis.com

CONTAINS WHITE MUSKS, MIMOSA, BLOND WOODS ACCORD, AND RICE STEAM ACCORD

$180

"This perfume is more upscale but a good pick for artists: a paper-and-ink scent by Diptyque."

MARTINE SYMS'S
CUSTOM MATCHBOOKS
foryourparty.com

Starting at $37.45

"My recent best gift was to give some custom matchbooks to a friend. She is a fellow weedhead and it went over well."

FRITZ HAEG'S
2025 HURRAH TODAY CALENDAR
clarecrespo.com

$47

"The only holiday gift I have been giving for the last few years is Los Angeles artist Clare Crepo's Hurray Today Calendar. Each loose-leaf monthly page is a playful celebratory illustration of an annual theme (cakes, vegetables, etc). It is a gift that friends and family can actually live with. We look at it daily, marking time and the seasons together."

KRISTIN FARR'S
INSTANT AUDIENCE
mcphee.com

$10.95

"No one's around to cheer for all that work you just finished. Press the buttons for reactions you truly deserve."

SHAWN HARRIS'S
HOBBY BLADES
excelblades.com

$25.37 (pack of 100)

"No one has ever used more than five blades—a twenty-lifetime supply!"

TADÁSKÍA'S
LADYBUGS
naturesgoodguys.com

LIVE DELIVERY GUARANTEED

PRE-FED
Ladybugs
HIPPODAMIA CONVERGENS | GENERAL PREDATOR
Predator to: Aphids, Mealybugs, Spider Mites, Thrips, and other soft-bodied insects.
Package Contains: 36cc | Approximately 750 Ladybugs

LIVE!

$17.50 (approximately 750 ladybugs)

"I often encounter animals, insects, and shadows and sometimes feel like they're trying to tell me something mysterious. At the beginning of 2023, a ladybug landed on my hand when I was traveling to Austria. When I got there, I saw the shadows of rabbits jumping in the woods at the airport. In 2024, I arrived in Oakland, California, and spotted a flying yellow ladybug. Later, in the same city, a red ladybug landed in front of me while I was talking to a friend. The ladybug landed in the path of four small spiders; each one tried to eat the ladybug's head. After escaping the four spiders, the ladybug disappeared. In Reno, Nevada, I learned the nursery rhyme 'Ladybug, Ladybug, fly away home. Your house is on fire, your children are gone.' Soon after, a woman dressed in red told me that it was common to buy semi-frozen ladybugs and toss them, after heating and reviving them, in gardens to eat the pests. I returned to Rio de Janeiro, Brazil, as the forests in the Montreux area of Reno began to burn."

REBECCA MORGAN'S
WALLACE BERRIE FIGURINES
etsy.com

All I Did Was Ask For A Raise

Starting at $9

"Wallace Berries are ubiquitously stamped in the cannon of kitsch: exaggerated features with dreamlike, sometimes nightmarish qualities—unsettling or grotesque, overly happy, awkwardly positioned characters. I like thinking about them as a departure from the sleek and polished midcentury aesthetic of the 1950s. In my own work, I think about forms and images that are 'accessible'—the tchotchke cannon from my rural identity and upbringing has always been critical to my visual vernacular."

MICAH LEXIER'S
PINA ZANGARO MACHINA PRESENTATION BOX
pinazangaro.com

$82.50

"It is a perfect object. I always bring one (or more) with me when I go to an art-book fair so that I have a safe place to store/carry the zines and out-of-print ephemera that I purchase. Nothing ever gets bent that way."